HEMP — AMERICAN HISTORY
REVISITED

HEMP — AMERICAN HISTORY REVISITED

The Plant with a Divided History

Robert Deitch

Algora Publishing
New York

ISBN: 0-87586-213-6 (softcover)

ISBN: 0-87586-214-4 (hardcover)

ISBN: 0-87586-230-6 (ebook)

Library of Congress Cataloging-in-Publication Data

Deitch, Robert, 1950-
  Hemp: American history revisited : the plant with a divided history / by Robert Deitch.
    p. cm.
ISBN 0-87586-205-5 (soft : alk. paper)
ISBN 0-87586-206-3 (hard :alk. paper)
ISBN 0-87586-226-8 (ebook)
  1. Marijuana—United States—History. 2. Hemp—United States—History. I. Title.

HV5822.M3D45 2003
362.29'5—dc21

2003011513

Printed in the United States

TABLE of CONTENTS

INTRODUCTION

This is not a book exclusively about hemp. Both hemp and marijuana are by-products of the Cannabis plant — an extraordinarily useful plant, a plant that mankind has exploited in virtually every way, for thousands of years. What is it about hemp, or Cannabis, that causes such a diversity of opinion about it today? You would think that by now we would know everything there is to know about it and long ago would have come up with a way of minimizing any potential danger so that we could enjoy its many benefits — just as we do with all the other potentially dangerous products and commodities (from fire, guns and corrosive chemicals to alcohol, tobacco, and automobiles) that we use in our everyday lives.

Unfortunately, the exact opposite is true because in 1937, despite Cannabis' beneficial history, an unwitting U.S. Congress and President (Franklin Delano Roosevelt) essentially outlawed the cultivation and use of hemp, for virtually any purpose. Ostensibly, they were motivated by fear of the harmful effects of an intoxicant; in reality, they were serving other interests. Most of them had been duped into believing they were taxing the use of an allegedly harmful drug — "*marijuana*," to discourage its use. In fact, few if any of the congressmen who voted in favor of the Marijuana Tax Act had ever heard the word "marijuana" before and didn't know what it meant. They certainly didn't know that hemp and marijuana came from the same Cannabis plant, and they were never told they were actually outlawing hemp — a crop they were very familiar with because most of them grew up with it on their family farm.

Now, more than 65 years later, we are socially, environmentally and economically suffering from the results of that failed and foolish decision, which has trampled on our civil rights and directed the flow of capital out of the United States and even undermined the value of the US dollar. Worst of all, it has left the population generally unaware of how deeply rooted Cannabis is in American and world history, how important it was to mankind's development — and why. Hemp was important to the economy of the American colonies and was still a valuable commercial commodity up until the Second World War. Most people are unaware that our use of Cannabis as fuel, fiber, paper and food, could solve a number of the environmental and economic problems we face today.

"Rooted" is an extremely apt word because throughout history the Cannabis plant has shown its importance in countless aspects of human life. The story of hemp also illustrates that history is not preordained; it is molded by the various discoveries and events we experience and by the interests of those who are in a position to choose the path we travel.

The history of mankind reflects the struggles of common people to survive in a world of atrocities committed by those with wealth and power. Of course, all those atrocities are conducted under the auspices and supposed righteousness of the law, be it the king's law, god's law, or any other law that is convenient.

The rules under which a society operates dictate whether that society progresses or declines. Two thousand years ago, people believed the gods controlled man's destiny. Modern man is more inclined to believe that we live in a world of "cause and effect," and that everything we do has both positive and negative aspects. The Chinese long ago recognized the natural phenomenon of opposing realities, referring to it as Yin and Yang. A similar realization may well have led Sir Isaac Newton to his "Universal Force" theory, which says: "For every action, there is an equal and opposite reaction." The simple truth is that our problems (environmental, social and economic) are manmade, not "acts of god."

In the chapters that follow, we will see how beneficial the plant has been; we will see whose interests were served by outlawing this remarkable plant; and we will see how eliminating this valuable natural resource has negatively affected the economy, the environment and our personal well-being. It will be shown that the far-reaching effects of the 1937 Marijuana Tax Act, which itself was found unconstitutional, has gone far beyond what Congress originally intended.

First, what do we mean by "hemp"?

The Cannabis plant is the source of both "hemp" (indicating its industrial uses) and "marijuana" (indicating its medicinal and intoxicating properties). While it grows like a weed (and is often referred to as "weed"), it is actually an herb. Cannabis may be the fastest growing plant on the planet. It grows virtually anywhere, whatever the climate and soil condition; it is easily grown from seeds, requires very little care or attention, and does not need any chemical pesticides whatsoever. Its deep root system breaks up and aerates the soil and even adds nutrients. It is almost the perfect plant.

There are basically two species of Cannabis: *sativa* and *indica*, both of which are grown for their fiber and intoxicating properties. Cannabis sativa is the most common around the world, while indica is most prevalent in and around India. It may be known as "India hemp" or "Indian hemp," but those names have also been applied to jute and dogbane (*Apocynum cannabinum*), which are unrelated to Cannabis but add to the confusion. The name "Indian Hemp" was also used by colonial Americans, both to acknowledge the difference between sativa and indica and to refer to Cannabis seeds imported to America from India by the British.

The quality of the fiber (hemp) or its medicinal potency (marijuana) depends entirely on seed heritage and how the plants are grown. When cultivated for its industrial uses (fuel, paper, fabric, plastics), the seeds are planted four inches apart and allowed to grow has high as thirty feet, because the fiber and cellulose is derived from the stalk of the plant. The cellulose is used to produce a variety of products, most commonly paper and animal feed. The long fibers have traditionally been used to produce rope, canvas and even fine quality "linen." (A common misconception is that "linen" means cloth made specifically from the flax plant; in fact, linen cloth has always been made from a group of fibers, known as "bast fibers," from a range of plants including flax, cannabis, and nettles, among others. The most common, easiest to grow, most abundant, and usually least expensive was hemp, which probably means most of the linen was made from hemp.) Even the seeds and seed oil of the Cannabis plant have many commercial and industrial uses — paint, varnishes, fuel, even as food — flour for bread and cake, porridge (hot cereal), and vegetable oil. From colonial times to the Civil War, Americans commonly smoked hemp leaves, like tobacco.

In recent decades, we have come to identify the medicinal and intoxicating properties of Cannabis as "marijuana." Chemically, the active ingredient in marijuana has been identified as Tetrahydrocannabinol (THC); but, in fact, over 400 different cannabinoids have been found in marijuana. These cannabinoids contain both the medicinal and the intoxicating properties of marijuana. Cannabis (marijuana) has a long distinguished history of medicinal use, dating back some five thousand years. Its use as an intoxicant has also been traced back to the beginning of civilization.

Unlike hemp, marijuana is taken from female plants grown more like bushes. They develop resinous buds on their branches, and inconspicuous flowers that produce few seeds. They are cultivated specifically for their THC content; in contrast, hemp plants contain only a minute amount of THC.

Unfortunately, despite its long beneficial history the hysteric fear of the intoxicating properties of marijuana that developed in the 1920s and 30s became the excuse on which all forms of Cannabis were made illegal in the United States.

The version of American history taught in our schools is not meant to educate; it's designed to inspire patriotism. Unfortunately, it produces somewhat of an inaccurate understanding of our world and leaves us with more questions than rational answers. For example: Why was there no interest in colonizing America until 100 years after Columbus proclaimed its discovery, and what was the impetus that suddenly caused millions of Europeans to risk their lives crossing the Atlantic and to endure the hardships of a strange, unsettled, uncivilized new land? What was it about colonial America's agrarian-based society that allowed it to grow and prosper so quickly when, in the history of the world, no other agrarian-based economy ever prospered nearly as well or as fast? What really caused the break-up between colonial America and mother England? "No taxation without representation" may have been the rallying cry, but it's not likely that taxation was a sufficient reason for going to war against Great Britain - then the world's premiere military might.

Cannabis is part of the answer. This is a plant that mankind found extraordinarily useful for thousands of years, a plant that played an important role in colonial America's prosperous economy and remained a valuable commercial commodity up until the Second World War. Today, the importance of Cannabis, particularly as hemp, because of its illegal status, is almost forgotten. Why was this under-appreciated plant outlawed, what were the effects of that ban, and are we really better off without it?

4

In the following pages, the history of America is re-examined from the perspective of mankind's many uses of Cannabis -- past, present, and future.

The establishment of the United States was a social experiment. It was the first time in history that a government was founded to empower "the people," not a king or some other potentate. The deceptively simple concept of "government of the people, by the people, and for the people" articulated in the Declaration of Independence and the US Constitution echoed around the world. These monumental documents, like their predecessor the Magna Carta (signed in England in 1215), and like the Communist Manifesto, sought to dramatically improve the lives of the common people; but such changes always have to be forced on the established powers. And even now, there is an ongoing debate in the United States over how much power should be invested in the central (federal) government and how much should be left up to the states and local jurisdictions.

Sometimes, what looks good on paper doesn't quite work out as expected, in practice. The US Constitution has evolved, due to our need to keep it relevant to the needs of ever-changing society; a number of amendments have been added — some good, some not so good. The 18th Amendment banned the manufacture and sale of alcohol, but after a decade that decision was widely recognized as a dismal failure and it was repealed. Less than a decade later, that same failed policy was applied to marijuana, and subsequently to the cultivation and use of all Cannabis products — and that ban has not repealed.

People familiar with the benefits of the industrial use of hemp (and, certainly, those who appreciate its recreational uses) strongly feel that outlawing the use of Cannabis was a monumental mistake -- even worse than Alcohol Prohibition. That is not only the belief of tens of millions Americans, it is fast becoming the position of hundreds of millions of people around the world.

The problem is not that we have made a mistake; it is that we have failed to learn from our mistakes -- and we have failed to recognize America's drug war as a mistake. It is probable that Alcohol Prohibition contributed to the 1929 stock market crash and the Great Depression of the 1930s; if we don't rationally address the economic and other issues that relate to hemp, there may be more trouble ahead. Hemp can reduce our dependence on petroleum products, and hemp-based technologies are cleaner than many in use today.

We should not be afraid of change. Change is healthy; the alternative is stagnation. As Thomas Jefferson once wrote, "A little rebellion now and then is a good thing." He also spoke of revolution as "the medicine necessary for the sound health of government," and said, "God forbid that we should ever be twenty years without such a rebellion.' It is natural for government bureaucracy to become entrenched and stagnated, and the responsibility for keeping it a vital and useful part of society lies entirely with the people it is entrusted to serve. (Let's just be glad we have elections every four years, instead of bloody revolutions every twenty years.) But government by the people requires "the people" to stay informed about the issues, to think through the consequences of imposed changes, and to call for change where change is needed.

CHAPTER 1

HEMP'S IMPORTANCE TO MANKIND'S EARLY DEVELOPMENT

The hemp trade was a fundamental driving force in the early colonization of America, but its importance to mankind was established long before, at the dawn of civilization. The Cannabis (hemp) plant was valued early on for its strong fiber, used for cordage, rope and cloth (linen), and for its seeds, used in food, and their oil. As fiber, food, fuel, medicine, and unquestionably as an intoxicant, Cannabis has been used by people in every part of the world. Carl Sagan even suggested that the rudimentary beginnings of civilization may well have started with the cultivation of Cannabis — since food was already plentiful, it is likely that people started cultivating crops for other reasons.

In the Neolithic Revolution period, approximately 12,000 years ago, a series of dramatic social and technological changes occurred, effectively marking the end of the Stone Age and the beginning of civilization. These changes included the cultivation of previously wild plants, the building of permanent settlements, the domestication of animals, and the manufacture of pottery and cloth; all of this permitted a huge increase in the human population and began the human domination of the earth. Ernest L. Able, perhaps the foremost authority on the history of hemp, noted:

The first record of man's use of Cannabis comes from the island of Taiwan, located off the coast of mainland China. In this densely populated part of the

7

world, archaeologists have unearthed an ancient village site, dating back over 10,000 years to the Stone Age.

The discovery that twisted strands of fiber were much stronger than individual strands was followed by developments in the arts of spinning and weaving fibers into fabric — innovations that ended man's reliance on animal skins for clothing. It was hemp fiber that the Chinese chose for their first homespun garments.[1]

During the course of its long history in China, hemp found its way into almost every nook and cranny of life. It clothed the Chinese from their heads to their feet, it gave them material to write on, and it became a symbol of power over evil. W. Eberland and Able also note the importance of hemp for bowstrings, as a military weapon;[2] — but those bowstrings helped provide meat, as well.

The plant has fed mankind directly, too. Hemp seeds used to be served as porridge or gruel ("gruel" usually meant a porridge made from the cheapest available ingredients), or ground into a flour and used to bake cakes and bread; they could even be made into a nutritious and good-tasting butter.[3] In the early 1990s when there was mass starvation in Africa due to armed conflict, it was reported that the Red Cross, CARE, and other charitable organizations were feeding people "gruel," specifically because it had more protein than oatmeal or cream of wheat. The report did not say it was hemp-based gruel, but of all the grains, hemp produces perhaps the highest amount of digestible protein and is very high in essential fatty acids.[4] It could very well be that historical references to "gruel" more often meant hemp-based porridge than oats or wheat or any other grain, and that it has become an obsolete word specifically because hemp is no longer part of our diets — in large part because of its illegal status.

The versatility and strength of the fibers of hemp made it one of the raw materials most used by primitive man; and for well over 10,000 years practically everything people had was made from hemp. It was hemp cloth that replaced animal-skin coverings. It was strong hemp (later called "manila," when it had to be imported from the Philippines) rope and sail that enabled man to capture the

---

1. Able, Ernest L. *Marijuana, The First Twelve Thousand Years.* Plenum Press, New York: 1980, p. 4.

2. Able, p. 6.

3. Erasmus, Udo. *Fats and Oils, The Complete Guide to Fats and Oils in Health and Nutrition.* Alive Books, Vancouver, Canada: 1986, p. 232

4. *Ibid.,* p. 231

power of the wind to explore and inhabit the world — without it, even the discovery of America would have come much later. Even the word "canvas" is derived from Cannabis.[5] Hemp-based paper (rag bond, made from tattered hemp cloth) appears to have been the paper that first enabled humanity to create books and communicate ideas over time and distances. Paper money, first developed by the Chinese, was made from hemp, and most of the world's paper money today is still linen-based. Oil extracted from Cannabis seeds was used to waterproof the hulls of wooden ships, as lamp oil, and as the base for paints and varnishes. Medicinally, Cannabis has an equally prestigious history. It was used as commonly as we use aspirin today, to soothe pain and suffering.

The usefulness of hemp was probably discovered simultaneously in many parts of the world, but the Chinese were the first to mass produce a wide variety of hemp-based products, leading to wide scale commerce and rapid development of their society. It may be their extensive use of hemp that enabled the Chinese to become the most cultured, the most civilized and most sophisticated society on earth at one time.

MAN'S EARLY KNOWLEDGE OF CANNABIS AS MEDICINE

It's not exactly clear when or where man first discovered the Cannabis plant, but the earliest reference dates back to the first millennium BC. According to Dr. Robert P. Walton, a noted American physician and authority on marijuana, hashish (the yellow resin-like substance excreted by the upper leaves of the Cannabis plant) was known as early as 1200 BC. Others believe it is considerably older. The Chinese Emperor Fu Hsi (ca. 2900 BC), whom the Chinese credit with bringing civilization to China, seems to have made reference to Ma, the Chinese word for Cannabis, noting that Cannabis was a very popular medicine that possessed both yin and yang. Hemp was so highly regarded in ancient China that the Chinese historically called their country the land of mulberry and hemp.[6] It is probably pertinent to note that Cannabis, hemp, is part of the mulberry family of plants. The Chinese Emperor Shen Nung (2737 BC) is also said to have espoused Cannabis as a cure-all for common ailments. The stories of Fu Hsi

---

5. *Webster's Third New International Dictionary (Unabridged)*. G.C. Merriam Publishing, Springfield, Mass: 1981, p. 329.

6. Able, p. 5.

and Shen Nung are most likely folklore that was used as a vehicle to pass on the knowledge of the medicinal benefits of Cannabis from one generation to the next; Cannabis may have been used as a common medicine in China long before the reigns of either one.

The first undisputed mention of the intoxicating properties of marijuana is found in "Researches" (450 BC) by the Greek historian Herodotus, known as the father of history, who describes a Scythian burial ceremony in a small hut with a pit for hot stones. The Scythians threw Cannabis on the stones, producing smoke, which they inhaled.[7] This description of the Scythian burial ceremony was confirmed in 1937, when Professor S.I. Rudenko, a Russian anthropologist, unearthed the remnants of a Scythian burial site and found a bronze cauldron filled with burnt Cannabis seeds; — the intoxicating effects may have been seen as the cleansing of their minds.[8] Rudenko also found shirts woven from hemp fiber and metal censers, designed for inhaling marijuana smoke. To Rudenko, the evidence suggested that inhalation of smoldering marijuana occurred not only in a religious context but also as an everyday activity, one in which Scythian women participated alongside the men.

In the second century AD, the Chinese surgeon Hua To developed an anesthetic made from cannabis resin and wine, called *ma-yo*, that he claimed enabled him to perform painless surgery. Among the operations he performed under this anesthesia were organ grafts, resections of intestines, laparotomies (incisions into the loin), and thoracotomies (incisions into the chest).[9] As Chinese physicians became more and more familiar with the properties of drugs, *ma* continued to increase in importance as a therapeutic agent.

SUCCESS BREEDS IMITATION

While Europe went through the period of feudalism and war known as the Dark Ages, the Chinese were reaping the rewards and prosperity of three thousand years of relative peace and freedom. It was the most advanced and inventive civilization on the face of the earth. They invented gunpowder, the crossbow, paper and even the lowly noodle, as well as a myriad of hemp-based products.

---

7. Goldman, Albert. *Grass Roots*. Warner Books: 1979, p. 59-62.

8. Rudenko, S.I. *Frozen Tombs of Siberia*. University of California Press, Berkeley, CA: 1970, p. 285.

9. Able, p. 12.

When Europe began to pick up speed as well, emerging from the Dark Ages late in the 10th century, it was in Venice and Genoa that the progress was first seen. And coincidentally, it was the Venetian Republic that was the first Western European country to industrialize around hemp.

In fact, it was Venice that elevated the art of processing raw hemp into rope, sails and fine linen-like cloth. Even today, fine Italian linen is the standard by which all linen products are judged. The high quality ropes and sail cloth they produced allowed Venetian merchants to travel farther than others before them, increasing their markets and influence beyond Southern Europe and the Mediterranean so that they dominated trade between all the countries bordering the Adriatic, Aegean, and Black Seas from the 11th century to well into the 17th century.

The Venetians were extremely meticulous about the quality of hemp they used — they even developed a hemp grading code that was legally enforced and righteously administered by the Hemp Guild. Hemp was known as "Quello Delle Cento Operazioni," meaning the basis of a hundred operations. Their skill in processing hemp helped make the Venetians the world's preeminent economic and military power. That prosperity gave them the leisure and resources to develop an increasingly inventive, creative, progressive civilization, bringing on the "Renaissance."

THE BRITISH CONTRIBUTION

The cultivation and exploitation of hemp spread quickly throughout Europe, and like the Venetians before them, the British became rich and powerful by mass-producing high quality hemp-based products. The British contribution was their ability to produce machinery that processed the raw hemp into finished goods of a uniform consistency and quality. That was especially important in the production of rope, which before then, varied in consistency — and, of course, a chain or rope is only as strong as its weakest link. Once rope could be produced of a uniform consistency, it was easy to determine how thick the rope had to be in order to lift a particular weight or perform a particular job.

Quality rope and sail were particularly important to Britain which, as an island nation, depended on shipbuilding. Without a large merchant and naval fleet, England would have been isolated and insignificant. Because of their utilization of hemp, by the mid-14th century England became the industrial goliath of Western Europe. To compete with Spain, Portugal and the Dutch in the exploration and exploitation of the world they built and outfitted a large merchant and navel fleet, further whetting the appetite for raw hemp.

The Spanish had an apparent advantage in its enormous fleet of enormous warships, the Armada, but even so, the British managed a victory (1588). In essence, the Spanish Armada was intended to be the vehicle for a devastating sneak attack on England. But, in a long day of fighting, the rapier will outperform the broadsword because it is lighter and easier to swing — especially after the first hour. Similarly, the British with their fleet of small ships were able to gain the advantage over the heavy, awkward ships of the Spanish Armada — and the quality of their sails and ropes contributed to the victory by giving them better speed. The large warships were slow to get underway, and when at rest had to be slowly maneuvered into position by the oars of galley slaves. The British not only defeated the Spanish Armada, they annihilated it — in a matter of days.

The need to build and maintain ships created a "boom" in the hemp market. Each ship required more than two hundred tons of rope and sails — and much of that needed to be replaced every couple of years.

While England could build all the machinery she needed to produce the finished products, she had a very finite land space on which to grow hemp in the first place. In 1533, King Henry VIII issuing a law requiring British farmers to grow hemp; thirty years later, Queen Elizabeth I increased the amount farmers were required to produce and increased the penalties for not growing enough hemp. The British were quickly running out of space to produce both the food and the hemp they needed — and that fact was a dominating motive behind England's colonization of the world, starting particularly with Ireland and ending only after she secured control of India in 1760.

It is also worth noting that England did not split from the Catholic Church simply because King Henry VIII wanted a divorce that the Catholic pope would not grant. There was enormous resentment of the Catholic Church left over from the Spanish Inquisition, and there was a power struggle between England, Spain and the Roman Catholic Church. By 1611, the British had their own bible — the King James version — a far more forgiving Protestant bible; and England no longer officially considered itself a Catholic state. As political competition spilled over into religious conflict, life in England became increasingly difficult for the more religiously inclined — particularly the Roman Catholics and Puritans (Calvinists). Many members of religious groups came to America in search of "religious freedom."

America's phenomenal and quick successes can best be explained by what attracted people to its shores, especially early on. Obviously, people came for many different reasons — some, because of philosophical and religious differences, some to escape the almost constant wars in Europe and persecution by the state, and many for the economic opportunity. People risked their lives crossing the Atlantic to make a new life for themselves free of the edicts of the aristocracy or religious domination, and many came with hopes of making their fortunes.

The British Crown mounted the Roanoke expedition (1582; it failed) and established the Jamestown Colony (1607) in an effort to explore possibilities in America. However, the real effort to populate and colonize America didn't come until the early 1630s. The fundamental reason for America's predominately Protestant British heritage is that Britain encouraged its people to colonize America — and they did that primarily because Britain's domestic hemp-based industry, the lifeblood of the economy, desperately needed a stable, reliable, and relatively cheap source of raw hemp.

The Age of British Colonization

The British realized their economic survival depended on controlling a large land mass. As early as 1582, the British had sent a ship of colonists to North America (the Roanoke Expedition), but the whole colony disappeared. No miracle hemp farm seemed to be in the offing.

Queen Elizabeth I and her generals were brutal in obtaining complete dominance of Ireland, which until then had still enjoyed some independence. England needed the Irish farmers to feed their factories with hemp; but the Irish had ideas of their own. Of course, they also knew the value of hemp, and were using it to build their own textile industry — they already had a reputation for producing high quality linen and linen-like fabrics. And, of course, the Irish were solidly Roman Catholic, whereas by then the British were solidly Protestant. The zeal to rid England of anyone who was not an enthusiastic part of the Anglican (Protestant) Church drove even some Englishmen who were less religious Protestants to Ireland.

In the interim, most of the hemp England needed was imported from the Baltic countries and later Russia. Russia quickly became the world's leading producer and exporter of hemp, helped by its vast, thinly populated lands and cheap peasant labor force. Hemp was bought and sold by weight, and everyone from the farmer to the longshoremen who loaded the ships would throw in rocks, wood, or other "fill," or wet it down, just to add weight. They even shipped rotten hemp. The British bitterly complained, but even the threat of immediate execution for anyone found adding weight failed to improve the purity of the shipped product. Efforts to secure hemp elsewhere — Poland, France, Holland, Italy, and Prussia (Germany), still left England dependent on Russia, and England's insatiable need kept growing. By 1630, 90% of their hemp came from Russia, and by 1633 that figure rose to 97%.[10] The British decided it was imperative to secure another source. As Able notes, this abject dependence on Russia left England terribly vulnerable.[11]

It wasn't only the navy that needed hemp. The British built their economic empire by exploiting the commercial properties of hemp. The worldwide demand for British-made fabrics and cordage outpaced their production capacity, even with Ireland securely under their control. In 1607, they sent more ships and more colonists to America, and established the Jamestown Colony. By now, they knew that a large land mass did exist in America, and they also learned that it was only sparsely populated by native Indian tribes (who were "uncivilized," and therefore didn't count).

In 1611, formal orders arrived from England instructing the colonists to raise hemp. The Spanish also cultivated hemp, when they first arrived in the Americas;[12] and so did the French, who colonized the northern parts of America. In 1616, Jamestown colonist John Rolfe reportedly boasted of growing hemp even better than that produced in England or Holland.[13]

It seemed that America could well be the answer to England's longstanding problem of hemp supply, and they continued their efforts to populate North America. At the same time, they turned their attention to India. However, establishing the British East India Company (1612) sparked a 150-year-long war for control of India. The Portuguese had enjoyed a 100-year monopoly on trade with

10. *Ibid.*, p. 73, quoting H. Zinn, *England and the Baltic in the Elizabethan Era* (Manchester University Press, 1972) p. 232.

11. *Ibid.*, p. 75.

12. The earliest Spanish explorers of Central and South America are know to have brought Cannabis seeds with them from Spain.

13. *Ibid.*, p. 77, quoting from *History of Agriculture in the Southern United States to 1860*, by L.C. Gray (1:25).

India, and later the Dutch, the French and a variety of India's local leaders contested their supremacy. The British gained a precarious hold on India in 1687 but it was not until 1760, when they defeated the French and Islamic army, that they were able to fully take control. (Ironically, by the way, hemp was both the reason the British went to India and the weapon Gandhi later used to destroy England's economic hold on the subcontinent.) Once India was securely theirs, the British quickly turned their attention and resources back to North America.

That might seem a bit tardy, given that Columbus arrived in 1492 (in Cuba and the surrounding islands, at least), and apparently the Chinese discovered California some seventy years earlier; and Leif Erickson arrived on the East Coast four centuries before that. Until there was a clear economic purpose, no one from the outside world had the abiding interest required to establish a permanent foothold in North America.

COTTON-PICKIN' COMPETITION

Cotton is an alternative to hemp in many applications, including but not limited to cloth; but it has short fibers, and is neither as strong nor as durable. However, once Eli Whitney invented the cotton gin (1793), cotton fibers became much cheaper to process than hemp — especially American cotton which was cultivated and picked by enslaved Africans. The cheap American product helped kill off Britain's hemp-based textile markets; the British, in fact, converted to using American cotton well before the US Civil War. That put many British textile workers out of a job.

It also devastated India's economy and caused extreme economic hardship there: hemp was India's most important export and England was its one and only customer. This left India dependent on England for finished goods, including fabrics, but with no way of paying for them. Mahatma Gandhi figured out that India's massive poverty was largely due to her dependence on British-made fabrics, now made from cotton that was not grown in India. He also realized that India would never be free of British rule until she began developing her own industries and became economically self sufficient. Gandhi began a boycott of all British products, particularly textiles, and as an example to his followers he abandoned his store-bought European-style suits and dressed himself in simple cloth — hemp cloth, which he spun and wove himself. India's hemp-based textile industry quickly became a reality and the importation of British made fabrics immediately declined. Gandhi's strategy proved extremely effective. The British realized that without a market for their products it was not economically feasible to continue their domination of India, and they left — relatively uneventfully.

THE GROWTH OF INFANT AMERICA

America's connection with Cannabis (hemp) is both interesting and ironic. The cultivation of hemp was a primary reason for America's colonization, yet the United States has led the worldwide effort to criminalize the cultivation and utilization of Cannabis.

Initially, the British didn't expect much hemp from its fledgling Jamestown colony; but they did expect, as much as possible, that the colony would begin paying its own way. The Virginia Company, by decree of King James I in 1619, ordered every colonist (property owner) to grow 100 plants specifically for export. Thus, England's only colony in America began to grow hemp in order to meet this obligation and, soon, to serve a growing demand in other colonies. Around 1629, a ship-building facility was established in Massachusetts that used a great deal of hemp. There were rope-walks producing rope and cordage, too, and many farms had small spinning operations to produce fabrics. Of course, every family's clothing and household linens were also routinely made at home.

The colonists began to grow (and export) tobacco, as well. The colonists had learned to smoke tobacco from the local Indians, and smoking quickly became fashionable both in the Virginia and in Europe. Tobacco was exclusively an American product, fostered by Virginia's warm climate, and it soon became the colony's number one export. Still, the colonies grew hemp as an alternative source of income to balance out those times when a glut of tobacco drove down prices.

After 1663, the Jamestown colony concentrated on tobacco and the bulk of Virginia's hemp cultivation moved to Kentucky and the Carolinas. The massive cultivation of Cannabis is reflected in town names like Hempstead and Hemp Hill, which can be found in many states east of the Mississippi.

The success of the Jamestown colony encouraged more settlers to come to America, and some of the next wave were Dutchmen. The Dutch represented a real economic threat to the British. Coming from a relatively small, industrialized country (like England), they established their New Netherlands settlement (later renamed New Amsterdam, and later, New York) in 1624, which quickly became a thriving, prosperous little community. The British responded to the Dutch presence by substantially increasing their efforts to populate and establish a dominant influence in America. To entice even more migration, the British Crown offered free transportation, free land — and free hemp seeds. England even made a standing offer to purchase the hemp the colonists produced, which gave them more economic security than they would have had at home.

The British Crown also increased the number of colonies in America by issuing a royal grant to Lord Baltimore to establish the Maryland Colony in 1632 and similar grants to Captain John Mason to establish the New Hampshire colony in 1635 and to Roger Williams to establish the Rhode Island colony in 1636. The Dutch weren't their only concern: in 1638, the Swedes established a settlement in Wilmington, Delaware. Unfortunately for the Swedes, they made a fatal mistake in taking over a Dutch outpost in 1654, and the New Amsterdam Dutch retaliated a year later by ousting the Swedes.

The Dutch were astute businessmen and traders. By 1650, they were doing more business with the colonies than the British were. The British Parliament responded by imposing the first of several trade restrictions on its American colonies, which forbid the colonies from trading with foreign merchants without a special license. In 1651, they went a step further and passed the Navigation Act, forbidding their colonies from importing or exporting goods via non-English owned ships. Given the lack of British ships, this caused shortages in the colonies. War actually broke out between the British and Dutch (1652-54) because of the Navigation Act. The British won, enabling England to again dominate trade with the colonies. In 1660, the British Parliament expanded the Navigation Act, regulating colonial commerce to suit England's needs. Specific commodities including "indigo" (which seems to have been a colloquial name for Indian hemp), sugar, and tobacco could only be shipped to British ports.

England's need for hemp continued to increase, which meant they were willing to pay more for it. They began offering a pound of tobacco for every pound of hemp, an offer they doubled in 1662. That was obviously meant to encourage the cultivation of hemp in the Northern colonies, where tobacco was considered something of a luxury. It was also meant to encourage exportation. The vast majority of America's colonial farmers grew hemp but most of it was used domestically. That did not help the mother country.

In Britain, the hemp industry continued its rapid growth but ran into a labor shortage caused by so many people migrating to America (and by the dispersion of its army and navy all over the world). London took advantage of unrest on the Continent to begin enticing people to cross the Channel and move to England. Again, from Ernest Able,

> To induce hemp workers who were fleeing persecution in Europe to seek refuge in England, Parliament passed a law in 1663 that any foreigner who settled in England or Wales and established a hemp related industry within three years would, upon taking the oath of allegiance to the king, be accorded the same rights and privileges as natural-born citizens.[14]

The British expanded their settlements on America's East Coast, but they were slow to move west. This allowed the French to settle the area around what would become Chicago, and from there the French explorer LaSalle moved south, along the Mississippi, to the location of today's New Orleans, claiming the Mississippi River and all the land surrounding it for France in 1682.

At the same time Spain was consolidating its grasp on large areas further west and to the south, including much of what we know as California, Colorado and the other southwestern states, and of course Mexico. However, neither the French nor the Spanish were settling or farming the land in great numbers; the Spanish were searching for gold and the French were primarily trapping for fur. Only the British and Dutch made a concerted effort to colonize America. All of Europe and Asia were using hemp, but they all had enough land to grow what they needed. All except the British and Dutch.

Two years after the British established the Carolina colony in 1663, Charles II ordered a 300-man force of British troops to seize the New Amsterdam settlement from the Dutch. Once that was accomplished, Charles II renamed it New York in honor of his brother James, the Duke of York and future English King. The Dutch recaptured New York in 1673 but ceded it back to the British in 1674, leaving England in virtual control of colonial America. The British went on to establish Pennsylvania in 1681, Delaware in 1682, and Georgia, the last British colony in America, in 1733.

The founder of Georgia, James Oglethorp, recommended settling the area along the Savannah River, saying:

> It is proposed the families there settled shall plant hemp and flax to be sent un-manufactured to England, whereby in time much ready money will be saved in this Kingdom, which now goes out to other countries [Russia] for the

---

14. *Ibid.*, p. 77, quoting Moore, B. *The Hemp Industry in Kentucky.* p. 12.)

purchase of these goods, and they will also be able to supply us with a great deal of good timber. 'Tis possible too they may raise white mulberry trees and send us good raw silk. But at the worst they will be able to live there, and defend that country from the insults of their neighbors, and London will be eased of maintaining a number of families which being let out of jail have at present no visible way to subsist.[15]

In 1705, the English Parliament passed the Trade Act, expanding the number of colonial products that could be exported only to English ports; these again included hemp, described as "naval stores." The Trade Act expired in 1713, but the bounties continued on naval stores for another eleven years, and the subsidy on hemp continued for an additional 16 years.[16]

Many of America's founding fathers became wealthy by producing hemp or hemp products, including George Washington, Thomas Jefferson and one of America's richest colonists, Robert "King" Carter. (Jefferson later abandoned his cultivation and spinning of hemp because he felt it was too hard on his slaves.) Jefferson received the first US patent for his invention of a machine that would break hemp (that is, start the process of extracting the fibers). Even Ben Franklin's wealth was derived from hemp — he was America's leading paper producer, and it was all made from hemp. Alexander Hamilton wrote a Treasury notice about the commodity in the 1790s: "Flax and hemp: Manufacturers of these articles have so much affinity to each other, and they are so often blended, that they may with advantage be considered in conjunction."

The value of hemp was universally recognized and the colonists commonly used raw hemp as a barter medium. Even the colonial governments, Virginia in 1682, Maryland in 1683 and Pennsylvania in 1706, allowed farmers to pay one-fourth of their taxes in hemp. This further encouraged the cultivation of hemp and promoted the economic well-being of the colony.

HEMP IN THE COLONIES

While most historians agree that colonial America was prosperous well before the mid-18th century, they do not really explain the source of that pros-

---

15. Boorstin, Daniel J. *The Americans: The Colonial Experience.* Vintage Books, New York: 1958, p. 77-78.

16. Schlesinger, Arthur M. Jr. *The Almanac of American History.* Barnes & Noble Books, Greenwich, CT: 1993, p. 73 & 76.

perity. Colonial America was an agrarian society, with 95% of the population involved in farming. But agrarian societies historically do not produce widespread wealth and prosperity. A cash crop like tobacco can produce prosperity; but far from all colonial farmers were producing tobacco and, although smoking quickly became fashionable, not enough people were smoking to account for the prosperity that existed in the colonies. Tobacco may have been America's premier cash export, but it was hemp that fueled the economic machine.

British colonial policy was meant to discourage industrialization; colonies were supposed to provide raw materials and serve as new markets for English finished goods. Hemp was the raw material England most needed, and they basically established their colonies worldwide as hemp farms. The plan backfired, however, and most American hemp was retained for local use. Just like their Chinese, Venetians, and English predecessors, colonial-era Americans processed the raw hemp into finished goods — rope, cloth, and paper. These industries rose up like an evil genie to compete with Britain's own domestic industries.

The Crown did everything it could to prevent competition — including forbidding the exportation of any machinery or machinery plans or parts to the colonies. Unfortunately for the British, the colonists didn't need British-made machinery, plans, or parts, as many of them had grown up in England and learned through apprenticeship all they needed to know to make their own.

The industrialization of colonial America began innocently enough. The first industry in America was textiles. The people of the Jamestown colony, which started in 1607, as well as the Pilgrims who arrived in 1620, needed clothing and household linens. Soon, fed by the abundance of lush forests, America's first shipbuilding facility was established in the Plymouth colony by the Massachusetts Bay company in 1629, and the need for rope and sail to outfit those ships quickly created a burgeoning domestic market for all the local hemp. The abundance of wood also encouraged craftsmen to establish cottage industries producing furniture and cabinetry. Gradually, the thriving domestic industries made America independent from England; and so, very little raw hemp was ever exported to England despite the fine words. For more than two centuries, in economic terms hemp was the most important agricultural crop America produced.

Colonial America was rich in natural resources, but in those days there was not much of a cash economy. People grew, made, or traded for what they needed. Farmers' wives and daughters would spin and weave their own cloth, from which they made the family's clothing and linens (bed sheets, towels, napkins, handkerchiefs, and tablecloths). The weekly gathering of the local women ("spinning bees" or "quilting bees," where many hands would help make quick work of a big project or, at least, pleasant conversation would mask the drudgery of endless repetitive tasks) was about the only social contact most colonialists had with their neighbors. An individual or a sewing circle that produced better work than others might lead to a small business in the trading or bartering of cloth and/or clothing, which might bring a family a little more money. Before long, some of the larger hemp farmers started large scale spinning operations, thus establishing America's fledgling textile industry.

The British were not particularly concerned about colonial housewives producing homemade fabrics for their own use, but they did become extremely concerned by around 1718 when a group of professional spinners and weavers arrived in Boston from Ireland. In the years following, the quality, quantity, and variety of America-made textiles dramatically improved. This really marked the beginning of America's textile industry. That was a genuine threat; but the British were tied up in Ireland and India and were fighting almost continually with the French.

At just this time, American colonists also began producing their own paper — hemp-based paper — which they went on to use to produce their own newspapers and books. Until 1883, 75-90% of all the paper the world produced was made with hemp fiber.[17]

All this still left England hungry for hemp. The British were at war with the people of Ireland — for some 160 years; they were fighting the Portuguese, Dutch, French and Indians for control of India. And they were involved in the very costly endeavor of colonizing and defending their America colonies from the Spanish, French, and native Indians to ensure their dominance in North America. The extraordinarily bold and aggressive manner in which the British pursued their interests is a sign of their desperation. Either they underestimated the cost of acquiring control or they decided the alternative was too grim.

And, although their resources were stretched to the limits, they were extraordinarily successful in their efforts — taking control of Ireland in 1690, and India in 1760; and they were very much in control in America. In fact, most Americans were happy living under the protection of the British Crown. For most, living conditions in colonial America were good (far better than in England), taxes were reasonably low; and with the British busy in Ireland and India, there were few British soldiers roaming the country enforcing the king's

---

17. Herer, Jack. *The Emperor Wears No Clothes*. Hemp Publishing, Van Nuys, CA: 1985, p. 7.

will. The British did maintain a token force in the colonies, but even in the French and Indian Wars it was predominantly American colonists, not British troops, who did the fighting.

RELIGION IN COLONIAL AMERICA

Most of the early settlers came to America because there was no opportunity and no work for them back home. They wanted the chance to own and farm their own land instead of working as serfs (or sharecroppers). Many came to escape the wars and religious strife. Thousands of Englishmen and women migrated to North America after 1610, making the Jamestown Colony and surrounding area a thriving community long before the pilgrims landed at Plymouth Rock on December 21, 1620. By the time of the American Revolution, Virginia had grown to an enormous size (five or six times bigger than the State of Virginia today).

Although a great deal of mythology is attached to the Pilgrims' landing at Plymouth, it was actually a rather insignificant event that had little to do with the colonization of America. According to Pete Skirbunt, "The Pilgrims...were 102 people who sailed from England. Of these, only 35 were actually seeking religious freedom. They were 'Separatists' from the Church of England. The others, called 'Strangers,' simply wanted to leave England for a variety of reasons and start life over in America."

(By the way, "Pilgrim" is just a name that was applied some 170 years later to the first groups of Puritan migrants.) The Puritans were fanatics, as exemplified by the Salem Witch Trials. Although quick to criticize the morals and work ethics of others, they gave no evidence of being any more productive or prosperous than anyone else. In fact, quite the opposite is true. They arrived in New England on the first day of winter, totally un-equipped to survive in the wilderness. The Pilgrims were focused on their religion; they weren't farmers and they were not great hunters or fishermen; but they were determined. Apparently, they survived the first winter by finding and stealing caches of food the Indians had put away for themselves. It is quite possible that the Indians showed the Pilgrims how to grow corn and to fish and hunt for themselves just to keep them from stealing their food (what else could they do, kill them?). Thanksgiving celebrates the meeting of these two cultures but in truth, Thanksgiving speaks more to the humanity and generosity of America's native Indians. Inviting the Indians to dinner to share their first harvest was the Pilgrims' way of thanking them for teaching them how to feed themselves. However, the Pilgrims don't seem to have been fast learners, and they may not have wanted to do more than feed themselves and pray — in general, the Plymouth colony did not prosper, compared to other colonies, and by 1629 it was on the verge of collapsing when the Massachusetts Bay Company took control and put the Pilgrims to work building ships, and fishing. So that, in a sense, it was hemp that saved them, too.)

The reason the Puritans did not face the same discrimination in America as they did in England was that religion, particularly organized religion (the Church), was much less important in the colonies. There were, of course, plenty of churches and congregations supporting them, but those were almost entirely in well-established communities, not on the Western frontier (which was not very far "West" at that time). Actually, most colonial Americans were not all that religious. They were not regular church goers, and they were not forced to leave England or Europe in order to be free to express their religious beliefs — to the contrary, many of them came to America in part to escape the imposition of religion in their lives.

Yes, the 35 Pilgrims and the religious cults that followed them were a small minority of the 11,000-plus other colonists.[18] The rapid colonization of America was driven by something other than religion. And rapid it was: from slightly over 4,000 Europeans in 1620, America grew six-fold to 24,000 by 1640, then doubled by a decade later, then doubled again by 1670 and again by 1690, to a population of 192,000. All but a small minority of these 17th-century colonists were Protestants — the dominant religion in both England and colonial America. These were the same Protestants who, only decades earlier, had made life miserable for Catholics, Puritans, Quakers and others, forcing them out of England. Religious freedom was not a primary motivating factor for the overwhelming majority of American colonists.

Life was hard and most of the colonists were single young men, who spent nearly all their time on the farm or on the outskirts of civilization, trying to eke out a living by trapping, or trading with the Indians. They rarely saw a white woman, and they drank large quantities of beer, rum, wine and hard cider (partly because much of the water and [unpasteurized] milk was not safe to drink, and coffee [first introduced in the colonies in the 1660s] and tea were either too expensive or not available at all). Even the Pilgrims apparently drank beer.

---

18. Kurlansky, Mark. *Cod, A Biography of the fish that Changed the World.* Penguin Books, 1998.

"Aboard ship [the Mayflower], the voyagers ate bread, biscuits, pudding, cheese, crackers, and dried meats and fruits. Instead of water, they brought barrels of beer — a standard practice in the days before refrigeration, because beer remained potable longer than water."[19]

The general belief in colonial America was in an "almighty God," but there was widespread skepticism about organized religion, which was considered a real social threat — especially with the memories of the Spanish Inquisition and the Salem Witch Trials still fresh in people's minds. Most colonists, including most of America's founding fathers (including Washington, Jefferson, Franklin, and Samuel and John Adams) disassociated themselves from organized religion and referred to themselves as "Deists" — not Protestants, Catholics or anything else. Deists were freethinkers of the 17th and 18th centuries, who felt that their belief in God was compatible with the rationalism of the "Enlightened Age." They held that one's belief in God should be a personal rather than public matter, and they believed that morality was derived from natural law, not from revelation. "Deists," today, are generally known as "Agnostics." Apparently, the colonial era "Deists" didn't feel threatened enough by organized religion to pass laws restricting the practice of any religious belief — perhaps because they, along with the outright atheists, were in the overwhelming majority.

Unfortunately, many religious cults, and many quite fanatical ones, established churches in colonial America — churches that not only demanded their followers live according to their teachings but that sought to impose their will on the surrounding communities, as well. Push came to shove when a number of town councils, dominated by church members, passed laws that imposed additional taxes intended to financially support the local church. Forcing people to support the church through taxes outraged the majority of colonists and reaffirmed their skepticism and/or resentment of religious influence. Organized religion came under heavy public criticism, exemplified by Thomas Paine's very popular and often quoted book, *The Age of Reason*. (Too bad Paine did not have greater success: We still suffer from the imposition of extreme moralistic views, including when it comes to the question of recreational intoxicants.)

This encroachment by the church may well have been the primary reason America's founding fathers included the concept of separation of church and state in the Constitution. Constitutional scholars have variously framed the

---

19. Skirbunt, Peter. *The Pilgrims' Real First Thanksgiving*. From the US Dept. of Defense website, http://www.defenselink.mil/news/Nov1999/n11221999_9911221.html, accessed Dec. 1999.

intent of the First Amendment as either to protect religious people from government, or to protect government from religious people. However, since the constitution only speaks of the rights of the people — not the government's rights or religious rights — it is far more likely that the actual intent was to protect the American people from being dominated by organized religion, any religion.

According to the first official census (1790), when the Constitution was debated (1787) there were approximately four million people in colonial America, with a variety of religious backgrounds. It would have been impossible for the founding fathers to officially sanction any one religion for the whole nation — the Constitution never would have been ratified. In fact, chances are that a civil war would have broken out. Including the separation of church and state as part of the constitution reflected a "live-and-let-live" philosophy. It also ended the ability of the church to impose taxes, and it diminished the church's influence on the society.

THE USE OF CANNABIS, OTHER THAN AS HEMP

We know colonial Americans were aware of the medicinal properties of Cannabis. It was one of the few medicines they had, and they used it as commonly as we use aspirin today. That means that in addition to farming hemp for fiber they cultivated "garden varieties" of Cannabis with a high Tetrahydrocannabinol content — marijuana. They either smoked it, brewed it as tea, or ingesting it. Washington's diary entries indicate that he grew hemp at Mount Vernon, his plantation, for about 30 years.[20] According to his agricultural ledgers, he had a particular interest in the medicinal use of Cannabis, and several of his diary entries indicate that he indeed was growing Cannabis with a high Tetrahydrocannabinol (THC) content — marijuana. "Sowed hemp [presumably Indian hemp] at muddy hole by swamp" (May 12-13, 1765), indicates he was growing it away from the hemp he grew for fiber. "Began to separate the male from female plants at do [sic] — rather too late" (August 7, 1765), and, "Pulling up the (male) hemp. Was too late for the blossom hemp by three weeks or a month" (August 29, 1766), indicates that he was trying to grow female plants, which produce a high THC content.[21]

---

20. *Washington's Diary Notes*, Library of Congress (Volume 33, page 270).

21. *The Diaries of George Washington*, Houghton Mifflin Pub., 1925.

Like all farmers, Washington probably sampled the quality and potency of what he grew, and he may have used this hemp to treat his chronic tooth aches. Jefferson (also a hemp farmer) noted in his diary that he smoked hemp for relief from migraine headaches.

Actually, it was a common practice for colonial Americans to smoke Cannabis, of varying degrees of potency, in lieu of tobacco, for recreational and for medicinal purposes, and the practice probably lasted until well after the Civil War. It was readily available, and free — you could simply pick it, dry it, and smoke it. Unless it is grown specifically for its medicinal or intoxicating properties, ordinary hemp contains relatively little Tetrahydrocannabinol, the intoxicant. African-Americans and Hispanic-Americans, too, have a long history of using Cannabis as a recreational intoxicant. Later, the US lost the knowledge and appreciation of the pleasure of smoking Cannabis, because after the Civil War the use of hemp as a raw material dramatically declined; later, the end of segregation marked a rejuvenation of that practice and included the White community.

The primary market for hemp was the ship-building industry and the appearance of the "Iron Clads," the steamships Monitor and Merrimac, drastically changed the way ships were built. Also, tobacco products increasingly supplanted Cannabis, particularly after the introduction of pre-made cigarettes and the development of sophisticated distribution networks.

In the early days, even wealthy gentleman farmers and businessmen commonly smoked Cannabis, sometimes the ordinary kind, sometimes more potent. No fewer than eight US presidents (Washington, Jefferson, Madison, Monroe, Andrew Jackson, Taylor, Pierce, and Lincoln)[22] have been identified as Cannabis (hemp) smokers. Washington reportedly preferred a pipe full of "the leaves of hemp" to alcohol, and wrote in his diaries that he enjoyed the fragrance of hemp flowers. Washington and Jefferson, both known to have grown medicinal hemp (marijuana), are said to have exchanged smoking blends as personal gifts. In a letter, Washington wrote, "The artificial preparation of hemp, from Silesia, is really a curiosity." It has been suggested that this may be a reference to hashish. Monroe apparently began smoking Cannabis while he was Ambassador to France and continued using it to the age of 73. Andrew Jackson, Zachary Taylor

---

22. Chris Conrad, *Hemp, Lifeline to the Future*, p. 193, quoting from a June 21, 1975 article in *Green Egg Magazine* entitled "Pot and Presidents," that told of the research of Dr. Burk, president of the American Historical Reference Society and a Smithsonian Institute consultant.

and Franklin Pierce reportedly smoked Cannabis with their troops and wrote home of the pleasures of smoking hemp. Pierce, a reformed heavy drinker, is said to have written home that smoking hemp was the only good thing about the Mexican War. And Abe Lincoln, who grew up poor and probably couldn't afford tobacco, reportedly said he liked nothing better than sitting on his front porch smoking from his hemp pipe.[23]

These realizations raise the quirky question of whether America's founding fathers and several of our early presidents were "pot heads"? (The Clintonesque answer, of course, is that it depends on what your definition of pot head is.)

These men never would have attained their leadership roles if their peers had thought the use of Cannabis negatively affected their mental or physical capacities. In fact, judging from the extraordinary accomplishment of drafting the Declaration of Independence (written by Jefferson) and the Constitution (in which Madison played a primary role), the two principle documents upon which the United States is founded, it is hard to imagine that their abilities were impaired in any way.

Furthermore, Washington, who was unquestionably the man who brought life to the Constitution, couldn't have been more beloved by the people. Washington's widespread popularity was legendary; however, it is important to note that he did not attain the love, respect, and loyalty of his troops or the American people because he was a military genius. In fact, Washington had not distinguished himself as a military strategist or leader before being appointed Commander-in-Chief of the Revolutionary Army. He was put in charge mainly because he attended the Continental Congress meetings, day after day, wearing his former military uniform, the uniform he had worn during the French and Indian Wars, leaving the impression that he was more experienced than the other candidates — and, of course, he looked great on his white horse! But looks alone were not good enough, and since Washington did not immediately produce meaningful results there were efforts afoot within the military and in Congress to replace him as Commander-in-Chief. His only military victory was the surprise attack on Trenton, New Jersey, on the morning of December 25, 1776. Even the final battle of the Revolutionary War, the defeat of Cornwallis at York-

---

23. The Hohner Harmonica Company found a letter in its archives from Abraham Lincoln, stating that he liked nothing more than sitting on his porch, playing his harmonica and smoking hemp from his corncob pipe. Also, Michael Meyer's video, *The Drug Cartel, The Control for World Economics,"* Copyright 1993, Len Bauman Productions.

town, Virginia, on October 19, 1781, was due primarily to the unexpected but timely arrival of the French fleet.

That is not to imply that Washington was not a man of substance; he clearly grew into the position of responsibility he had taken on. What the people really loved about Washington was that he truly was a man-of-the-people. He treated everyone as equals — he was there, like everyone else, to help win America's independence from England. He was the ultimate role model, the kind of man they all wanted to be. And what is most important, many of them, just like Washington, were hemp farmers — so that there was a commonality of concerns, ideals and feelings about the events of the day.

When Washington finally agreed to become the first president, the United States was already beginning to fall apart. The Articles of Confederation under which the Continental Congress was organized and operated had numerous flaws that especially hindered interstate commerce. The Constitutional Convention that took place at Philadelphia's Independence Hall in 1787 was convened specifically to address and fix those problems (not to scrap it and start over; that was Alexander Hamilton's idea, and when he proposed it a lacerating war of words broke out).

The US Constitution that was eventually produced was bitterly debated and was not at all popular because it created and empowered a federal government, when most Americans felt allegiance to the individual states.

Washington's support of the Constitution and his reluctant acceptance of the presidency were the keys to its ratification, implementation, and ultimate success. His virtual coronation as President of the United States simply reflected his popularity. He could have made the presidency into a monarchy, but told those addressing him as "Your Majesty" to simply refer to him as "Mr. President." He also felt that it would not be consistent with the best interest of the people to create a dynasty, so he served only eight years as president — thus setting a precedent for his successors. Actually, Washington didn't want to serve a second four-year term at all, but there did not seem to be anyone else available who could moderate the almost constant bickering between Jefferson and Hamilton, and Washington believed both men were important to America's future.

These men had very good minds; no one can claim that any of them was in any way impaired by smoking Cannabis, of whatever kind. Their insight, vision and ideology set high new standards.

It is also significant that, while people all across colonial America took up the habit of smoking, the cultivation of tobacco was pretty much confined to

Virginia. Farmers living in the northern colonies more commonly smoked hemp leaves. Some people like to think that smoking hemp leaves rather than tobacco may have contributed to the development of more liberal Northern attitudes. The most hotly contested issue at the Constitutional Convention in 1787 was slavery, and the opposing sides were undeniably split along geographical lines — North and South — and this was years before Eli Whitney invented the cotton gin and well before cotton and slavery became major economic issues for the South.

But the slavery issue was not resolved in 1787, and in 1793 Whitney did invent his cotton gin; cotton became far cheaper than hemp to turn into cloth. Gradually it supplanted hemp as America's textile industry standard. Cotton farming was much more profitable, especially in the Southern states where slavery was predominately practiced.

We also know that many of the colonists who inherited and kept slaves — including Washington and Jefferson, who are believed to have smoked hemp/marijuana regularly — were actually opposed to slavery, and in their wills many bequeathed their slaves their freedom. They did use slaves to build their mansions and tend their vast farms, and regularly slept with their female slaves; but they seem to have treated them better than many others did. Jefferson's long-term relationship with his servant Sally Hemings was a common practice in those days, and mirrored similar relationships his father and grandfather had with their servants.

It is also worth noting that while slaves rarely had access to alcohol, they did have access to hemp; and they had knowledge of the intoxicating properties and medicinal properties of Cannabis. They brought that knowledge with them from Africa, and easily recognized the unique leaves of the plant they knew as "dada." Actually, the use of marijuana as an intoxicant was a well-established practice long before the white man ever discovered Africa, and the Africans probably used it as commonly and as long as their Arab neighbors have used hashish — another form of the same intoxicant. African women reportedly smoked it to stupefy themselves during childbirth. They would grind the seeds into a mush (gruel) that they used to wean children on, and they made it into bread. African tribes historically treated anti-social behavior by forcing the transgressor to ingest large quantities of marijuana smoke; they had an almost nonexistent repeat rate. South African mine owners even supplied "dada" to their workers because it helped them work harder with less fatigue. That situation dramatically stopped after the Boer War, when the British took control —

the British saw the use of "dada" by the blacks as a threat to their supremacy. Undoubtedly, the African slaves passed that knowledge on to American-born slaves, but rarely to white Americans, whom they distrusted and rarely spoke to.

THE SPLIT IN BRITISH-AMERICAN RELATIONS

Historians still debate what exactly caused the split between colonial America and "Mother England"; one possibility is that historians have grossly overlooked the importance of hemp to both sides. Jefferson envisioned America always remaining an agrarian-based society. Many historians find that puzzling and they simply dismiss it as an intellectual error. However, when we consider the importance of hemp to the prosperity of colonial America — including Jefferson's personal wealth, before he became involved in politics — his vision of an agrarian society makes a great deal more sense. (By the way, in a letter to George Fleming, December 29, 1815, Thomas Jefferson noted, "Flax is so injurious to our lands and of so scanty produce that I have never attempted it. Hemp, on the other hand, is abundantly productive and will grow forever on the same spot."[24] George Washington instructed his men to: "Make the most of the Indian hemp seed, and sow it everywhere!"[25]

There are many reasons why historians have not acknowledged the importance of hemp to the development of colonial America; for one thing, there was relatively little record keeping and what there was now seems vague or misleading. Most of our knowledge about commerce in those days comes from shipping records, meaning exports. That leaves us in ignorance about domestic consumption, and most of the hemp the colonies produced was used domestically.

We also need to recognize that the colonies were home to settlers from all over, and hemp was known by various names in different parts of the country. References to "Indigo" — from India or Indian — may have been a colloquialism used to refer to Indian hemp, meaning hemp produced from seeds imported by the British from India. We certainly weren't shipping England large quantities of blue dye; "Indigo" must have meant something other than today's dictionary definition. Then there is the vague label of "Naval Stores," of which hemp in the

---

24. Conrad, Chris. *Hemp, Lifeline to the Future.* Creative Xpressions Publications, Los Angeles, CA: 1993, p. 304.

25. Note to the gardener at Mount Vernon, 1794. *The Writings of George Washington.*

form of rope and sail must made up a large proportion. Tobacco, by way of contrast, was a rather new discovery, and it had only one name; everyone identified it as tobacco, and we shipped it to Europe as tobacco.

Until the mid-18th century, Britain ruled its American colonies more by consent than by force, and the Americans were generally comfortable being part of the British Empire. The token military presence was mainly to protect the colonists from Indians, to insure against encroachment by the French, Spanish, and Dutch, and to back up British-appointed colonial governors. They were predominantly stationed in port cities and on the frontier; the overwhelming majority of colonists rarely saw British troops. The farms were spread out over the countryside and people lived simple, mostly self-sufficient lives; they rarely went to town, much less the cities.

The British Crown, however, was not particularly happy with its American colonies. They hadn't provided men or financial support to fight its many wars and weren't really contributing as expected to the wealth of England. Instead, they were fast becoming a competitor and a threat to England's future as a world economic power. The British were not getting the hemp they expected and British merchants were bitterly complaining that the colonies were not purchasing British-made finished goods. The Americans were also flagrantly ignoring many of Britain's laws, like the Navigation Act. To the British Crown, the colonies they had nurtured and protected were now shirking their responsibilities. The population had grown in 150 years. The colonies no longer needed nurturing, and it was time they started contributing to the treasury.

Actually, Britain's aggressive military policies around the world had been quite costly and they were heavily in debt. Now, they demanded the colonies pay in gold or silver for everything they imported from England. The British did not really want to go to war with their cousins; they had been in an almost constant state of war for hundreds of years and were tired of it. The British government, however, felt it needed to act decisively or risk being perceived as weak by enemies around the world.

The colonists, however, believed they had built America and they were angry with the British (and the French as well) for stirring up the Indians and endangering their lives in the French and Indian Wars (1754-63) that were part of the "Seven Years War" between England and France. The colonists weren't fighting for British supremacy; they were fighting for their lives and property. With colonial wealth in the form of gold and silver being shipped to England, the colonies were experiencing a massive economic slowdown. Hemp producers and processors were particularly unhappy with the shipping restrictions because they allowed British merchants to control the market and dictate the price they paid colonial producers. Indeed, many colonists came from the bottom rung of English society, or even jails; some had come to America to escape British persecution in one form or another, and some were religious outcasts — they felt little loyalty to "Mother England." Also, by this time, there were hundreds of thousands of colonists from all over Europe (Holland, Germany, Sweden, France, Spain and more).

The relationship between England and America dramatically began to change after 1760 when the British finally established their dominance of India, and particularly after 1763 when they defeated France. Now, the British definitely turned their attention to America, intent on correcting a number of issues that they were too busy to address earlier. The first thing they did was to substantially strengthen their military presence, to back up their demands — which included the Sugar Act (1764), the Stamp Act (1765), and the Townsend Acts (1767), which further restricted shipping and imposed additional taxes on the colonies, followed in 1774 by another series of laws known locally as "The Intolerable Acts." The colonists retaliated with an outright boycott of British products — of which the Boston Tea Party was a memorable, if misrepresented, part.

Life in colonial America drastically changed as the number of British troops increased. The population became very much aware of the political leanings of their friends and neighbors, identifying them as either patriot or Tory (British sympathizers), indicating whether or not they could be trusted. Boston was a hotbed of anti-British sentiment, stirred up by the writings of Thomas Paine and the oratory of Patrick Henry. The real rebel, the "instigator," was Samuel Adams, the leader of a group of Boston rowdies known as "the Sons of Liberty." Sam Adams was the original political "spin doctor." In 1770, Adams took a minor incident in which a squad of British soldiers, in self defense, fired into a mob that was taunting and stoning them, and turned it into "the Boston Massacre." Actually, the soldiers were not ordered to fire; it was more a panic reaction by one soldier that quickly spread to the others. It suited Adams better to highlight it as "the first shedding of blood in America's Revolutionary War." Adams even had Paul Revere come up with a now famous engraving depicting the British troops firing on an unarmed group of civilians, creating an image of British intolerance in the minds of the colonists. Adams also planned the Boston Tea Party in 1773, wherein the Sons of Liberty (dressed as Indians) boarded British merchant ships and dumped their cargo of tea in the bay in retaliation for an imposed tea tax.

Perhaps the most important thing Adams did was to get his cousin John Adams involved in the revolution.

America became a nation of coffee drinkers in part because of a deep-rooted contempt that developed for the British, from before the Revolutionary War until well after the World War I. Drinking tea identified one as a Tory, a possible British sympathizer.

THE WAR FOR INDEPENDENCE BEGINS

With all the taxes and tensions mounting, 56 delegates representing twelve colonies gathered at Carpenters Hall in Philadelphia on September 5, 1774 to write King George III a letter. They took the trouble to outline the colonies' grievances, in the faint hope of securing more fair treatment from the King — and thus to avoid having to do anything more drastic. It is unlikely they expected a direct written response from King George, and indeed they did not get one.

Anti-British sentiment had been building and it didn't take long before the tinder was lit. The confrontation at Lexington and Concord, the proverbial "shot heard around the world," was almost accidental. The colonists were afraid that British troops might set out from Boston to seize a large "rebel" stockpile of weapons and munitions that was being stored sixteen miles away in Concord, Massachusetts, but no one knew when, or whether, that would happen. The colonial "rebels" had a network of people watching for British troop movement and signals established to warn of impending danger; of course, the signal was "one if by land and two if by sea." Six companies of British infantry under the command of Major John Pitcairn set out from Boston on the evening of April 18, 1775, and that night two lamps shown from the steeple of the Old North Church in Boston, indicating that the British were crossing the Charles River. That sent Paul Revere and William Dawes riding out to warn the citizens of Lexington and the surrounding towns that the "British are coming."

At dawn the next morning, seventy armed colonial militiamen gathered at Lexington Square to take on the British troops en route to Concord, several miles up the road; but realizing they were badly out-numbered, they started to disperse. Nobody knows which side fired the first shot, but at the end of a five-minute battle there were eight dead and ten wounded militiamen. The British troops continued on to Concord. Word of the incident quickly spread and by the time the British arrived at the Old North Bridge there were several hundred angry militiamen ready to engage them. The British retreated after about five minutes of fighting and started marching back to Boston. The colonial militia followed them all the way back, picking them off one by one from behind trees, boulders, and buildings. Reportedly, many of the militiamen went home for lunch or to take care of a few chores, then came back to shoot a few more "redcoats," still marching in formation. The British column arrived in Boston late that afternoon, short by 273 men; 95 colonial militiamen also died that day.

Three weeks later, 56 delegates met again, representing the same 12 colonies, in a large room of the Pennsylvania State house in Philadelphia, known now as Independence Hall, for the Second Continental Congress. Georgia, which did not send a delegation to the first Continental Congress, was again not represented directly but indicated a willingness to be party to whatever decisions were made, as they had for the first Congress. A delegation from Georgia finally did show up in July. The delegates had mixed feelings about what course of action to take. Some delegates wanted to declare independence no matter what the cost, and some, although unhappy with the British regulations and taxes, still considered themselves loyal British subjects. Some wanted to send King George another letter. Most were not yet prepared to go to war with Britain, the greatest military power on earth.

Meanwhile, British troops were methodically seeking out militiamen to take their revenge for the Lexington and Concord debacle and many other sniper shootings. It could only be a matter of time before they showed up in Philadelphia. Time was running out. Without quite working out the more irksome details, such as how to pay for it, on June 17, 1775, the Congress officially established the Continental Army and selected George Washington as Commander-in-Chief. It was also about this time that Thomas Paine's book Common Sense was published and circulated, aiming to convince the colonists that there was no way for England and the colonies to resolve their differences peacefully.

When news of the formation of the Continental Army reached King George, he officially declared the colonies in rebellion — meaning that England was declaring war. When his declaration of war was read to the delegates, Ben Franklin stood up and said, "Gentlemen, if we don't all hang together, we will surely hang separately." The delegates quickly agreed to declare independence and Jefferson was given the task of drafting the document, which he did with talent, clarity and speed. The Declaration of Independence was officially adopted on July 2, 1776.

The 56 men who signed it were pledging their lives, their fortunes, and their sacred honor to the cause of independence for the colonies. These were not adolescents, delinquents or fools; they were serious, well-educated men, among the more successful of their peers, who weighed the risks and decided this was their best chance going forward. Defeating the British would be an enormous challenge, but it seemed feasible.

For the record, five of those who signed the Declaration were captured by the British, who tortured and then executed them as traitors. Over a dozen were victims of British retaliation; their homes, businesses, and property were vandalized, looted, seized or burned to the ground. Nine fought and died of wounds or hardship relating to the war. Two lost their sons in the Revolutionary Army; another had two sons captured. Many of these men were hounded and hunted by the British and many died penniless. Twenty-four were lawyers and jurists, eleven were merchants, and most of the rest were simply hemp farmers and/or manufacturers of hemp-based products.

Most of America's founding fathers were hemp farmers and/or operated businesses that converted raw hemp into finished products. These men took a leading role in establishing the new government, both in the legislature and in the field, because they felt they had the most to win or lose. The rallying cry may have been "No taxation without representation" but, realistically, the Revolutionary War was an economic war to determine which country, England or America, profited from America's bountiful resources — especially hemp.

The Declaration of Independence was a statement of intent. To draft a document establishing a government, the Articles of Confederation, took another seventeen months. Essentially, the first two years of the Revolutionary War were fought without a legitimate government in place and without any means of paying for the guns, uniforms, blankets, tents, horses, food, and everything else. Haym Solomon, a Jewish businessman and broker, sold bonds to support the revolution. The bonds were redeemable after the war, with interest, if and only if America won. America did win; but everyone involved was more or less bankrupted by the events — Solomon included.

However, the war dramatically increased the need for hemp, so that the price of raw hemp rose tenfold. Canvas tents, uniforms to transform the rag tag men into a unified force, blankets for the soldiers, and drafts for documents including the Declaration of Independence were all made of hemp. Betsy Ross purportedly made the first flag from hemp cloth and until 1937 all American flags were made from hemp.[26] The only men exempted from military service were those involved in hemp-related businesses, but still most of those who fought in the war must have been either farmers or otherwise related to the hemp trade. Hemp's military importance was dramatically pointed out in 1781 when the traitor Benedict Arnold led a force of British troops in attacking and destroying hemp farms along with a public rope-walk (a hemp-rope manufacturing facility) in Warwick, Virginia, which supplied America's navy.

WHY HEMP WAS NOT A MAJOR REVOLUTIONARY ISSUE

Contentious as the commercial competition over hemp and finished goods had been, by the time of the American Revolution the British no longer needed America's hemp. What they needed was a share of the profits it produced, to pay off their war debts. By 1760, the British had secured control of both Ireland and India, which provided all the hemp they needed. Their relatively wealthy America cousins were still restricted from selling or shipping hemp either as a raw material or as naval stores to anyone but the British, but the colonies were using most of their hemp domestically, anyway. On the other hand, the British Crown had invested a great deal of time, effort, and money colonizing and protecting America and they expected a return on their investment, which is why the British began imposing taxes on commodities like sugar, stamps, and tea that the colonists used every day.

THE WAR ENDS AND HEMP USE DECLINES

The Revolutionary War ended on September 19, 1781 when Washington defeated Cornwallis at Yorktown. The Tories disappeared and even many British soldiers shed their red coats and blended in, as life in the colonies was far better than life at the bottom of the heap in England. And the value of hemp plummeted.

As the jubilation wore off, the idea of independence lost a little of its shine when everyone settled down enough to consider the fact that England was the marketplace of the world. The British had defeated their competitors — the Dutch, Spanish, and the French — either militarily or economically, and there

---

26. Herer, Jack. *The Emperor Wears No Clothes*, p. 5.

was only a limited market for the products America produced. The French were in the throes of their own revolution. Domestically, the need for hemp dropped dramatically after the war.

But the influx of hopeful new immigrants went on unabated. Between the end of the Revolutionary War and 1810 the population almost doubled, and by 1830 the population approached 13 million. The inflows of people and investment enabled America to continue growing at an extremely rapid rate.

Meanwhile, both the textile and paper industries were looking for cheaper alternatives. Before Eli Whitney's invention of the cotton gin, which mechanically cleaned the cotton and prepared it for spinning, cotton was insignificant — it accounted for less than 5% of all the fabrics produced on this side of the Atlantic. The rest was mainly from hemp, which produced warmer, softer, more durable fabric. Suddenly, cotton had a technological and economic advantage.

Preparing hemp for spinning required separating the fibers from the hemp stalks, an onerous and time-consuming task. Raising and harvesting cotton was more difficult, but with the advantage of slave labor the South kept costs low. Most of the hemp was grown in the Northern states, where slaves were few. America's textile industry made a strictly economic decision when it decided to make cotton the industry standard. Of course, it made the Southern plantation owners enormously wealthy, and that is why in the South they call it "King Cotton."

In 1790, the South was producing a thousand tons of cotton per year. By 1860, it was a million tons. In the same period, 500,000 slaves incresaed to 4,000,000.[27]

It was also strictly an economic decision when the paper industry switched from hemp to wood. Trees, from the new land's plentiful forests, were essentially free for the taking. The quality of the paper wasn't as good, nor did it last as long as hemp-based paper; but it was so much cheaper to produce that the benefits outweighed the disadvantages.

The loss of the textile and paper markets was a blow to hemp farmers, and it did affect the fortunes of many Americans, probably including Thomas Jefferson. Like most wealthy American farmers, his income was primarily derived from the cultivation of hemp. Jefferson's many years in France and in government no doubt contributed to the deterioration of his farming operations, and with

---

27. Zinn, Howard. *A People's History of the United States, 1492-Present*, HarperCollins Publishers 1980, 1995, p. 167.

the dwindling hemp market he could not recover. He was only able to hold onto Monticello because his creditors respected him so much they hesitated to throw him out.

However, the major market for hemp was still the shipbuilding and outfitting trade. As late as 1850, hemp was holding on as America's third most important agriculture crop, yielding only to cotton and tobacco, with more than 8,000 farms actively engaged in the cultivation of hemp.

And so it went until 1862, some thirty years after Jefferson's death. In a certain sense, hemp was killed in the Civil War. When the sailing ship was dramatically outclassed by the new Ironclads, the Monitor and Merrimac, hemp became obsolete overnight.

REORGANIZATION UNDER THE CONSTITUTION

The Articles of Confederation drafted in the early days before the Revolution were idealistic but they were not very practical. In fact, they proved cumbersome and often unworkable — especially when it came to inter-colony (or interstate) commerce — and the Constitutional Convention of 1787 was called specifically to address these problems. Alexander Hamilton (who had been George Washington's military aide) pushed for the adoption of a whole new founding document, and we got our Constitution as the result.

The years between the defeat of Cornwallis at Yorktown in 1781 and the opening of the Constitutional Convention of 1787 was a period during which all sorts of people, for all sorts of reasons, were trying to shape America's character. Hamilton was the leading proponent for an elitist society that, like everywhere else in the world, would place its reliance on (and serve the interests of) those with the most resources. Today, to suggest that the wealthy are better qualified to run things smacks of elitism. Back then, it was reasonably assumed that only men with money could have access to education and a wider knowledge of the world, and only they would have the leisure to think through and work out larger problems. Success is also, sometimes, a measure of ability, after all. In this spirit, Hamilton and those who thought like him decided to exploit the flaws in the Articles of Confederation and suggest it was beyond repair. In fact, they managed to replace the Articles of Confederation (under which the individual states retained power) with a document that gave power to a central government — the federal government.

Probably because of his influence with the banking and financial leaders, Hamilton attended the convention as a New York State representative. Hamilton was a difficult, ambitious man, and many — including John Adams and Thomas Jefferson — neither trusted nor liked him. Hamilton was later killed in a duel with Aaron Burr, a former Vice President of the United States; but Hamilton had Washington's trust.

When Hamilton revealed his proposal, a vicious debate broke out. (It is still going on.) People generally felt allegiance to their states, not a central government. The delegates quickly fell into two camps and created competing political parties. The Hamilton forces were known as the Federalists (creators of a federal government) and the opposition, led principally by Samuel Adams, became known as the Anti-Federalists. Hamilton, however, had done his homework, and the government he proposed was far better organized than that which was sketched out or hinted at under the Articles of Confederation. After all, the other side had not prepared for such an event as this. In the end, even Sam Adams agreed with the new plan. Under the Articles of Confederation, the ultimate power was in the hands of the people, whereas under the Constitution the three branches of the federal government — the legislative (Congress), judicial and the executive — held the power. One compromise that was made was the inclusion of a Bill of Rights, which essentially protected people's rights and set limits on the government's power.

The birth of the US Constitution was a long drawn out and very democratic process that lasted from February through September. Many of the delegates would go home for weeks at a time, but they always returned. Near the end of that lengthy and trying process another fight broke out over the issue of slavery, in large part because a number of black slaves had won their freedom fighting side-by-side with white colonists for freedom from England. There was some sentiment that the rest of them should be freed as well; but the greatest priority was to keep England at bay, and that meant avoiding any public display of weakness or dissension in the ranks. It was essential to demonstrate that the colonies were able to govern themselves — or perhaps the British would have tried to take back its colonies before 1812! The primary goal now was to craft an agreement on a new form of government which could be sent to the individual states for ratification.

Southern delegates exploded when confronted with the idea of ending slavery. Most of them supported Hamilton's vision and considered themselves part of the "Federalist Party." They threatened to walk out. It wasn't an idle threat. In the late 1780s, slavery was still permitted under British law, and during the Revolutionary War the British found the colonists in Virginia and points south considerably more hospitable and agreeable than their Massachusetts brethren. And the South stayed closer to Britain for a long, long time. During the Civil War almost one hundred years later, the British bought Southern cotton and probably provided the Confederacy with weapons — a vital support, given that the Southern states had very little industry.

The slavery issue was threatening final passage of the Constitution and the foundation of a viable new nation. That would suggest to England that the colonies were fragmented and perhaps were militarily vulnerable. The Northern delegates abandoned their anti-slavery position, for the moment, because they believed the birth of the United States was more important. Of course, in the ensuing decades the slavery-based cotton industry was increasingly an economic threat to the Northern hemp farmers, and that helped lead to the Civil War.

Not everyone agreed that the Constitution should be ratified, particularly given its provision for shifting power to a central (federal) government.[28] Many people saw that as a betrayal that would lead to creating an American aristocracy. In 1792, in fact, Jefferson ran for the presidency as the nominee of the (liberal) Anti-Federalist Party — and did so specifically to counter Hamilton's influence on George Washington.

The Federalist Party candidates, Washington and Adams, trounced Jefferson. By the 1796 elections, the Anti-Federalist Party had reinvented itself twice — first, ironically, as the "Republican" Party, probably reflecting George Clinton's influence, and later as the Democratic-Republican Party, reflecting Jefferson's influence. (George Clinton was a member of the Second Continental Congress. During the Revolution he was charged with defending the Hudson River Valley, which he failed to do; he was more successful as governor of the state of New York, where he developed a strong state-based power center in the course of seven terms, and as Vice President under Jefferson and Madison.)

After the Constitution was ratified and Washington was inaugurated as president, the focus quickly changed to the establishment of the government. Washington needed the cooperation of the financial powers to help build and

---

28. State-by-state ratification of the Constitution by date: Delaware, December 7, 1787; Pennsylvania, December 12, 1787; New Jersey, December 18, 1787; Georgia, January 2, 1788; Connecticut, January 9, 1788; Massachusetts, February 6, 1788; Maryland, April 28, 1788; South Carolina, May 23, 1788; New Hampshire, June 21, 1788.

finance the government, and Hamilton (Secretary of the Treasury) was essentially his conduit. Hamilton eventually became the de facto leader of the Federalist Party. But Jefferson, as Secretary of State, distrusted Hamilton's proposals and motives, and suspected that he and others in the emerging Federalist Party were secretly plotting to implant monarchist ideals (an aristocracy) and institutions in the government.

Hamilton also became a political enemy of Aaron Burr; as Treasury Secretary, Hamilton imposed some early regulation on Wall Street brokers like him. Aaron Burr had all sorts of ambitions. He wanted to start a bank but didn't want his name associated with it, so he founded a water company and opened a bank through that company. The bank grew to become the Chase Manhattan Bank; Burr went on to become a popular New York Senator.

Washington, fed up with politics and anxious to get home, was reluctant to run for a second term but did so for two reasons. There was still a long way to go in creating the government the Constitution called for, and he believed the country needed both Hamilton and Jefferson, his two most trusted (and most incompatible) advisors. Hamilton probably also encouraged Washington to run for a second term, knowing that without him he would lose his power base. Washington won reelection by nearly a 2-1 margin and Adams again came in second, making him vice president under the rules of the day.

Jefferson and Hamilton did have deep-seated philosophical differences. Jefferson believed the government should operate for the benefit of the average people, and Hamilton believed that those who invested their money in America should be rewarded. Hamilton believed in what we have come to know as "trickle-down economics" and a ruling class.

Jefferson's philosophy was extremely progressive for his time, and clearly not everyone shared his belief that, as stated in the Declaration of Independence, "all men were created equal" or that the United States government should be created as a "government of the people, by the people and for the people." Many of his contemporaries, especially those of wealth, were not willing to give up their advantages. They believed that people of means were more capable and more entitled to leadership than others. Obviously, this basically left out the working class, women in general, blacks, and Indians. Of course, among the "non-elite," Hamilton's views were not very well received. Average Americans were glad to have got the snobbish Brits off their backs; they were not about to foster a new elitism among their own neighbors. Jefferson's vision, breaking with that sort of tradition, drew on new notions of equality and rights that were beginning to cir-culate in Europe in the 1700s.

Washington often sided with Hamilton, which angered a great many peo-ple including John Adams. Adams ran as a Federalist, hoping to regain the vice-presidency and to challenge Hamilton's growing control of the Federalist Party. Jefferson, George Clinton,[29] and Aaron Burr all ran as Anti-Federalists, directly challenging Hamilton and his cronies. Washington's popularity won out, allow-ing him, Adams, and the Federalists to remain in power. Unfortunately for Washington, the bickering continued; it became almost constant. Washington made clear his intentions to return to his Mount Vernon home and live the rest of his life as a private citizen, when his term ended. The search for his replace-ment revealed that the population was just as ideologically split as were Jeffer-son and Hamilton, and the opposition between the two political parties became even greater. Upon leaving office, Washington noted that his biggest disappoint-ment was his inability to resolve these ideological differences.

Although Adams and Jefferson liked one another and were not very far apart ideologically, a deep rift developed in their relationship during the election of 1796, when they competed for the presidency. In fact, they did not speak to each other for quite a few years. Adams beat Jefferson by a margin of only three Electoral College votes, which meant Jefferson served as Adam's vice-president. This was the first election that Jefferson ran as the nominee of the Democratic-Republican Party. Adams didn't like Hamilton and did not invite him to serve in the administration. Hamilton's career in "public service" abruptly ended, although he was still very influential within the Federalist Party.

John Adams was a fairly good president, but he simply could not win reelection as the nominee of the Federalist Party, which was now totally con-trolled by Hamilton and his supporters. In fact, the Federalists never won another election (which is hardly surprising since, during the War of 1812, they supported the British).

After Adams and Jefferson retired from politics, they renewed their friend-ship by mail, and that friendship lasted until the day they both died, within a couple of hours of each other, on July 4, 1826 — the fiftieth anniversary of the passage of the Declaration of Independence and the birth of the nation.

The presidential election of 1800 ended in a virtual electoral tie between Jefferson and fellow Democratic-Republican Aaron Burr; Adams (the Federalist)

---

29. George Clinton actually received 50 electoral votes to Jefferson's meager 4-vote total.

finished a close third. The House of Representatives decided the winner, and that was Jefferson. Here again, Hamilton played a decisive role as an influential Federalist Party boss. The House Federalists preferred Burr; but Hamilton, now living in New York, disliked Burr even more than he disliked Jefferson. At least, he respected Jefferson. Burr became Jefferson's vice-president; but Jefferson didn't trust him and, in fact, Burr did begin cultivating his federalist friends and trying to boost his own position of power. Burr was dropped from the ticket in the 1804 election and he entered New York gubernatorial race. Heavily involved in New York politics, Hamilton did everything possible to undermine Burr's political chances. The bad blood between Burr and Hamilton deteriorated into an ongoing exchange of derogatory comments and name calling, and some of Hamilton's remarks were printed in New York's newspapers. Burr demanded Hamilton retract his comments; Hamilton refused. The confrontation escalated into a duel, and Burr shot and killed Hamilton.

With or without Hamilton, and despite all their money, the Federalists were politically dead. Still, committed Federalists ran presidential candidates against Jefferson's enormously popular successors, James Madison and James Monroe; they were soundly defeated. There was really only one viable political party in America and that was Jefferson's Democrat-Republican party — which consisted primarily of a coalition of groups who found a common ground in their opposition to Hamilton and his wealthy elitist cronies.

While Jefferson and Hamilton are long gone, the basic class struggle between the haves and have-nots, and the bases of their philosophical differences, are still with us. In his landmark book *The Radicalism of the American Revolution*, historian Gordon Wood points out that "America's 1776 Revolution was not seen as radical by the French. It was not a class-based uprising of the downtrodden. The American Revolution was, and continues as, a revolt against the misuse of government by elites to promote their own interests against the people's."[30] What's that got to do with hemp? The demise of hemp as an essential part of our economy and daily life was also the result of elites promoting their own interests, as will be discussed in later sections.

---

30. As described by Kevin Phillips in his (1994) book *Arrogant Capital*.

JOHNNY APPLESEED

There are many aspects of history where our understanding is lessened, or is completely distorted, by the general silence on America's historical use of marijuana and other hemp-related products. Even the mythical folk hero Johnny Appleseed might be a "cleaned up" version of a typical character from the turn of the last century. Appleseed portrays a carefree young man with a devil-may-care attitude and a complete disregard for material wants — if his tattered clothes, bare feet and the use of a cooking pot for a hat are any indication. Supposedly, Johnny Appleseed traveled across America planting apple seeds everywhere he went. Unfortunately, there is no sign of a string of apple trees stretching across the nation that would even remotely indicate the route he might have taken. The story of Johnny Appleseed most likely represents a composite image of the young men who would have been making their way westward in the early 1800s. While it may seem far-fetched, the pictures of Johnny and his easy-going, gentle (stoned?) manner are strikingly reminiscent of the hippies of the 1960s. Could it be that he and his fellow unencumbered wanderers were, in fact, pot-heads literally and figuratively?

Alcohol cost money, but hemp and the more intoxicating forms of Cannabis could be propagated for free, from seeds. We know colonial America was aware of and used Cannabis for medicinal purposes. They cultivated hybrid species of Cannabis with a high Tetrahydrocannabinol content. Chances are, it wasn't apple seeds Johnny was planting, but intoxicating Cannabis seeds; and he was doing it for the same reason the hippies did — hoping to ensure the availability of a pleasurable smoke.

The story of Johnny Appleseed probably survives because it contains an inkling of the truth; but, like so much of our history and our folklore, the facts have been altered. Maybe he should have been called Johnny Hempseed; but, if that is what he was up to, today this same lovable folk hero would be arrested.

CHAPTER 2

THE CRUSADE AGAINST MARIJUANA

People have been using Cannabis (marijuana) in one form or another since the beginning of time, and often it was used for its intoxicating powers as part of religious rituals. The Sufi sect, in 13th-century Persia, was one prominent example. Sometimes, religion apart, it was simply an integral part of a culture, and it was certainly part of the Arab culture. While there were plenty of cultural difference between Christians and Arabs, one of the starkest differences was in the recreational intoxicants they used — the Christian world used alcohol almost exclusively, and the Arab world primarily used hashish, a concentrated form of marijuana. And so, at the height of the Church's fight for dominance in Spain and northern Africa (where the Moors were well entrenched), and in the Middle East, hashish was vilified because of its association with the Arabs.

Of course, not all Arabs are Moslems and not all Moslems are strict fundamentalists anyway — far from it; but it is ironic to note that the Quran specifically prohibits the use of any kind of mind-altering substance at all. When the Christian-Moslem clash was at its hottest, however, the Church was not making such fine distinctions. As the followers of the prophet Mohammed (who was born in the latter half of the sixth century) gained momentum in the 8th, 9th, and 10th centuries and Islam grew into a major religion, Christians and Moslems met principally on the battlefield. In AD 1095, Pope Urban II declared a religious war, the start of the Crusades, against the Arab/Moslem world with the stated goal of recapturing control of the Holy Land for Christianity. The battle went on for two hundred years.

As far as the church was concerned, the use of marijuana or hashish was evidence that individuals or groups were followers of competing religions, that is, "pagans" or "heretics" — and heretics were considered mortal enemies of the Christian Church, which justified killing them off. Christians could be excommunicated for using marijuana.

Contributing to Christendom's fear of the Moslems (and Cannabis) was the story of Hassan-Ibn-Sabbah, or Hashishin, better known as the "Old Man of the Mountain," and his cutthroat cult of assassins. The story was originally part of the 11th-century poet Omar Khayyam's "A Thousand and One Nights," but was introduced to the Western world in 1297 by Marco Polo. Given that legends often contain a kernel of truth, the idea of a large and widespread army of hashish-smoking killers must have given Christians the shivers.

In 1484, Pope Innocent VIII officially outlawed the use of marijuana.

THE OLD MAN OF THE MOUNTAIN

The story of Hassan-Ibn-Sabbah probably contains some truth, but it was also probably greatly embellished as it was passed from generation to generation. Essentially, Hassan, the son of a wealthy Shiite merchant, became a powerful, ruthless and unyielding religious zealot, whose 70,000 followers terrorized the Middle East from the 11th to the mid-13th century. Hassan would send one or more of his followers into his enemy's camp and within a short time that person would be assassinated. In fact, the word assassin is of Arabic origin and is believed to be derived from Hashishin, "hashish-eater."

Hassan supposedly used hashish (a processed form of the yellow resin that Cannabis leaves excrete) to win the loyalty of his followers. Hashish had been used throughout the Middle East for centuries or more. Under the guise of a religious ceremony, Hassan would induce his male followers to eat and smoke hashish until they passed out. While unconscious, they would be carried to an area best described as a Shangri-la, and for weeks they would indulge themselves with the finest food, wine, and women and, of course, more hashish. (That must have been intoxicating, in itself.) When the time came that Hassan needed them to assassinate someone, there was no question: Their reward for committing the deed was to be able to return to Hassan's Shangri-la. Perhaps not many lived long enough to make the return visit, but they must have died happy in the expectation, nonetheless. Even after his death, Hassan's assassins continued purging the countryside of infidels (until Genghis Khan killed off 12,000 of them, around the middle of the 13th century).

Just to be clear: it wasn't the hashish that put the idea of murder into the minds of those men; it was only part of the reward. Considering the difficulty of life in those times, plentiful food, wine and women would certainly have been more than enough to allure most men. Exactly when or how hashish became associated with the story of the old man in the mountain is unknown, and of course, medieval readers (or story-tellers' audiences) unfamiliar with the effects of Cannabis had no reason to doubt it. Furthermore, because of inconsistencies in the story, there is even some doubt that it was hashish that was used. Marco Polo never actually identified it and he may not have been in a position to know what hashish was — he traveled through the Middle East but spent most of his time in the Far East. And people simply don't pass out under the influence of Cannabis — although, because it has a mellowing influence, people sometimes do get sleepy. Also, the use of Cannabis, either as marijuana or hashish, is difficult to associate with violent people; it is more likely to induce a lax, placid, and infinitely tolerant mindset than to spur anyone to violence. The Beatniks of the 1950s and the Hippies of the 60s and 70s were passivists and espoused nonviolence.

RELIGION & ALCOHOL: THE BEGINNINGS OF ALCOHOL PROHIBITION

For as long as mankind has known about the intoxicating properties of alcohol, there have probably been people trying to stop others from using it excessively. Public drunkenness has always been a social problem, especially since some people become nasty, dangerous and destructive when they drink. However, the vilification of alcohol and the drive to stop people legally from using, manufacturing, or distributing it is unique to the United States. This originated among the staunchly religious minority sects — like the Puritans, Amish, Shakers, Quakers, and Baptists, whose religious convictions forbid the use of alcohol. There was a religiously-inspired crusade for alcohol temperance in colonial America but it represented a very small percentage of the population — it was not taken seriously by the majority of Protestants or Catholics.

There were sporadic attempts to curb or restrict the use of alcohol throughout the 17th and 18th centuries, always religiously inspired.[31] In the Georgia Colony, populated almost entirely by criminals released from British jails, "the paternal interest of the London Trustees, *dominated by the Protestant church,* led them beyond land and labor to morals."[32] "To preserve the colonist against luxury and indolence, they sought to protect them against strong drink. Soldier-settlers had to be sober to defend the borders." The London Trustees passed the Act of 1735, declaring that, "no Rum, Brandies, Spirits or Strong Waters could be brought into Georgia"; and that "kegs of such liquors found in the colony should be publicly destroyed, and the sale of liquor should be punished as a crime."

The Georgia colony was, in fact, a British social experiment. It was an effort to make these people productive, and, of course, useful to England — the British Crown even saw it as a philanthropic effort. But these were people who had no particular motivation to adhere to the edicts of England's moral fanatics, especially after being shipped off to fend for themselves in a wild frontier land. Restrictions on the importation and availability of alcohol (in the 1730s—early 40s) were simply ignored by most Georgia colonists who, hidden from the eyes of the authorities, built their own stills and breweries.

Daniel J. Boorstin gives many colorful examples of the controversy. He quotes,

> In their plans for Georgia's morals, the Trustees had no more success. It was one thing to pass a well-phrased Act 'for Suppressing the odious and loathsome Sin of Drunkenness' but quite another to enforce it on a population sparsely spread over hills and swamps. One correspondent reminded the Trustees that poverty, distress and frustrated hopes always drove men to drink 'to keep up their Courage.' Even in England most people had nothing to choose but either to be quite Forlorn without hopes or Mad with Liquor. Now to bring them [the Georgia settlers] to a proper medium would be to give them Sound & Strong reason to hope for better times and by degree to humor them with proper Notions Such as are the most useful to them.

Boorstin points out that even in terms of trade relations, a ban on rum was absurdly detrimental to Georgia, which had nothing but timber to sell and noth-

---

31. Primarily, the Massachusetts Bay Colony (1633) forbade the sale of "strong water" to any Indian and Georgia's Governor James Oglethorpe forbade the importation of rum and other spirits (1733).
32. *The Americans: The Colonial Experience.* Daniel J. Boorstin, p. 82, Vintage Books 1958.

ing to obtain from the nearest customer, the British West Indies, but sugar and rum. It was also argued that the addition of spirit was healthy in a region where the water quality was less than satisfactory. Finally, everyone knew very well that such unenforceable laws would divert the profit from the sale of liquor from "legitimate" business to the bootleggers, "as it is the nature of mankind in general, and of the common sort in particular, more eagerly to desire, and more immoderately to use those things which are most restrained from them; such was the case with respect to rum in Georgia."

Enterprising Carolinian rum-runners proved more decisive than any other argument, and the Georgia Trustees, over Oglethorpe's loud objection, beat an ungraceful retreat. In 1742, while still keeping the Act against rum on their books, they ordered their agent to ease enforcement. Later that year they repealed prohibition, but they still allowed only rum imported from another British colony in exchange for native Georgia-made products.

In fact, the strict regime seems to have hindered Georgia's development rather than promoting it. It flourished neither in population nor in wealth. The Georgia colony failed, not because of its people but because of the rules under which they were forced to live. What took place in the Georgia colony mirrored the moral hypocrisy of the Quakers who, in this experimental society, imposed unrealistic, irrational and unwanted ideological beliefs under the guise of moral righteousness. Moral fanaticism is neither godly nor representative of true humanitarian religious beliefs.

In 1784, Dr. Benjamin Rush (one of the signers of the Declaration of Independence), with a particular interest in mental diseases, wrote "An Inquiry into the Effects of Spirituous Liquors on the Human Mind and Body," a scathing account of alcohol's ill effects. It clarified for the world the effects of alcohol abuse and gave moral support to those who saw alcohol as evil. The staunchly religious Prohibitionist crusaders promoted Dr. Rush's findings as conclusive evidence — although not many doctors in those days agreed with all his conclusions. They did inflict a degree of concern and fear in the minds of the general public. The temperance movement grew because people came to realize that indeed their daily use of alcohol affected their lives and because common drunkenness had become an ongoing social problem. America's first organized attempt at temperance (moderation) was started by Dr. Billy J. Clark, a New York physician, in 1808. Clark's 44-member group was not intending to change the world; they were concerned only with their own desire to stop using alcohol. They signed a non-binding pledge to stop drinking, except by advice of a physician or in case of actual disease. This may have been the first "self help" encounter group.

Life in infant America had its good times and bad, and during times of extremes, like wars, the consumption of alcohol substantially increases. That was particularly true of the period preceding and following the War of 1812, which produced a noticeable increase in the use of alcohol and public drunkenness. That particularly offended the sensibilities of the Calvinists (formally the Puritans) — the dominant religion in New England and the surrounding areas. Although well intentioned, they had a reputation of being both clannish and hostile to strangers, in part because they lived their lives according to their strict interpretation of the scriptures.[33] They considered themselves righteous (true believers) and faithful, and they were intolerant of people of different religious faiths or those who opposed organized religion altogether. On the other hand, the holier-than-thou Calvinists with their anti-alcohol opinions were quickly and easily dismissed as religious fanatics. And it was from this milieu that John D. Rockefeller, who became "the most hated man in America," emerged.

The anti-alcohol rhetoric dramatically changed after 1810, when Lyman Beecher, an East Hampton, Long Island pastor, took up the temperance crusade. Beecher was preaching an extremely conservative political ideology — referring to Jeffersonian Democracy (liberalism) as ungodly. (Jefferson's party later evolved into the Democratic Party.) He professed a desire to save the State from "rum-selling, tippling folk, infidels and ruff-scruffs." Much of alcohol's negative image came from the rantings of fire-and-brimstone preachers like Beecher, who claimed that alcohol was an instrument of the devil — "the devil's brew." Beecher used the organized religious network of churches to spread the word and establish temperance groups throughout New England and New York. Among these groups, in 1813, was the Connecticut Society for the Reformation of Morals, espousing the suppression of drunkenness, gambling and general lawlessness — the goodie-two-shoes crew.

In 1825, Beecher and the Boston group declared themselves a national organization under the banner of the American Society for the Promotion of Temperance (even though they were preaching total abstinence, not temperance). Essentially, Beecher created the temperance movement right in the middle of a network of Christian churches supported by thousands of extremely conserva-

---

33. *Colonial British America: Essays in the New History of the Eearly Modern Era*, edited by Jack P. Greene and J.R. Pole, p. 184.

tive, religiously conscious crusaders. Their mission in life was to get the rest of the world to readjust its perspective of right and wrong, to match theirs. Many parishioners supported the temperance movement only because otherwise they would have been ostracized. However, it is also reasonable to assume that a great many people started avoiding church or at the very least lost some of their respect for it due to this unrealistic and fanatically moralistic attitude. Outside the network of Christian churches, the Prohibitionist movement was going nowhere. Public opinion could hardly be expected to rally to such a cause.

In 1834, the American Society for the Promotion of Temperance changed its name to the American Temperance Society, and claimed a million supporters (one out of every thirteen Americans). However, at their 1836 annual convention, the membership total rejected abstinence and overwhelmingly supported *temperance* — they entirely excluded wine and malt beverages from the ban. Actually, the delegates fought over three proposals: (1) To denounce the anti-slavery reformers while placating the Southern temperance societies — The Southern States were devoutly religious, strong supporters of abstinence, and determined to keep their slaves. (2) To sponsor legislation against the liquor traffic. — This was the first time the temperance movement attempted to use legal coercion to force their ideology on the general public. (3) To adopt a pledge of total abstinence from all intoxicants. Now, they were showing their true colors and questionable moral foundation — demanding total abstinence and laws to inflict punishment on those who did not comply, while supporting the continuation of slavery.

Following that convention, its membership and the number of affiliated groups substantially declined. Perhaps they heeded Nietzsche's warning: "Mistrust those in whom the urge to punish is strong."

In the 1840s, there was a revival of the reform movement but now, ironically, it was reformed alcoholics known as the "Washingtonians" who spoke out in favor of temperance. This group was apparently the forerunner of Alcoholics Anonymous, but it too was heavily influenced by ordained ministers. Among the boldest was Father Theobald Mathew, who won worldwide acclaim trying to woo his fellow Irishmen away from whiskey. Reacting to the rising tide of the temperance movement, Maine passed a weak prohibition law in 1846 and a much stronger one in 1851. By 1855, thirteen other states had followed suit. However, before the Civil War, political opposition, court challenges and enforcement difficulties caused nine of these states to repeal their prohibition laws, declaring them unconstitutional. Temperance took a back seat to the events in the run-up to war, but became active again when it was over.

ANDREW JACKSON V. JOHN QUINCY ADAMS

The presidential election of 1824 ended up, after some shenanigans, with John Quincy Adams as president. He promptly named Henry Clay (who had had a hand the shenanigans) his Secretary of State. The theft of the election was so bald-faced that it left John Quincy Adams a lame duck from the get-go.

After the demise of the Federalist Party, there was essentially only one political party in America — Jefferson's Democrat-Republican Party. That meant that in this 1824 election all the candidates had the same party affiliation. However, the natural diversity of opinion was too much for one political party, and it was breaking apart. The nominating caucuses, the mechanism used to nominate the party's presidential candidates, had fallen into disrepute and there was not a great deal of trust anywhere. By the election of 1828, there essentially was no Democrat-Republican Party, with the possible exception of John C. Calhoun. It had been replaced by two completely separate political parties — Jackson's Democrat Party and the National Republicans Party, who nominated Adams for reelection.

John C. Calhoun became a political oddity. He served as vice president for eight years, but under two different presidents — John Quincy Adams (1824-28) and Andrew Jackson (1828-32). Calhoun and Jackson developed philosophical differences on trade tariffs and Calhoun resigned as vice president before the 1832 election, and was reelected to the senate.

HEMP AND PRESIDENTIAL POLITICS

After the election of 1824, a clear political split developed between the Jackson and Adams supporters, especially in Congress. Jackson's supporters essentially passed a bill that their opponents labeled Tariff of Abomination — a term coined by Calhoun, which placed heavy duties on specific imported raw materials — particularly hemp. The tariff punished the textile manufacturing New England states, which overwhelmingly supported John Quincy Adams, and favored mid-Western hemp farmers where Jackson was popular. As Paul F. Boller, Jr., describes the situation:

> In drawing up the bill they ignored New England, which was solid for Adams; they also risked antagonizing the anti-protectionist South on the assumption that it would never choose Adams over Jackson. Their main objective was to win Ohio, Kentucky, and Missouri (which had gone for Adams in 1924), as well as such important states as Pennsylvania and New York. To please farmers in those states they placed heavy duties on imported raw materials, especially hemp, flax, molasses, iron, and sail duck (hemp canvas). New Englanders screamed; but they didn't matter. Southerners were also incensed; but they were planning to support Jackson in the hope his administration would reverse things. Some of the Adamsites realized what the Jacksonians were up to. "I fear this tariff thing," warned one of them; "by some strange mechanism, it will be changed into a machine for manufacturing Presidents, instead of broadcloths and bed blankets." He was right. It was a shrewd move by Jackson's supporters in Congress.[34]

That the weapon of choice was a tariff on imported hemp shows that even thirty years after the invention of the cotton gin, America was still economically very dependent on hemp-based textiles — especially in the Northern and Mid-western states. Although cotton was cheaper to produce, it lacked many of hemp's desirable attributes — strength, warmth, durability. Cotton was also cheaper in part because of the very high demand for hemp. That economic reality, after 1800, forced both the growing textile and paper industries to seek out alternative materials. As the textile industry turned to cotton, it caused a dramatic increase in the use of slaves. And the paper industry began producing wood-based paper, made from the plentiful forests.

Jackson really didn't need political trickery; he trounced Adams in the 1828 election, both in the popular vote and the Electoral College. The American people finally got what they had wanted four years earlier — and they loved Jackson, because he acted in opposition to the money interests. Even more, Jackson was the first US president who didn't come from either Virginia or Massachusetts, and since the union had grown considerably from the original 13 colonies Jackson was seen more as a president of all the people.

---

34. Boller, Paul F. Jr. *Presidential Campaigns*. Oxford University Press 1984-85, p. 48. Boller was, in part, quoting Minnigerode's *Presidential Years*, pp. 168-69 and Remini's *Election of Jackson*, p. 162.

The National Republican Party was not the short-lived Republican Party of the late 1780s, the former Anti-Federalists Party, nor was it the Republican party of Lincoln that evolved in the mid-1850s. John Quincy Adams' National Republican Party represented a rebirth of the old elitist Federalist Party. The National Republican Party was essentially created to oppose Andrew Jackson's economic policies; it lived only long enough to run candidates in two presidential elections (John Quincy Adams in 1828 and Henry Clay in 1832); both of them lost badly to Jackson. By the 1836 election, the National Republicans reinvented themselves as the Whig Party. The truth, however, is that although the party name changed, neither the ideology nor the party's leadership did. The 1852 election was the last election in which the Whig Party ran a presidential candidate.

Jackson's anointed successor, Martin Van Buren, was the first president to spend a good deal of his time defending the United States against the slander of the British, who had outlawed slavery by then. America was considered an uncivilized country, in part because it still enslaved people. The British ban on slavery encouraged and emboldened the Northern Abolitionists and helped persuade the population that their cause was just — and that it was possible to put an end to the inhumane practice. Before 1836, it was principally Northern blacks (Negroes) who helped their Southern counterparts to escape along the "underground railroad." After 1836, more white Americans became involved with that mission.

BUILDING THE RAILROAD

The discovery of gold in California in 1849 caused a massive migration westward and spawned the expansion of the railroads. The railroads proved extraordinarily important to the industrial North shortly thereafter, during the Civil War. The North had a far more extensive railroad system in place and was better able to quickly move troops and supplies — making the railroad companies and their owners phenomenally rich in the process. Cornelius Vanderbilt, owner of the New York Central Railroad, became the richest man in the country because he was the largest shipping and railroad operator. But the real robber baron railroad tycoons were people like Jay Gould and Jim Fisk, who made their money manipulating stock prices. In 1867, Vanderbilt decided to add the Erie Railroad to his vast shipping and railroad holdings and started to buy up all the outstanding stock. The Erie Railroad was controlled by Daniel Drew, its director, Jay Gould, and Jim Fisk, who conspired to bilk Vanderbilt by printing more stock certificates. When Vanderbilt discovered the swindle, he paid off a judge and got his money back. When the news of this little game became public, the government decided it was time to implement somewhat more stringent disclosure regulations. Every now and then, they get that message.

The Civil War delayed completion of the transcontinental railroad, which was finally celebrated on May 10, 1869 when the Union Pacific and Central Pacific railroads met at Promontory Point in Utah. That same year, Gould and Fisk attempted to corner the gold market, which they were able to do by convincing then President US Grant not to sell any government gold. The price skyrocketed and most of the available gold in America was now in the hands of these two men. Now, that brought business to a standstill — the United States and the rest of the world were on the gold standard, meaning everything had to be paid for in gold. There was panic in the streets, especially Wall Street. Finally, Grant ordered the Treasury Department to make enough gold available for sale to bring down the price. Millions of dollars worth flooded back into the market and the price plummeted, ruining many of the people who had been forced to buy it at the high. A mob gathered at Fisk's offices; Fisk was personally assaulted and his life was threatened. Jay Gould was nowhere to be found. He got out of town fast. Probably took a train.

KING COTTON

After the introduction of the cotton gin, the demand for cotton exploded. Hemp was replaced as the textile industry's standard, and that is what made cotton king. This brought untold wealth to the Southern states, enticing plantation owners to substantially increase production. That meant significantly increasing their labor force (that is, slaves). It also helped set the stage for the 1820 Indian Removal Act, under which five Indian nations were ejected from their homelands in the South and forced to move west. All in all, instead of easing man's burden, the cotton gin accelerated the worst human rights abuses in US history.

Opposition to slavery increased as fast as the number of slaves did. While many people found slavery repugnant and inhumane, wars are generally fought over economic issues, not humanitarian ones. In the case of the Civil War, one of the leading issues was who would get the profits from the textile industry — the

Northern hemp farmers or Southern cotton farmers. Due to the lower cost, cotton virtually took over the textile industry between 1800 and 1850; and so, despite the thriving shipbuilding market, hemp farming was becoming less profitable and much more competitive. Still, until the beginning of the Civil War, the demand for hemp rope and sail cloth had been sufficient to keep the cost of raw hemp relatively high.

Why was the Civil War fought? It was the South that took the offensive, firing on Fort Sumter, and then, state by state, the South formally seceded from the Union — a determined and defiant act. To say the war was about slavery is to ignore the facts. There was a popular movement in those days known as the "Copperheads" (referring to the copper in pennies), who supported the Union's war with the South for economic reasons, specifically with regard to controlling various markets. And more important, Lincoln orignally offered to allow the Southern states to *keep* their slaves if the states would rescind their succession.

The Emancipation Proclamation was issued almost a year and a half after the Civil War started. It states,

> That on the 1st day of January, A.D. 1863, all persons held as slaves within any State or designated part of a State the people whereof shall then be in rebellion against the United States shall be then, thenceforward, and forever free; and the executive government of the United States, including the military and naval authority thereof, will recognize and maintain the freedom of such persons and will do no act or acts to repress such persons, or any of them, in any efforts they may make for their actual freedom.
> — *Abraham Lincoln*
> *The Emancipation Proclamation*
> *September 22, 1862*

In fact, it did not even free all slaves. It only freed those slaves in territories still under Confederate control.

Much as we might like to think so, it was not public revulsion at the institution of slavery that drove the North and South to war. It was the seeking of economic advantage, as usual. Slavery became an issue because cotton was an issue. The Northern hemp farmers couldn't compete with cotton, and skilled working class people saw slavery as a means of justifying their own low wages. Most Southern plantations had skilled, trained slaves working as carpenters, masons, buggy makers, leather workers and, of course, general laborers, and if they didn't have a slave with the skills they needed they would borrow one from a neighbor who did. One reason the Southern states failed to develop an industrial base (which is what cost them the war) was because skilled workers could not earn a decent living in the South. It was slavery that kept the South economically viable.

In the decades leading up to the war, efforts to find common ground and resolve the problem proved futile. As additional states began entering the Union, the debate turned to maintaining a parity between the number of free and slave states — exemplified by the Missouri Compromise of 1820, which allowed Maine statehood as a free state and the territory of Missouri statehood as a slave state. Many of Missouri's citizens were not pleased, and an all-out war broke out in the territory.

THE BRITISH OUTLAW SLAVERY

Obviously, after America's Revolutionary War, relations with Great Britain were severely strained and they deteriorated even further after the War of 1812 (during which the British took over parts of the Midwest, and Washington DC — they burned down the White House).

By the early 1830s, American industry had grown to the point that it threatened British industrial supremacy, particularly in textiles. America's exportation of cheap cotton fabrics was destroying England's textile markets around the world, and the British had to take drastic steps to stop it. What they did, in 1833, was to outlaw slavery throughout the British Empire. This had many effects, but one of them was to embarrass America and show the world that the United States was an uncivilized and brutal society.

In the long run, the British ban encouraged the US to end slavery, too — which would eliminate the economic advantage it gave to cotton. Given the British were still using their military might to effectively enslave the people of Ireland and India, this might be seen as a somewhat hypocritical position. But it did succeed: with the British Empire out of the slave trade, the US became the world's leading purveyor of slavery and the focus of the world was on the Southern cotton plantations, where the treatment of slaves was particularly appalling.

Unfortunately, instead of ending the British propaganda by ending slavery, the US government initially defended the Southern plantation owners' use of slaves. That was the position of both the Whig Party and (after the 1852 elections) the Democratic Party. Although ideologically different, at the time, the elitist Whigs and the Democrats were not very far apart politically, and both were in the pockets of the wealthy Southern cotton plantation owners. Actually, the reason the Whigs lost the 1852 election and were dead politically is that they did nothing to end slavery, which the public was calling for. Unfortunately, the Democrats weren't any better than the Whigs and were quickly heading down that same path.

Slavery was fairly pervasive in the Northern states as well, before the British abolition. One of the principal employers of slaves in the North was the hemp industry, because harvesting, cleaning and processing hemp was labor intensive. Working at a Northern hemp farm or factory was no easier and maybe harder than working in the cotton fields of the Deep South, but slaves there were generally treated far more humanely. They might work side by side with white workers or free "negroes," and they were paid a weekly salary — there was little in the way of "slave quarters" in the Northern states.

Still, abolishing slavery throughout the British Empire did bring the issue of slavery to the forefront in America. In the Northern states the use of slaves precipitously declined, and Northern abolitionists seriously began to organize. Until that point the fledgling "underground railroad" consisted primarily of free blacks, many of whom had themselves escaped the South and now worked to help their fellows northward to freedom. It is estimated that more than 100,000 blacks traveled North on the "underground railroad" before the start of the Civil War — most after the mid-1830s, when more white abolitionists became actively involved.

The growth of the Abolitionist movement indicates that people had given up on waiting for the government to settle the matter. By the mid-1850s, voters had had enough of the Democrats as well and began supporting third parties like the Free Soil Party and the newly-formed Republican Party, both of which said they would end slavery. At the same time, abolition extremists like John Brown were becoming bolder. Many admired Brown for taking over the Federal arsenal at Harpers Ferry in an insurrection aimed at the slaveholders, and were just as angry about slavery as he was. Slave-owners, of course, were appalled, and Brown was hanged. That incident probably cost the Democrats the 1860 election, and it may not have mattered whom the Republicans nominated.

THE 1860 ELECTION — A FOREGONE CONCLUSION

The almost unprecedented emergence of the liberal and liberating Republican Party and particularly the election of Lincoln represented a refreshing change from the kind of politics that preceded it all — a lot of politicking and no action. The Republican landslide indicated the public's desire for change. Lincoln won the 1860 election by better than 2-to-1 margin, and the Republicans also won control of both the house and senate by huge margins. The Democrats knew they were going to lose, but they didn't know by how much. The South knew that the Republican Party was controlled by Northern Liberals; they knew it meant the end of slavery if Lincoln and the Republicans won, and they probably also knew the Democrats didn't have a chance of winning — which is why they threatened to secede from the Union if Lincoln won.

In the minds of the Southern oligarchy, slavery was a states' rights issue (there's that debate again over central versus local government), not human rights; or maybe they just didn't see their slaves as human beings. The question of whether state law should supersede federal law or federal law supersede state law remains unanswered, even today, but slavery was not an issue on which the Southern states could have won their argument. In any case, the slave-owning states seceded from the Union and abandoned their argument at that time.

The Southerners, having lost at the polls, risked losing everything by seceding. Without public debate the Southern state legislators, all Democrats, brought the nation to the brink of war. Even before Lincoln's Inaugural Address, the fledgling Southern Confederacy attacked Fort Sumter. Thus began the Civil War (The War Between the States) that pitted brother against brother. But, like all wars, the Civil War was fought over economic issues, not moral niceties. Even after delivering his Emancipation Proclamation, Lincoln said that the Civil War was not being fought over the issue of slavery but that it had evolved because of economic issues; and those issues included the economic advantages the Southern cotton plantations had over the Northern hemp farmers. Of course, Abraham Lincoln believed slavery was wrong, but he certainly wasn't an abolition extremist (except in the eyes of wealthy Southern slave owners).

Actually, the Emancipation Proclamation did not sit well with many, perhaps most, Northerners either; they had no interest in improving the status of black men and women.

THE IRONCLADS

As noted above, hemp was a casualty of the Civil War. It was killed in a battle that was not, in fact, conclusive for North or South. The fateful event took place March 9, 1862 between the steamships Monitor and Merrimac, and it was actually a victory of steam over sail. Both the "Ironsides" wreaked havoc on their respective enemy's fleets of wooden sailing ships. The Ironclads introduced a new level of ship-building technology to the world — a technology that didn't depend on the wind, and didn't require miles of rope, acres of sail, or large crews to rig and run them. The Ironclads were vastly more effective and cheaper to build, maintain, and operate. In little more than a year, all the major navies in the world converted their fleets to Ironclads, and merchant fleets soon followed.

That naval battle was the very decisive end of the hemp industry's best customer: military and commercial sailing ships. Although sailing ships continued to play their trade in a limited way for the next 50 years, the shift toward steam was economically devastating to hemp farmers and created extreme hardships. Having already lost the textile and paper industries, losing the ship building industry was a catastrophic blow to America's hemp-based agrarian economy.

Most hemp farmers packed up and moved West in search of a new start in life, probably in Conestoga wagons covered with hemp canvas. Those who stayed were able to scratch out a living supplying hemp for rope and canvas and the seeds for paint and lamp oil. Many Civil War veterans, North and South, found little left for them to go home to. The fact that not much hemp farming took place in the Western states probably reflects the general feeling that hemp was no longer much of a cash crop.

During the Civil War, the South was cut off from the textile mills in the New England states, and exported most of its cotton to England — whom most Americans still considered an enemy.

With the war lingering and the 1864 election approaching, Lincoln felt the need to make the point that Union represented more than the North trying to impose its will on the South, and that peace meant the inclusion of the South, not dominance. To show that unity, Lincoln selected Andrew Johnson, a Tennessee Democrat, the only Southern Democrat to remain in the House of Representatives after the outbreak of war, as his vice-presidential running mate. However, when Lincoln was assassinated (April 14, 1865) only five days after Robert E. Lee surrendered to Grant at Appomattox, Union supporters were infuriated — Lincoln was their hero, their knight in shining armor. Both in the house and senate they took their anger out on Andrew Johnson, Lincoln's suc-cessor. Although he attempted to implement Lincoln's plans for a peaceful non-retaliating reunion of the nation, Jackson was still a Southerner. The "radical Republicans" were particularly angry about the "Black Codes" laws passed by several former slave states meant to restrict what blacks were able to do with their newly won freedom.

Not only did the radical Republicans' Congress pushed through the 13th Amendment, which abolished slavery, they were intent on destroying the South's white power base. They passed the Freeman's Bureau Bill, which gave medical, educational, and financial assistance to impoverished blacks, and the Civil Rights Act of 1866 which gave blacks the right to vote.

Since there were more blacks in the South than whites after the Civil War, the Civil Rights Act definitely did threaten the white power base. That spawned the Ku Klux Klan, which reportedly played a key roll in driving out any rem-nants of the Republican party in the South. For a hundred years after the Civil War a Republican candidate couldn't get elected dog catcher in any former Con-federate state. Although most blacks joined the Republican Party, the white Southerners stayed staunch "Dixie Democrats" well into the middle of the 20th century. They could not forgive Lincoln and the Republicans for freeing the slaves and ruining the whites.

(Politically, the "Dixie Democrats" represented the far right, ultra conserva-tive, wing of the Democrat Party. Lincoln's Republicans were the liberals of the day, and those liberal Republicans, with the exception of two non-consecutive Grover Cleveland administrations, held total control of the US government for over 50 years. The parties switched roles in the 1912 election, when the Republi-cans became the conservatives and the Democrats became the liberals, as we know them today. In the late 1960s, most of the "Dixie Democrats" bolted the party to support the Republican nominee Richard Nixon. In the 1980s, the rest of the ultra conservative "Dixie Democrats" bolted the party to support Ronald Reagan, the Republican candidate. Today, the expression "Dixie Democrats" is simply a cute term that denotes delegates to the Democrat National Convention from Southern states — it doesn't mean they are (conservative) right-wingers.

After Lincoln's assassination, a power struggle developed within the Republican Party and the wealthy, the Federalists, eventually won control of the party. The liberal bent of the Republican Party was still intact but it was little more than a façade. The Republican Party bosses held the real power and they were in the pockets of the industrialists, like Rockefeller, who practiced "government by the rich." Lincoln, a liberal, resisted the financial mafia and Andrew Johnson, his successor, tried to hold true to Lincoln's dream. That was his undoing.

Congressional Republicans were called radicals because they had gone too far, too fast — ending slavery was one thing, but giving blacks welfare and voting privileges was something completely different — especially considering that nobody else received public assistance from the federal government and not even white women were allowed to vote. Andrew Johnson vetoed the Freeman's Bureau Bill and the Civil Rights Act because he believed both would provoke Southerners and inhibit the reunification of the nation. Congressional radicals overrode Johnson's veto on the Freeman's Bill: the first time any presidential veto had been overridden. A month later they overrode his veto of the Civil Rights Act. Four months later they pushed through the 14th Amendment, which solidified blacks' voting rights.

They also passed a number of laws that placed restrictions on what the president could do, and when Johnson dismissed Secretary of War Edwin M. Stanton, he allegedly violated those restrictions. The US House passed eleven separate articles of impeachment; however, he was acquitted in the US Senate trial — by one vote. A few months later, the Republicans nominated Ulysses S. Grant, which ended Johnson's presidential career. Two years later, the people of the State of Tennessee returned Andrew Johnson to the US Senate.

Ulysses S. Grant, however, was a much better general than a president. He was easily manipulated by the party bosses and influential industrialists. Grant was a popular figure; he easily won reelection, but the legacy he left was that of an incredibly corrupt administration. For almost a half-century the robber barons got away with anything they wanted, simply by putting enough money in the right pockets. The railroads were extremely predatory. Carnegie cut wages at will. Rockefeller used the opportunity to destroy his competition and create a monopoly on oil and refining. That is, until McKinley was assassinated and vice-president Theodore Roosevelt ascended to the presidency.

It is somewhat ironic that, although the North won the war and slavery was abolished, economically the real loser was the North and its robust hemp industry. As in the Revolutionary War, hemp products, especially rope and canvas, were still vital war materials used on naval and merchant ships, on supply wagons, for tents, for uniforms, and of course for the flag. Hemp was so important to the war effort that hemp farms and processing facilities became major military targets and many were destroyed during the Civil War. These facilities were generally not rebuilt because the end of the war dramatically reduced the demand for hemp — especially after the stunning debut of the Monitor and Merrimac.

America certainly didn't stop cultivating and utilizing hemp; but it curbed production noticeably. After the war, there was an attempt to recapture at least part of the textile market by importing hemp seeds from China that produced a much finer fiber, but the Chinese declined to provide the seed, thanks in part to a little interference by the British, and in part in reaction to the brutal treatment (including beatings and murder) Chinese railroad workers were being subjected to on America's western frontier.

In hindsight, all things considered, maybe we would have been better off without that cotton gin at all.

THE CHINESE OPIUM WARS

The strange and wondrous world of the Middle and Far East came to the attention of Europe through the thoroughly exotic and incredible tales of Marco Polo, which were told and retold over the centuries. His stories told of inventions the "enlightened" world of Western Europe had never seen or heard before — fireworks against a black sky, rockets, noodles, paper money, and even unknown intoxicants. The Western world acquired knowledge of these things only indirectly, through the Russians, Arabs, and others, because until just before the beginning of the 19th century China was very much a closed society. The Western world first "discovered" the panda bear in 1869!

It wasn't that the Chinese were hostile to the rest of the world; they had learned, through early experiences with Europeans and others, to mistrust outsiders. China desperately needed to open its markets to the world, but on terms that would not "give away the store." Trade relations, as the British defined them, tended to trap the weaker partners in a cycle of dependency. China did not want to import finished goods; to make China economically independent, would require putting the Chinese people to work producing the finished goods that were needed and wanted. Rather than trading, the Emperor was willing to sell virtually anything for gold or silver.

But if the British or any other nation paid for all the tea, silk, and jade they wanted in gold or silver, they would have bankrupted themselves in a very short time. The British merchants devised a plan to get around what they considered

China's unreasonable trade policy without actually breaking the law. The use of opium was not illegal in China. The British East India Company began shipping opium to China in 1767;[35] and the so-called "China Trade" was extraordinarily lucrative. Essentially, British merchants would exchange British-made goods in India for opium, which they sold on the black market to Chinese drug dealers for gold or silver. Then they legally bought whatever they wanted — silks, jade, porcelain, artistic treasures, and especially tea — which they exported to England and sold at premium prices. Part of the reason they selected opium was that the "white powder" could not be identified as being imported, although it was no real secret. The British merchants operated openly because, at least at first, they were not creating much of a social problem. The use of opium was a widespread practice in China and in many part of the world, including India, for thousands of years. Unfortunately, the dramatic increase in the amount of opium available in China created a massive opium addiction problems, which eventually led to the Opium Wars (1839-42).

The British, because they controlled India, a major opium producer, dominated the "China Trade." American merchants weren't standing on any moral high ground; they simply couldn't compete with the British because they did not have access to a cheap source of opium. Instead, they were indirectly involved, often financing (brokering) their British counterparts, and they too used their profits to legitimately purchase Chinese goods to export to America. Commodore Kearney, visiting Hong Kong in 1842, found evidence of extensive American participation. Notorious among the American firms were Russel & Company and Augustine Heard & Company, both of Boston.[36] Other countries — France, Germany, Holland, Japan and several others also joined in. A second Opium War broke out in 1856 and subsequently ended with the Treaty of Tientsin in 1858.

It is important that we understand what took place in China because it ties in to the outlawing of opiates and cocaine in the US in 1912 and, in turn, to today's worldwide drug war.

China's opium problem escalated in direct proportion to the exportation of silks, tea, art, porcelain and jade. The demand for Chinese products was immense, and opium was pouring in. By 1820, reportedly more than a thousand tons of smoking opium was being imported into China, not including what was

---

35. O'Brien, Robert and Colun, Sidney, M.D. *Encyclopedia of Drug Abuse.* Facts on File, New York: 1984, p. XIII

36. Anslinger, Harry J. *The Protectors.* Farrar, Straus, New York: 1964, p. 23.

grown in China itself, and by 1830 it more than doubled. The British and other foreign traders suffered few compunctions about the effects their business had on the local population; they lived and worked in gated and guarded enclaves (the largest of which was in Canton) and had very little contact with the Chinese people — most of whom feared and hated foreigners.

The Chinese government vigorously objected to foreign traders addicting their people to opium, but the British government refused to address the problem until China reconsidered its trade policy — which they were not willing to do. By the mid-1850s, perhaps half of the urban Chinese population was addicted to opium and the Chinese government had to create a "high commission" to investigate and eliminate the problem. This actually marked the start of China's "Opium War." Commissioner Lin's relatively short reign was brutal, starting with rounding up known Chinese opium dealers and publicly executing them. Then Commissioner Lin expelled all the foreign traders from China, raided their Canton warehouses, confiscated an estimated two tons of opium, and burned it. It was a decisive move by Lin, but it did nothing to resolve the opium problem; it only forced the trade further underground.

The British quickly reestablished themselves on the island of Taiwan, and then petitioned the British Crown to retaliate against the Chinese for their losses. In 1858, the British government sent a British man-of-war (a naval warship), which in a matter of days forced the Chinese government to capitulate. By the Treaty of Tientsin, the Chinese were obliged to reimburse the British merchants, actually all the foreign merchants, for their property losses — including the cost of the opium that was burned. It also removed foreigners from Chinese jurisdiction and required the Chinese government to surrender control of the island of Hong Kong to the British, in perpetuity; that was later renegotiated to a lease good for 99 years. The loss of Hong Kong was the end of Commissioner Lin, and the China trade, protected by British troops, operating from Hong Kong without interference from the Chinese government for another half century. China's economic condition did not improve and the situation erupted again in 1900, this time directly against the foreign embassies, in an event known as the Boxer Rebellion.

At the behest of President Theodore Roosevelt, the First International Opium Conference was convened at The Hague in 1911. The Chinese government finally had to "modernize" its trade policies, and the British agreed to stop importing opium. This did result in a substantial decline in the use of opium. But China's economy had completely collapsed long since, and so had the imperial dynasty. Early in the 20th century a republic was decreed, and a president installed. He died in 1916, and the country continued in a state of chaos or virtual civil war for the next several decades. Regions were basically run by various war-lords who financed themselves by selling opium after the British stopped.

The Kuomintang Party, founded in 1912 with a goal of establishing a parliamentary democracy and moderate socialism, was having internal battles of its own. With a little interference by Russian Comintern representatives, a communist group led by Mao Tse-Tung made attempts to gain control. Meanwhile, Japan could not resist the lure of her desperately weak neighbor; she bombed many of China's major cities and took over many territories. The use of opiates in China again skyrocketed, but it was now the Japanese supplying the opium and profiting from the addiction of the Chinese people. After the defeat of the Japanese in World War II, the ideological differences in the Kuomintang between Mao (the communist) and Chiang Kai-Shek (the capitalist) turned into an all out civil war. General Chiang's forces were greatly outnumbered and desperately needed the financial support of the United States. Reportedly at the insistence of Madame Chiang, the General severed his relations with the opiate producers and conducted a campaign to suppress the drug trade. He also emphasized the fact that Mao was trafficking in opium to finance his military campaign.

Chiang Kai-Shek did get US support, but he was unable to win the support of the Chinese people — mostly they were poor, uneducated farmers only surviving on the opium profits. They understood the complex global politics enough to know that if Chiang and the Nationalists won, they would not get any help from the government, anyway; and their lives would be in danger because Chiang was waging the war on opium only to please his American backers. In contrast, Mao and the communists dangled extraordinary promises to treat and help everyone equally. Inevitably, Chiang and his Nationalist followers were forced to leave. They took refuge on the island of Taiwan (knlown in earlier times, under Portuguese occupation, as Formosa), where even today their anti-drug laws mirror those of the United States. And they still enjoy US protection.

For the next many years, Mao and the communists were far too busy establishing their government on the mainland to worry about the Nationalists in Taiwan. However, the rhetoric coming out of Washington, DC, especially from the Federal Bureau of Narcotics and suggesting that the Red Chinese were trying to addict America's youth to heroin, helped create and promote anti-communist hysteria. This reached a frenzy in the 1950s during the era of McCarthyism, when a small number of people driven by a number of other agendas destroyed the lives and careers of many prominent and not so prominent Americans by simply accusing them of being communists.

Once things settled down in China and the outside interests topped pumping drugs in, the use of opiates within China substantially declined — without a "drug" witch hunt. Today, China has no more of an opiate addiction problem than any other nation. The Chinese people generally are more optimistic about the future than they have ever been before. While the People's Republic of China clearly operates on a different notion of civil rights than what the US proclaims, it should be noted that the Chinese government has not stimulated the creation of a criminal subculture by making criminals out of hundreds of thousands, even millions, of its own people for minor indiscretions involving the use of potentially dangerous drugs.

PREJUDICE REARS ITS UGLY HEAD

If colonial America represents the nation's infancy, 19th century America represents our adolescence. In fact, the spate of unwise and aggressive actions seems particularly adolescent. Senseless killings, beatings and other acts fueled by bigotry took place in the form of a civil war, the slaughter of the Indian population, and the abysmal treatment of many of the Chinese and other immigrant railroad workers on the Western frontier. Life was cheap, and it was hard, but it was also literally hell for ethnic minorities.

The Civil War destroyed lives, homes, families, and whatever fortune many a man might have had. In large part, the massive migration West after the war represented millions of impoverished and devastated people desperately seeking to establish a new life for themselves. Many carried along everything they had in a Conestoga wagon, and usually traveled as part of a wagon train for their mutual safety. Most didn't own much, maybe a horse and a gun, and many who had not a dime to their name worked their way West by building the railroad.

As they moved, they ran into a mix of people of different races and completely alien cultures — blacks, native Indians, Mexicans, and Chinese — people who looked and dressed differently, spoke different languages, and had different customs and rituals. They had no education to take the edge off this lacerating strangeness. For all of them, it was a strange new world, and a very dangerous world with little or no law or lawmen. Here at the edge of survival, violence often broke out.

The United States had paid Napoleon $10 million for all the land West of the Mississippi, described in "the Louisiana Purchase," but it should be noted that the land never was Napoleon's to sell. While a good deal of the land was uninhabited, much of it belonged to native Indians and Mexicans who had been living there for decades, even centuries, before LaSalle or any other Frenchman first laid eyes on it. The French had not even attempted to settle the lands in question, except for Louisiana and a rather thin stretch immediately west of the Mississippi.

The United States recognized the French claim to the Louisiana territory because, 1) before the Revolutionary War, the British had limited westward expansion of the colonies to the Mississippi, and 2) it was a way of acknowledging France's help in the fight for independence from England. It remains debatable whether the amount of land identified as the Louisiana territory was vastly overstated so that Napoleon could flimflam the United States out of $10 million, or was an astute land grab on Jefferson's part.

The westward expansion was underlain by many gross abuses, financial and otherwise. Most appalling was the willingness of those who were doing the expanding to simply slaughter tens of thousands of Indians and Mexicans so they could steal the land and impose their authority over the territory. They justified the atrocities by claiming they were bringing civilization to the Western frontier. Other people have dealt with economic desperation without necessarily resorting to such barbarity.

Economic conditions have always been a determining factor in race relations: mass poverty generally increases the level of bigotry, while tensions decrease in times of plenty. Unfortunately, on the Western frontier, conditions were not improving and as the population grew, America's "melting pot" started to boil. The railroad owners, claiming poverty, convinced Congress that in order to complete the intercontinental railroad to the West Coast on time and without going over its projected cost, they would need to import thousands of less demanding Chinese workers. In truth, the US government gave very generous incentives to the railroad companies to build the intercontinental railroad and taxpayers were paying for every mile. Bringing Chinese workers in only further boosted the profitability of the project, lining the railroad companies' pockets — which is how they got the name "robber barons." Convinced of the importance of the intercontinental railroad to the nation's economy, and possibly by some small change spilling out of those companies' pockets, Congress permitted the robber barons to import Chinese workers. Employed under slave-like conditions, they quickly replaced almost all the white American workers and generally kept wages terribly low.

The public in fact hated the railroad companies, and they were angry at the Republican Congress for giving away their jobs. When Washington and Big Business failed to correct the situation, the public's anger and hostility flared. The uneducated and unskilled common laborers, replaced the unintelligible and alien Chinese workers, went on a rampage. On one occasion, 22 Chinese laborers were hanged in Los Angeles's Chinatown. By 1882, anti-Chinese sentiment forced passage of the Chinese Exclusion Act, prohibiting immigration for ten years. Not surprisingly, America's first "anti-drug" laws (early 1880s) were enacted to close the Chinese opium dens that sprang up in and around San Francisco, which had an enormous Chinese population. The racial upheaval added to America's dark image a racist society; the Chinese government retaliated by suspending trade and diplomatic relations with the United States.

THE ECONOMIC DEPRESSION OF THE 1890S

We mentioned Messrs. Fisk and Gould in an earlier section. In trying to corner the gold market, they had seriously destabilized the US dollar and the trouble continued for the next two decades. To relieve some of the apprehension, the US government started issuing gold certificates as currency — meaning that a dollar bill could be exchanged for a dollar's worth of gold, on demand. A strong US dollar backed by gold was very good for Wall Street, but not for Main Street. The worldwide production of gold was not keeping pace with rapidly growing industry, and created a money shortage that, in turn, caused a sharply lower demand for the products this country produced. The public debate over how to best resolve the problem divided the population into basically two camps — the "gold bugs" and the "silverites." Since there was sixteen times more silver than there was gold, it was reasoned, it would be much harder for anyone to corner the market (although it has been tried, even in the 1980s). The "silverites" believed that putting America on the silver standard would allow more money to circulate, which would stimulate economic growth; they demanded the free and unlimited coinage of silver — that, in effect, would mean spreading the wealth.

The Republicans backed by Wall Street prevailed and the nation's money problems were not resolved. Conditions deteriorated even more. Numerous attempts were made to bolster gold reserves through the sale of bonds, but each time the gold was replenished it would only be depleted again. The recession turned into a depression when, in 1893, nearly 15,000 companies failed, 500 banks went into receivership, and nearly 30% of the country's railroad system was declared financially insolvent. This caused a deep depression lasting well over three years. At one point the New York Stock Exchange closed for four months. Labor strikes intensified, and the future looked rather bleak. Why, things got so tough even Theodore Roosevelt, then Civil Service Commissioner, was forced to sell off four acres at Sagamore Hill to keep his family afloat. Or, so we are told.

Writing on the Panic of 1893, Lee I. Niedringhaus[37] stated that "the darling of the industrials was National Cordage, the most actively traded and widely held industrial security on the exchange. National Cordage was a combination of companies manufacturing rope and cordage principally for agricultural equipment." Presumably, that meant rope and cordage made from hemp, as there were no synthetic fibers at the time and jute and other fibers were still not making significant inroads in this industry.

The Re-emergence of the Prohibitionist Movement

Meanwhile, the Prohibition movement was still alive and well in the hearts, minds, and family values of righteously religious people. On September 1, 1869, the National Prohibitionist Party was established in Chicago, primarily by religious clerics and recovering alcoholics. They presented themselves as "Do-gooders," claiming the high road, but they took such an aggressive approach to imposing their moralistic ideals on the general public that one has to question their psychological motivation. This was still an idea whose time had not come and the Prohibitionist Party wallowed in relative obscurity, where it would have remained had it not been for the many contributions, totaling some $25 million, given to the Prohibitionist movement by industrialist John D. Rockefeller.

Relatively unknown before the 1870s, John D. was not a very likeable man. He was a thin-lipped penny-pinching tightwad with little in the way of personality and not much of an education. Rockefeller was seen as a hypocrite hiding

---

37. Museum of American Financial History. http://www.financialhistory.org/fh/1998/61-1.htm. Lee I. Niedringhaus has had a lengthy career in international banking and management consulting and for many years has specialized in late 19th century business and financial history.

behind the public façade of respectability — a self-promoting do-gooder, regular church-goer, and teetotaling pillar of society who always used front-men to do his dirty work. Rockefeller was raised by his mother Eliza in a strict Calvinist faith.[38] His father, "Doc" Rockefeller, was a traveling flimflam man and snake oil salesman, who was later discovered to have another wife in Livingston, South Dakota, where he lived for some 40 years.[39] Anthony Sampson describes John D. as "an extrovert character of doubtful reputation who was once, rightly or wrongly, indicted for rape, a background which doubtless encouraged John D. to withdraw into himself and into obsessive hard work.[40] Rockefeller attended his Baptist Church in Cleveland as devoutly as he attended his accounts,[41] and even taught bible classes. Rockefeller's social life revolved around his family, sprinkled with some church events, but he clearly shunned the other industrialists who were beginning to emerge. A prominent banker once complained: "We never see Mr. Rockefeller. He does not mingle with us in clubs and social gatherings, and so we have come to look upon him as a great spider sitting back in his web seeking whom he may destroy."[42] He was the Mr. Scrooge of the late 19th and early 20th century — but he was vicious, as well.

Although an avowed teetotaler and very much against anyone else using alcohol, Rockefeller's generous support of the Prohibitionist movement, which eventually lead to alcohol prohibition, may well have represented more of a business opportunity than personal conviction. Most people do not realize that Rockefeller had a financial interest in outlawing alcohol. The first automobile engines (the combustion engine, invented in 1876, and the diesel engine, invented in 1892) were designed to run on alcohol, derived from vegetation (biomass conversion), not gasoline. It is highly likely the only reason we ever started using petroleum-based gasoline to fuel our automobiles was because of John D. Rockefeller's devious, often unethical, business practices.

Rockefeller was clearly in a position to know early on that a number of people in Germany (Karl Benz, 1885), England, France, and the United States were trying to develop a practical motorized vehicle, and he probably knew that

---

38. Collier, Peter & Horowitz, David. *The Rockefellers, An American Dynasty*. Holt, Rinehart and Winston, New York: 1976, p. 9.

39. Collier & Horowitz, p. 8.

40. Sampson, Anthony. *The Seven Sisters*. Viking Penguin, New York: 1975, p. 31 - 32.

41. Josephson, Matthew. *The Robber Barons*. Harcourt Brace Jovanovich, New York: 1962, p. 47.

42. Collier & Horowitz, p. 32.

Henry Ford designed and built his first Model "T" to operate on alcohol. It didn't take a visionary to figure out that the automobile and airplane were significant inventions that would have an enormous economic impact, and it was obvious to Rockefeller that he would acquire immeasurable fortune if his gasoline fueled those wonderful inventions. Thus, in 1903, Standard Oil agents were at Kitty Hawk offering gasoline and lubricating oil to the Wright brothers. In 1904, their salesmen set up a service station for use by contestants in the first international automobile race from New York to Paris.[43]

Rockefeller wanted that market and he had to eliminate the competition, alcohol, by any means necessary — as he did in all his endeavors. By promoting the idea of alcohol prohibition, one could create serious doubts about the future availability of alcohol. Why tie the evolving automobile and aircraft industries to a questionable fuel? The adoption of gasoline as the standard vehicle fuel cata-pulted Rockefeller's wealth from $200 million in 1897 to the level of billionaire in 1913.[44]

People understand that businessmen have to be tough, but most likely Rockefeller's reputation as "the most hated man in America" (1880sC1920s) came about primarily because he was using his vast wealth to impose his skewed perspective of life on the American people: The majority of his charitable contri-butions went to supporting one church activity or another, many of which were promoting alcohol prohibition, which was extremely unpopular with the gen-eral public. More likely than not, Rockefeller financially supported Carry Nation and the campaign in Kansas's 1880 election that resulted in the state adopting a Prohibition Amendment to its constitution. Rockefeller was giving so much money to the Prohibitionist movement, particularly through the Baptist Church network, that in 1891 he hired Frederick T. Gates, an ordained minister, full time to administer his philanthropic gifts.[45] The money he gave the Prohibitionists Party rejuvenated the movement, enabling them to run candidates in a number of state elections as well as presidential candidates in 1884, 1888, 1892 and 1896. Those four elections were landslide defeats for the Prohibitionist Party[46] and

---

43. *Ibid.*, p. 39.

44. *Ibid.*, p. 53.

45. *Ibid.*, p. 51 & 52

46. No Prohibitionist Party presidential candidate captured more than two percent of the popular vote in any of the four elections in which they ran, and no viable Presidential candidate in those elections, Democrat or Republican, ever endorsed the idea of outlawing alcohol.

showed how opposed to Prohibition the American people really were. But that didn't stop Rockefeller.

Leading the Democrat Party toward progressive liberalism was, ironically, William Jennings Bryan, who also had a heavy religious orientation and Prohibitionist leanings. Bryan received the Democratic Party nomination in three elections — 1896, 1900, and 1908, but lost every time.

Along with the Prohibition Party two other organizations were formed, claiming to promote temperance but actually determined to outlaw alcohol. In 1874, the Women's Christian Temperance Union was established and spread throughout the Midwest, creating a direct link between women, the Prohibitionists, and organized religion and leaving the impression that temperance was an issue important to any woman. Many of the WCTU chapters would go into a saloon as a group and lecture the patrons about drunkenness and debauchery before dragging their tippling husbands home.

Every social movement has its fanatics, and the Prohibition movement had Carry Nation. In 1900, with hatchet in hand, she led a gang of militant WCTU women into a number of saloons and destroyed tens of thousands of dollars worth of furniture, fixtures and alcohol. Founder of Kansas' Medicine Lodge chapter of the WCTU, Carry Nation exemplified the lunacy and ignorance of the Prohibition movement. Of course, she was a victim of the world she was born and lived in. She was apparently raised by her mother, Mary Moore, closely related to Alexander Campbell, a religious leader in the 1850s. Carry's own education is described as brief and sporadic. Her first husband and only real love was Dr. Charles Gloyd, who died of alcoholism six months after their marriage. In 1877, Carry married David Nation (19 years her senior), a lawyer, minister and editor. They were constantly at odds, apparently because of Carry's extremist views on social reform (prohibition), which he disapproved of. David Nation divorced her in 1901.

Carry believed that her destructive antics were divinely inspired and that even her name (Nation) had been preordained.[47] Most newspaper reporters and editors described her as an ignorant, unbalanced and contentious woman of vast energies. Her followers had to be very much like her — uneducated, unworldly, lonely women whose husbands had either died or left them; and, of course, religious fanatics.

---

47. *World Book Encyclopedia.* 2003, Vol 14 (N-O) p. 26.

Carry's mother spent the last three years of her life in the Missouri State Hospital for the Insane. Carry's brother, sister, and daughter were also declared insane. During the last several years of her life Carry was diagnosed as suffering from psychotic delusions; she also "suffered episodes of paranoia and mystic seizures," "clouded and apathetic mind," and "increasing feebleness"; she died in 1911 at the age of 64 in a mental hospital in Leavenworth — eight years before alcohol prohibition was enacted into law.

The shock value Carry Nation provided showed the stubborn determination of America's Prohibitionists. It was also a serious setback to the women's suffrage movement. America was not an overtly chauvinistic society, by the standard of the day, as demonstrated by the fact that even before the Suffragette Movement was founded in 1848 several Western states passed laws giving women equal voting rights. It was highly likely that women would have gotten the right to vote long before 1920 had it not been for women like Carry Nation and the false perception they promoted: that women wanted alcohol outlawed. Actually, most women did not support Prohibition. The Suffragettes, in fact, advocated temperance (moderation), not abstinence; but it was perceived as a women's issue because women were prominent in the Prohibition movement — and, frankly, visions of a hatchet-wielding Carry Nation leading a herd of militant bible preaching women into a saloon and wrecking the place put fear in the hearts of many men.

Women were very much a prominent part of the speakeasy scene during the Prohibition Era. The Suffragettes, under the direction of Alice Paul (known as the mother of the Equal Rights Amendment), practiced a much milder form of militancy. They organized placard-carrying demonstrators and marched in front of the White House and through major cities. As often happens with nonviolent movements, many of the participants were beaten and jailed. The renowned historian Arthur Schlesinger noted, "The police, with Wilson's tacit approval, would respond with brutality. Women picketing the White House were roughly hauled off to jail, stripped naked and thrown into dirty cells with syphilitic prostitutes.[48] One woman, Ada Davenport Kendall, was put on bread and water for 17 days in solitary confinement for protesting against what she saw as injustice. But, in the end, they got what they wanted: the right to vote, in 1920 when enough states ratified the 19th Amendment.

---

48. Schlesinger, p. 433.

It is also worth noting that the issue of women's suffrage came to the forefront shortly after the US began experiencing a dramatic increase in the number of immigrants of diverse ethnic, racial and religious backgrounds. These people were becoming citizens and the men were acquiring the right to vote. Giving the vote to women of mainstream "American" heritage helped offset the demographic shift.

Perhaps the most effective of the anti-alcohol groups was what is known today as a PAC, Political Action Committee, calling itself "the Anti-Saloon League of America," founded in 1893. The Anti-Saloon League's stated objective was to close America's saloons, which they claimed represented a demoralizing force in politics. This was a reference to local Democrat organizations, particularly in Irish neighborhoods, that regularly conducted their business in the local saloons. The saloons were the hub of the community and usually the first building constructed in a new town. Like the pubs and taverns of merry old England, the saloons of America were restaurants and hotels. They also hosted town meetings and court trials, and many saloons had stages where touring theater groups entertained the community. More important, the local saloon was a place where men came to hear the latest news, to discuss local politics and decide local issues, and to conduct business. Most people at the time were basically illiterate and had very little, if any, education; community business and virtually everything else was communicated by word of mouth, not read in the daily newspapers.

The saloon was an oasis. It was also fundamentally a male bastion, catering to the whims of their adult male customers. That meant that some served as the local casino, too, and some served as the local brothel. The British have always been less prudish than Americans (perhaps because most of the fanatically religious groups left England and migrated to these shores!). In America, however, the "good women" of the community stayed far away from the saloons, especially on the Western frontier, lest their virtue be questioned. Men with strong religious convictions generally shied away, too.

Then there were those who were kept away not of their own choice. As a haven for the more affluent, that is, white, males, saloons often denied service to black, Indian, Hispanic and Asian men. That meant that they were effectively excluded from participating in deciding or influencing decisions such as hiring the local sheriff or how to spend community tax revenues. Using the local saloon was the way the "good old boys" maintained their control of the community. It also undermined the influence of the church in community affairs, and that is why the saloons became a prime target of the religiously inspired Prohibition movement.

The Anti-Saloon League justified its position by claiming that the mechanization of industry placed a premium on the sober employee, and that the taxpayers were footing the bill for poorhouses and prisons filled with victims of alcoholism. The Prohibitionist movement was dominated by white upper and middle-class suburban or rural Baptist women, with generally a very skewed and narrow perspective of the world — especially considering that before the beginning of the 20th century, most women were uneducated and stayed at home. These were women with the luxury of free time who saw themselves as crusaders on a mission. To them, the poverty ridden slums of America's large East Coast cities, primarily New York and Boston, which housed America's Irish and Italian Roman Catholic, German Lutherans, and Jewish immigrant populations, were dens of sin and drunken debauchery. They imagined that weaning these men off alcohol would "save" them. Perhaps they should have kept their focus on their own Baptist and Protestant men folk, who also frequented saloons all across America. Often, those taking the most vehement stand are blind to reality.

> Nothing so needs reforming as other people's habits.
> — Mark Twain, Pudd'nhead Wilson

One reason the poor immigrants stayed poor was because the more established families would not hire them in their communities, much less allow them to live there. In fact, the alcohol prohibition laws that were enacted state by state helped to control the spread and influence of those minorities just as the anti-opium laws of the 1880s were enacted to discourage Chinese railroad workers from settling in white Protestant and Baptist communities. As described by Joseph Gusfield, "native, Protestant, middle-class leaders, ideologically unopposed to moderate consumption of alcohol, joined the prohibitionist crusade to assert the continued superiority of their way of life."[49] Not surprisingly, after the 18th Amendment was ratified and alcohol prohibition went into effect, it was precisely these poor Italian, Irish, Jewish, and German immigrants who rose to positions of prominence within the bootlegging gangs of the 1920s, and economic survival was their underlying motivation. That is not to say that "pearly

---

49. Bonnie, Richard J. and Whitebread, Charles H. II. *The Marihuana Conviction, A History of Marihuana Prohibition in the United States.* University Press of Virginia: 1974, p. 25

white" Protestants and Baptists stayed out of the illegal alcohol trade; but it was easier for them to hide their illegal activities

The Prohibitionists, however, were fighting an uphill battle. Despite their organizational superiority and financial resources they were still considered the radical fringe, and the successes they did have were usually overshadowed by Teddy Roosevelt's dynamic personality. Roosevelt fascinated and dominated the news media after his ascension to the presidency — so much so that everything else was pretty much ignored.

THE TEDDY ROOSEVELT PRESIDENCY

The unexpected ascension of Teddy Roosevelt to the presidency definitely disrupted, at least temporarily, the plans of the industrialists who had controlled the Republican Party since Lincoln's assassination. The hero of San Juan Hill and former Governor of the State of New York, Theodore Roosevelt became McKinley's vice presidential nominee after Garret A. Hobart, McKinley's first vice president, died in November 1899. Essentially, Roosevelt's became McKinley's vice president at the insistence of New York's Republican Party bosses, who were anxious to get him out of New York. The Republicans had won the governorship because of Roosevelt's popularity but he was too much of a liberal reformer and they couldn't control him. Boss Platt, the Republican majority leader in the Senate, decided on installing Roosevelt as the vice president — a do-nothing job that was supposed to lead to political obscurity and usually still does.

To the chagrin of the Republican Party bosses, after McKinley's assassination Roosevelt attained the presidency. He became even more vocal about his liberal reformist ideals, very much to the distress of the railroad owners and Rockefeller. The Republican Party bosses argued almost constantly with Roosevelt, but the bulk of Republicans were still basically Lincoln liberals. They loved Teddy Roosevelt and what he was doing. The voters loved him even more, after he directed his Justice Department to prepare a case against the railroads and break up their monopoly. The victory over the railroads really made Teddy Roosevelt a stand-out American president — he became known as "the man who put a bit in the Iron Horse's mouth."

Teddy Roosevelt and John D. Rockefeller were the two dominant figures in the early 20th century and in the eyes of the public they easily fell into the good-guy/bad-guy image. They came to a clash when Roosevelt's Justice Department dragged Standard Oil into federal court for violation of the Sherman Anti-Trust Act. Rockefeller lost and was forced to break up Standard Oil into several smaller, independent companies. Roosevelt's popularity shot up again. Roosevelt easily won reelection in 1904, demanding that big business give the people a "square deal."

Most of what Roosevelt accomplished was done during his first term as president. He crippled himself in the second term by announcing prematurely that he would not seek a third term (in those days, it would have been perfectly legal). Knowing they would soon enough be rid of Roosevelt, and not wanting him to get any more credit than absolutely necessary, the Republican Party bosses, still in control of the US Congress and most of the state legislators, ignored Roosevelt's domestic legislative agenda. Even Roosevelt's liberal Republican supporters in Congress had to follow the lead of the party bosses. Essentially, Roosevelt accomplished three things in his second term, all without the help of Congress. He anointed William Taft (his friend, confident and Secretary of War) as his successor; he created the national forests by claiming millions of acres as a national treasure; and, in an attempt to insure his place in history, Roosevelt made a major effort to reestablish trade with China.

As Roosevelt's second term was coming to the end he was concerned, even obsessed, about his place in history. Reestablishing trade relations with China would be good for his image and good for the economy (creating new markets for American goods); it was also an opportunity to challenge British domination of the Chinese market. The British, still considered an adversary of the United States, were also still at odds with the Chinese government for continuing the "China Trade" with the attendant ruinous proliferation of opium. Roosevelt's initial attempts at diplomacy with China failed miserably; the Chinese were outraged by the brutal treatment and killings of its émigré workers and the Chinese Exclusionary Act that was promulgated only a few decades earlier.

Roosevelt sought the advice of some presumed "experts" — specifically, Dr. Hamilton Kemp Wright, a former Army physician (who made great advances in the treatment of beriberi), his wife Elizabeth, and their friend Bishop Charles H. Brent, an Episcopal missionary who described himself as "pursuing a lifelong battle against the opium trade." In winning the Spanish-American War, the United States inherited somewhat of an opium addiction problem of its own, in the Philippines. It was the policy of the previous Spanish government to legally supply opium to registered addicts. The Wrights and Brent apparently met in the Philippines, where Dr. Wright was stationed — probably at some church function. Bishop Brent was appointed to lead a War Department Commission of Inquiry studying alternatives.[50] These three people shaped America's drug policy and spearheaded the fight to criminalize drug use in America.

Dr. Wright and Bishop Brent were able to get close to Roosevelt only because of Wright's wife Elizabeth Washburn Wright.[51] Her father was US Senator (1889-95) William Drew Washburn of Wisconsin (Republican). The Washburn family goes back to Revolutionary times in Maine and Massachusetts. Two of Elizabeth's uncles were governors; her great-uncle was governor of Massachusetts; and another uncle, Elihu Washburn,[52] was a personal friend of Presidents Abraham Lincoln and Ulysses S. Grant. Elihu Washburn served as Secretary of State in Grant's administration and was seriously considered as Grant's successor — he probably would have been the Republican Party's nominee, had not a rift developed when Grant contemplated running for a third term. At least five of Elizabeth's uncles served in the House of Representatives, three simultaneously (one from Wisconsin, one from Illinois, and one from Maine), and two served as US diplomats. Elizabeth also had a cousin who attended school with Henry Cabot Lodge and later served as his private secretary, which led to an appointment as a Treasury Department lawyer. There's more. You don't get that far without being extremely wealthy and influential; the Washburns owned newspapers, railroads and a milling company (which became the Pillsbury-Washburn Mill Company), and several of the men served in various state legislators. The Washburns were very active in church affairs — one of Elizabeth's cousins became a missionary.

Although opium had no direct bearing on the strained relations between China and the United States, the Wrights and Bishop Brent essentially convinced Roosevelt that the best way of reestablishing trade relations would be to show the Chinese government that America was sympathetic to the addiction problem and wanted to help resolve it. They suggested the United States convene an international conference. Nothing else had worked, so Roosevelt thought this was worth a try. In 1906, he instructed Elihu Root, his Secretary of State, to start promoting the idea. Eventually, twelve nations interested in improving trade relations with China agreed to convene a conference on opium,

50. Brecher, Edward and the Editors of Consumer Reports. *Licit & Illicit Drugs*, Little, Brown and Co., Boston:1972, p.48.

51. Anslinger, Harry J. *The Protectors*.

52. *Dictionary of American Biography*. Charles Scribner & Sons, New York: 1936, Vol. 10, pp. 504-505

in Shanghai (1909). It was called the International Opium Commission and its agenda was specifically to address China's opium problem — not a worldwide problem. Roosevelt appointed Dr. Hamilton Wright as America's representative, with the title of US Opium Commissioner.

In discussing Dr. and Mrs. Wright and Bishop Brent, Director of the Federal Bureau of Narcotics, Harry J. Anslinger, in his book *The Protectors* said, "It was because of these three vigorous persons that President Theodore Roosevelt had convened the first meeting of the International opium Conference, in Shanghai, during the early 1900s."

The Shanghai conference was more show than substance, of course. None of the representatives had the authority to make decisions or sign any treaties. This was the first international attempt to discuss "recreational" drugs. China was pleased with the symbolic gesture; but she kept up the embargo on American trade. A second conference was held at The Hague, in 1911. America's participation in that conference had to be approved by Congress. The US Opium Commissioner, Dr. Hamilton Wright, presented his case, saying,

> Our move to help China [referring to the Shanghai Conference] in her opium reform gave us more prestige in China than any of our recent friendly acts toward her. If we continue to press steadily for The Hague Conference, China will recognize that we are sincere on her behalf, and the whole business may be used as oil to smooth the troubled water of our aggressive commercial policy there.

The International Opium Conference at The Hague proved far more successful than expected. The British agreed to end the "China trade" when China agreed to revoke its import ban. That agreement, however, did not include the United States. The Chinese were still furious over the Chinese Exclusionary Act. However, acknowledging the US government's efforts, the Chinese agreed to future talks about the possibility of reestablishing trade with the United States. But the Chinese really wanted nothing to do with any foreigners; they wanted the British to stop importing opiates, and they secured an agreement on that. Besides, China was in no position to make a major change of direction. The Emperor P'u Yi was a young child and the country was nominally being run by the wives of the previous Emperor, while real power was in the hands of warlords who were fighting each other for control. Wright's contact with the Chinese government was more diplomatic courtesy than substance.

PASSAGE OF THE HARRISON ANTI-NARCOTICS ACT

Frustrated by his failure to negotiate a trade agreement and encouraged by his bosses at the State Department to keep trying, Wright engineered a last ditch effort to show the Chinese that America was their friend and partner in the fight against opium addiction. The Harrison Anti-Narcotics Act of 1914 outlawed opium, under the delusion (created by Wright) that convincing the Chinese that America was serious about stopping opiate addiction would lead to trade relations. Perhaps more important to the State Department was the perceived opportunity to undermine British influence in China.

In truth, passage of the Harrison Anti-Narcotics Act was unnecessary, irrelevant, and did not lead to reestablishing trade with China. Technically, the Act did not outlaw opiates or cocaine; it only forced the people distributing them to register with the federal government, and heavily taxed the transfer of ownership. Enforcement of the Harrison Anti-Narcotics Act was given to the US Treasury Department; but, since no taxes were ever collected, it was worthless in that regard as well. The medicinal use of morphine and cocaine was exempt from the taxes, for humanitarian reasons, which effectively gave the pharmaceutical companies (the now "legitimized" former snake oil salesman) an exclusive market and huge profits. There was no practical reason to outlaw either opiates or cocaine, especially with the Pure Food and Drug Act of 1906 effectively curtailing their use.

The word "narcotics" is really an umbrella term, like "drugs." Webster's defines narcotics as "(a) a drug (as opium, belladonna, or alcohol group) that in moderate allays sensibility [dulls the senses], relieves pain, and produces [induces] profound sleep but that in poisonous [excessive] doses produces [causes] stupor, coma, or convulsions." (Bracketed italics indicate previous definition.)

For most Americans, that meant morphine — a liquid form of opium. Morphine was recognized as the most effective painkiller well before the Civil War (which was an extremely bloody conflict). The wounded were given large amounts of morphine to relieve their pain, and they quickly became addicted. Morphine addiction became known as "the Army's disease,'" and was considered this country's largest drug problem. In fact, alcohol has always been America's largest drug problem; but alcohol was not considered a narcotic. Including marijuana under that definition is a real stretch of the imagination.

Thus, while America was happy to pass laws against the use of opium by the Chinese, the abuse of opium derivatives (morphine and heroin) by "respectable" folk was totally ignored. Actually, before the turn of the century there were hundreds of elixirs, potions and cure-alls being sold all over America, even candy and "soft drinks," containing large quantities of morphine or cocaine. They were sold over the counter without any warnings or guidelines, and without the supervision of a doctor. A survey conducted between 1883 and 1885 in the State of Iowa revealed that, with a population of less than two million people, there were 3,000 stores selling products containing opiates. One nationwide drug distributor sold 600 different medicines containing opiates, all without the need of a prescription.

Concoctions like Ayer's Cherry Pectoral and Godfrey's Cordial were nothing more than opium sweetened with molasses and flavored with sassafras. There were also opiate-laden elixirs specifically marketed for children, like Mistress Winslow's Soothing Syrup, Mother Bailey's Quieting Syrup and Kopp's Baby Friend. If you couldn't get to a store, you could simply order Laudanum (morphine and alcohol) from the Sears and Roebuck catalogue.

Abbie Hoffman gave a colorful depiction of the scene:

> Doctors prescribed opiates for pain, cough, diarrhea, and dysentery. In fact, the nineteenth-century doctors prescribed morphine the way doctors today give out tranquilizers — with a shovel. One 1880 textbook listed fifty-four diseases that could be alleviated with morphine injections. Morphine was even given to alcoholics, in the belief that it was better to be hooked on narcotics than on alcohol. (This practice continued in the rural South until narcotics prohibition got serious in the late thirties.)
>
> Interestingly, the demographics of users back then differed greatly from users today: they were largely female, mostly white, and mostly in their forties. Women users, outnumbering men by nearly three to one, were an easy target for addiction — first, because opiates were prescribed for menstrual and menopausal discomforts; and second, because it was thought unwomanly to be seen drinking liquor in public, or to have it lingering on your breath. So while husbands were in town chuckin'em down at the local saloon, the wives were back home demurely taking their opium.[53]

And white women frequented the opium dens of San Francisco, shocking as that seemed at the time (and may seem, now). But they were addicted to the morphine in the elixirs they commonly used to relieve their common discomforts. It was also not uncommon for cowboys, while guarding their cattle from rustlers and

---

53. Hoffman, Abbie. *Steal this Urine Test. Fighting Drug Hysteria in America.* Penguin Group: 1987, p. 25.

wolves, to cuddle up to a bottle of "snake oil," which was soothing but left no tell-tale odor of alcohol on their breath; urban factory workers did the same.

Morphine, properly administered, undeniably had its place; obviously, the unregulated and irresponsible excessive use was the problem. The companies should have notified consumers their products contained drugs, and that if used excessively could be dangerous. Certainly, their addictive properties were not widely recognized until long after the Civil War; and, of course, companies see addicts not as problems but as "repeat customers."

Responding to the public's concerns over morphine addiction, the Bayer Company introduced heroin, in 1898, claiming it was as effective as morphine but not addictive. The only difference between heroin and morphine is the form it takes — heroin is a powder and morphine is a liquid. In the blood stream, they are one and the same. Yet, heroin was heralded as an amazing medical discovery by the enlightened scientific and medical community. Today, the medical community does not recognize heroin as a medicine at all.

This was not a problem exclusive to the medical and pharmaceutical industry. Opiates and cocaine were found in many products including liquor, candy and, of course, almost every "soft drink" on the market — Coca-Cola was only the most famous. Coca-Cola also marketed its cocaine laden "soft drink" as "brain food."[54] Coca-Cola substituted caffeine for cocaine only after its hometown (Atlanta) prohibited the drug's sale without a prescription in 1903.[55]

Cocaine also has a long history of use as a recreational intoxicant, apart from the Peruvian Indians who have been chewing coca leaves for centuries. Prominent people on both sides of the Atlantic[56] used cocaine in one form or another, and cocaine gained the reputation of being a rich man's drug. A cocaine-based wine, Vin Tonique Mariani, produced in Paris in the 1860s, was avidly endorsed by patrons including US presidents Ulysses S. Grant and William McKinley, Queen Victoria, the Prince of Wales, the kings of Norway and Sweden, the czar of Russia, the commanding general of the British Army, eminent writers — Alexander Dumas, H.G. Wells, Jules Verne, Emile Zola, Henrik Ibsen, Sarah Bernhardt, and inventor Thomas A. Edison, plus Statue of Liberty sculptor Bartholdi, Pope Leo XIII, Arthur Conan Doyle and Sigmund Freud. (Apparently, Freud's use of cocaine hurt him professionally, so he stopped using it.)

---

54. Falco, Mathea, *The Making of a Drug-Free America: Programs That Work.* Crown Publishing : 1994, p. 16.

55. *Ibid.,* p. 18.

56. *High Times Encyclopedia of Recreational Drugs.* Stonehill Publishing Co, New York: 1978, p.170.

The pharmaceutical companies were under no legal obligation to disclose the ingredients in their products, and naturally they kept their formulas secret to prevent competitors from copying them. If people became addicted, that was their problem. After all, this was simply the most effective pain reliever known to medical science. As a result, people were consuming large quantities of potentially dangerous drugs, almost daily, without knowing what or how much they were taking. Hundreds of thousands of people were unconsciously being addicted to opiates and made dependent on cocaine under the guise of a cure-all or thirst quencher.

Passage of the Pure Food and Drug Act not only forced companies to list the ingredients of their products; it also provided companies some legal protection by allowing them to patent their formulas. That legislation only addressed newly released products; companies like Coca-Cola were grandfathered in and were not forced to reveal their formulas. However, that legislation heightened public awareness of the inclusion of opiates and cocaine in the products they were using, and many simply stopped using them. Most of the elixirs and potions simply disappeared from the marketplace. The opiate problem immediately and dramatically declined.

That wasn't good enough for zealots like Hamilton Wright and his cohorts. They wanted to have opiates and cocaine outlawed. Because of the lack of any real substance, the argument used to justify outlawing cocaine quickly deteriorated into blatant bigotry. Setting the tone of Wright's anti-narcotic campaign was Dr. Christopher Koch, who testified before the US House Ways and Means Committee on December 14, 1910, stating... "There is little doubt that every Jew peddler in the South carries the stuff." Koch went on to point out the dangers the country faced at the hands of "cocaine-crazed Southern Negroes." He was later quoted[57] as saying, "Most of the attacks upon white women of the South are the direct result of a cocaine crazed Negro brain." Koch was certainly no expert on the subject, he was merely an opinionated Pharmacist, chairman of the Philadelphia Association of Retail Druggists Legislative Committee and former president of that organization. A graduate of the Philadelphia College of Pharmacy (1899), he later became vice president of the Pennsylvania Pharmacopeia Examining Board. Unfortunately, Koch's comments were not scientific, they were only bigoted and absurd. Few if any blacks, especially in the South, could afford cocaine.

---

57. *High Times*, p. 173

Sadly, Koch's statements went unchallenged — which doesn't speak well for the level of intelligence of our elected officials. Dr. Koch may have been a pharmacist but he wasn't speaking scientifically. His comments were a major part of Wright's strategy, meant to attract the support of Southern congressman for future legislation — specifically the Harrison Anti-Narcotic Act, already in the pipeline, which unquestionably would have failed without their support.

The situation with morphine exacerbated the hysteria over the presence of any potentially dangerous drug, especially in products children consume (soft drinks and candy). Harry J. Anslinger claimed that before the Harrison Anti-Narcotics Act (1914), "One out of every four hundred persons" were addicted and after it became law that figure dropped to "one in every four thousand."[58] Anslinger's assessment demonstrates either an obvious bias or total ignorance. He also drastically underestimated the problem, which Dr. John Morgan, Professor of Pharmacology at Mt. Sinai School of Medicine, more accurately estimated that 5% of the population was physically dependent on over-the-counter opiates.[59] That's twenty-five times greater than Anslinger's estimate. Both Anslinger and Morgan were describing the situation that existed in America before passage of the Pure Food and Drug Act (1906). However, it was the Pure Food and Drug Act that forced manufactures to list the content of their products, to inform the public of what they were actually ingesting. It also offered patent protection to manufactures, protecting their formulas from being imitated by competitors. That essentially destroyed the elixir/snake oil market and dramatically reduced the use of opiates (morphine), not the Harrison Act. Criminalizing the use of Opiates and cocaine, which is what the Harrison Anti-Narcotics Act did, was both unnecessary and ineffective. Realistically, the Harrison Act was little more then a message being sent to the Chinese, indicating that America was sympathetic to their addiction problem and even more important that America was their ally in fighting opium addiction problem worldwide. It was done primarily to encourage trade with the Chinese, which, because of the killing of Chinese railroad workers on America's Western frontier, had been outlawed by the Chinese government.

---

58. Anslinger, Harry J. *The Murderers*. Farrar, Straus and Co, New York: 1961 p. 6

59. Hoffman, p. 25.

TEDDY'S FINAL SHOT AT CORPORATE DOMINATION

One of the last things Roosevelt did as President of the United States was to take another shot at America's industrialists, and specifically William Randolph Hearst, America's leading paper producer. Using his wealth to influence the Republican Party, Hearst had acquired control of most of America's northwest forests. Roosevelt, by declaring millions of acres of wilderness land a national treasure, essentially thwarted Hearst's plans to cut it down for paper and forced Hearst to look elsewhere. Hearst then used his influence with the US government to cajole and bribe the Mexican government into giving him permission to cut down a Mexican forest.

That was essentially a done deal, but it did not strike everyone as being in Mexico's interest. Pancho Villa, with a group of like-minded compatriots, took control of the forest in 1914 and refused to let Hearst cut down any trees. This act of defiance is considered the beginning of the Mexican Revolution. It infuriated Hearst. Hearst vilified Villa and published diatribes against him almost daily, in his newspapers. This campaign, backed by Hearst's prowess as a major contributor to the Republican Party, caused the US government to pressure the Mexican government into taking action. Villa retaliated by raiding Columbus, New Mexico, and the US retaliated for that in March 1916 by sending General Pershing into Mexico. Thus began the Mexican Border Campaign.

Pershing failed to apprehend Pancho Villa, and with the United States on the verge of entering World War I, he and his troops were recalled in February 1917. Pershing was promoted to Major General and ordered to France, where he commanded America's Expeditionary Force. This left Hearst with only his newspapers to fire at Villa. After Pershing's withdrawal, the Mexican Revolutionary War began in earnest, causing the mass migration of Mexican nationals into the United States.

The American people weren't interested in attacking Pancho Villa — they saw him as a Mexican hero, and Hearst as a robber baron. Hearst had to change his tactics. He needed public opinion on his side, and as the country was being edged toward the Prohibition era, Hearst was able to exploit white America's bigotry toward the Mexican immigrants by artificially creating a fear of marijuana as a dangerous intoxicant. (The word *marijuana* was practically unheard of until after 1914 — it was actually Mexican slang meaning, "intoxicate." It was part of the lyrics to "La Cucaracha" (meaning "cockroach"!), which Villa troops adopted as their marching song. Actually, the Mexican word for the intoxicating properties of Cannabis is "Mota," not marijuana. The word *marijuana* was so obscure that Hearst was able to shape its meaning anyway he wanted.

Hearst didn't make his newspaper fortune by reporting objective facts or telling the truth. His success was based entirely on sensational journalism, a.k.a. "yellow journalism." Actually, the term "yellow journalism" derives from the cheap wood-based paper Hearst used for his newspapers, which turned yellow after a few weeks; it came to denote the dramatic and dubious style of journalism Hearst practiced. (Other newspapers worldwide also understood that this was a successful business model.) Sensational stories depicting marijuana as a dangerous drug became common fare in the US. It wasn't long before several Southern and Western states began passing laws outlawing marijuana. However, the fact that the question, "What is marijuana?" was asked on the floor of the House of Representatives in 1937, when the Marijuana Tax Act was passed, suggests that even then the word, the substance and the nature of marijuana were not widely known.

Hearst never mentioned that what he was calling marijuana was actually a form of hemp. Americans knew what hemp was, and they were aware of its many forms and many uses. Millions of farmers and manufacturers were still making a living cultivating and processing hemp into finished products — they weren't about to outlaw it. Hearst, of course, had a financial interest in outlawing hemp. Now that he owned so much forest land, he had no interest in returning to hemp-based paper. In fact, as early as 1916 the US Department of Agriculture was promoting the idea of using hemp to meet the nation's paper needs, noting also that at the current rate of paper consumption the forests would be used up by the year 2000. (And they would have been, if reforestation programs had not been implemented.)

THE LUDLOW MASSACRE

On April 20, 1914, in the midst of a strike for better working conditions and the right to join a union at the CF&I coal mine near Ludlow, Colorado, 24 people (including women and children) were killed and many more injured and burned by agents of the Pinkerton security agency. When word of the atrocity got out, and it was discovered that CF&I was owned by Standard Oil (Rockefeller), streets were jammed with people calling for Rockefeller to be lynched or assassinated. John D. Rockefeller, at the insistence of Jr., discretely retired and turned control of Standard Oil over to his son. John Jr. met with the striking miners and eventually settled the situation amicably; he also represented Standard Oil at the Senate hearings on the Ludlow massacre.

John Sr. retreated behind the high walls surrounding his mansion, also guarded by a large contingent of Pinkerton agents. His bad public image had finally crossed some limit. It was so bad that Jr. hired a public relations expert to help. Senior started carrying dimes in his pocket and giving them to people, particularly children. A dime didn't mean much to Rockefeller but, at the time, a child could by two pieces of hard candy for a penny. Giving dimes to kids really did not do much for Rockefeller's reputation with adults, but it did get him a lot of press coverage.

CHAPTER 3

THE 1912 ELECTION

Meanwhile, Roosevelt had succeeded in getting his chosen successor, William Howard Taft, elected in 1908. That was easy: the Democrats nominated the religious fanatic William Jennings Bryan for the third time. But almost immediately after becoming president, Taft simply caved into the Republican Party bosses, giving them free rein to put forth whatever "pork-barrel" legislation they wanted.

Here was corporate welfare at its worst, and it angered working men and women who were being denied any government assistance whatsoever. It also angered the more liberal/progressive wing of the Republican Party (remnants of Lincoln's Republican Party) and Roosevelt in particular. The party was selling out to big business interests. Roosevelt and Taft quickly became political enemies, and fought bitterly over the Republican Party's 1912 presidential nomination.

This power struggle made it apparent to the publc that the industrialists were attempting a takeover of the government through the Republican Party. In fact, they had been in control since the Grant administration. The voters were terrified, and were angry with people like Rockefeller and Carnegie. The Republican Party bosses either underestimated or ignored the political mood in the country, and they re-nominated Taft. That provoked Roosevelt and his followers, the Lincoln Republicans, to bolt the party and quickly reorganize as a third party, the US Progressive Party — the "Bull Moose" Party, with Roosevelt as presidential nominee. Without Roosevelt and his followers, the Republican Party had money but they had little or no constituency other than the industrialists, directed, as usual, from behind the scenes by Rockefeller and his men, with Taft acting as their front-man.

The party bosses in the Democrat Party were not as powerful, especially after the Tammany Hall corruption scandal. Wilson, a liberal, had denounced the Tammany Hall politicians and represented a threat to their power, which turned into a battle at the Democratic Party's 1912 nominating convention. The convention was deadlocked after 45 nominating ballots. Finally, on the 46th ballot, with the help of William Jennings Bryan, Wilson won the nomination, ending the long and arduous fight for the ideological control of the party. It should be noted that as President Elect, Wilson anointed Bryan as his Secretary of State.

The 1912 election represented an enormous victory for working class Americans — the have-nots. The Industrial Revolution of the late 19th century had created an all new and very scary phenomenon — the billionaire, with Rockefeller as the example. No one had ever accumulated so much wealth and power, or been so ruthless. The struggle between the haves and the have-nots was being played out at the ballot box in 1912, and that election can be seen as a referendum condemning Rockefeller and the other industrialists.

Not only did Taft (R) lose to Wilson (D) by a two-to-one margin, he also lost badly to Roosevelt, the third-party liberal candidate. Wilson received 6,286,214 popular votes (435 electoral votes), Roosevelt got 4,126,020 popular votes (88 electoral votes) and Taft got 3,483,922 popular votes (8 electoral votes).[60] Since the Republican Party had split, the Democrats also won control of the House and Senate for the first time in 52 years. It was a landslide victory for Wilson, but an even bigger landslide for the Liberal/Progressive movement. The popular vote was three times larger for the liberal candidates, Wilson and Roosevelt, than it was for Taft, the conservative.

Teddy Roosevelt then made the biggest mistake of his political life. After losing to Wilson, he went back to the Republican Party — who blamed him for their disastrous loss. Only a handful of Roosevelt's followers returned with him; most stayed with the Bull Moose Party, which later became part of the Progressive Party that united farmers with the Socialist party, the railroad unions, and the American Federation of Labor. The political battle lines between the wealthy

---

60. Brunner, Borgna, editor. *Information Please Almanac*, Houghton Mifflin Co, Boston: 1998, p. 62.

industrialists and the working class were starting to harden. The Progressive party grew in strength and momentum throughout the late teens and early 20s, and was quite successful, particularly in the state legislatures, instigating major policy reforms including conservation of natural and human resources, women's suffrage, popular election of US senators, and various popular initiatives.

Although victorious at the polls, the Democratic Party's hold on government was tenuous, at best. It had been a long time since the Democrats were in control of the government, and the Democrats themselves were somewhat disunited. Actually, what clinched the nomination for Wilson was his wife, Ellen, who invited Bryan to dinner. Several days later, Bryan threw his support behind Wilson.

Wilson was the most highly-educated president America ever had — with a Ph.D. His popularity grew in large part because he was keeping the US out of the war that was flaring up in Europe. But, Wilson didn't have much time for domestic issues. After the first year in office, he lost his beloved wife of 28 years. Ellen's death devastated Wilson; he withdrew into himself and avoided seeing anyone or doing much of anything.

In October 1913, about the same time Ellen died, Congress passed the bill that eventually created the 16th Amendment — for income tax. It was seen as a means to "soak the rich," but long before it went into effect the super rich protected their wealth by creating trusts and other financial instruments exempting them from having to pay heavy taxes. And even though the states were eager to "soak the rich," there is some controversy over whether the required number of states actually ratified the 16th Amendment. However, as the details and implications of the new income tax law started coming out, the working people and small businessmen realized the tax burden was falling on their shoulders — and blamed the congressional Democrats for letting it happen.

REPUBLICAN PARTY ADVOCATES ALCOHOL PROHIBITION

After the 1912 election, the Republican Party was in a state of disarray and possibly on the brink of political extinction. Without Roosevelt and his followers, the Republican Party — a shell of it former self — had little or no constituency, consisting only of the robber barons (Federalists), directed, as usual, from behind the scenes by Rockefeller and his cronies, with William Howard Taft acting as their front-man. What the Republicans did was announce their support for alcohol prohibition. It was pretty much understood that, in the foreseeable future, women would win the right to vote, and alcohol prohibition was seen as a "women's issue."

Supporting Prohibition was a blatant attempt to attract women to the Republican Party; but, in fact, what they attracted was mostly the religious extremists — fringe groups that were extremely vocal. The Prohibitionists were, at least, well organized and quickly filled the void left by the Bull Moose liberals. They were very effective at pushing Republican-backed legislation at the state level. In the four years after the Republicans announced their support of alcohol prohibition, 17 additional states passed laws prohibiting the manufacture, distribution, or importation of alcohol. In the previous eight years, 1905 to 1913, only 11 states had passed anti-alcohol legislation. By April 2, 1917, when the US declared war on Germany, there were 28 states with Prohibition laws.

Roosevelt and the few Lincoln liberals who did return to the Republican Party were hardly welcomed back into the fold — an inherent ideological conflict existed between Big Money and the religious fanatics, and the tiny "liberal Wing," which may have been the only voice of reason within the party.

WILSON'S COMEBACK

While the people understood Wilson's grief, they expected the congressional Democrats to place even more controls on big business. Instead, they got income tax and the Federal Reserve Bank.

Wilson was suffering — it has even been suggested that he told an aide he wished to be assassinated. Then, after about a year, his cousin Helen Bones introduced him to her friend, Edith Bolling Galt.[61]

Described as unusually pretty, and cheerful, Edith Bolling Galt came from one of the oldest families in Virginia. Edith literally brought Woodrow back to life — it was love at first sight for him, and before long he told his close advisor, Colonel House, that he was going to marry her. House told him that it would kill his reelection chances. Wilson shrugged off the advice, and married her on December 18, 1915, two months after they first met. Wilson's own campaign staff predicted he would lose and Wilson fully believed them.

---

61. Smith, Eugene O. *When the Cheering Stopped, the Last Years of Woodrow Wilson.* Morrow, William & Co.: 1964, p. 12 - 14

They had apparently given up on California, but when the vote was announced Wilson had eked out a few-hundred-vote victory, and the presidency was once again his. The do-nothing congressional Democrats, however, lost control of the House of Representatives and barely held onto their majority in the Senate.

Although America's participation in the war up to that point was limited to supplying weapons to the French, Germany saw that as an act of war and in January 1917 ordered its U-boats to sink America's merchant ships. When diplomatic efforts failed to stop that, Wilson asked and Congress agreed to declare war on Germany.

While Wilson and the Democrats were busy with the war, the Republicans were concentrating on domestic issues. Having won control of the House of Representatives in the 1916 election, they decided to push for a federal alcohol prohibition law, which they promoted as the "Great Social Experiment" meant to raise the moral fiber of America, and as that "extra little effort needed to win the war." (Interestingly, Edith had a herd of sheep brought in to graze on the White House lawn — thus freeing the gardeners for more important government or military duty.) Congress proposed and then passed the 18th Amendment on December 18, 1917 and sent it out to the states for ratification. President Wilson opposed Prohibition, realizing it would make America look ridiculous in the eyes of the world. However, the Senate Democrats, probably at the behest of William Jennings Bryan, as a symbolic gesture to women and probably believing it would fail to get enough states to ratify it anyway, also passed a similar bill. As a constitutional amendment, it did not require the president's approval nor was it subject to his veto. That created a rift between Wilson and Bryan that soon led to Bryan resigning as Secretary of State.

By late 1917, the Germans indicated that they wanted to end the war. It was simply a matter of negotiating the terms for peace. President Wilson was busy putting the final touches to his famous "Fourteen Points" proposal, which included the establishment of the League of Nations; this became the basis for negotiating an end to the war. In January 1918, Wilson presented his "Fourteen Points" to Congress.

All the major countries involved in World War I found something not to like in Wilson's Peace Program. However, when negotiations began in October 1918, Wilson insisted that the Fourteen Points should serve as a basis for the signing of the Armistice. And the Armistice was signed, on November 11, 1918. The major allies agreed to hold a conference in Paris to discuss the post-war world, culminating a year later in the signing of the Treaty of Versailles, which created the League of Nations.

However, after the 1918 congressional elections, the Democrats paid the price for allowing the bill calling for the 18th Amendment to pass and go out to the states for ratification — they lost control of the US Senate. That meant both houses of congress were controlled by the Republicans, who were not about to let Wilson push through his agenda. And that is part of the reason why they opposed America's participation in the League of Nations. Leading the opposition was Senator Henry Cabot Lodge, the Republican majority leader. It was a bitter fight; Wilson and Lodge grew to despise each other, so much so that Edith Wilson later asked Senator Lodge not to attend Wilson's funeral.

Realizing that the opposition had the power in Congress, Wilson took the issue of US participation in the League of Nations to the people, touring the country to promote membership. While on that tour, four months before Prohibition went into effect, Wilson suffered a paralyzing stroke, on October 2, 1919.

It left him largely incapacitated. For the last seventeen months of Wilson's administration, until Harding's inauguration in March 1921, the "first lady" basically ran the country. Unfortunately, only those things necessary to keep the government functioning were addressed; there was no attempt at resolving existing social or economic problems or issues, and Prohibition simply lingered. Congressional Republicans labeled Edith the "petticoat president." It was a responsibility thrust on her, not one she desired; and during that period all the government's employees and bills got paid, but nothing new was really initiated.

Although it was proposed as that "little extra effort to win the war," Prohibition actually went into effect over a year after World War I ended. Ratification of the Eighteenth Amendment was announced on January 29, 1919, two and a half months after hostilities ended on November 11, 1918. The war had been won and there was no longer a need for that "extra little effort." But without a referendum by the people, and with President Wilson attending the Paris Peace Conference, Prohibition became the law of the land — it went into effect on January 16, 1920.

After the World War, America dramatically increased the size of its standing army. DuPont became the US government's primary manufacturer of munitions. DuPont later created Rayon, the world's first synthetic fiber, from stabilized guncotton.

The presidency wasn't exactly kind to Wilson; he lost his first wife, struggled with the war, and was unable to get Congress to authorize participation in the League of Nations. The only good thing was finding a new love, Edith. At least, Wilson did have the respect of the people. He was seen as the principal architect of a negotiated end to the War — he brought peace to the world and for that, he was beloved throughout America and Europe. Even after suffering his debilitating stroke, Wilson remained a very popular president. He spoke out against alcohol prohibition (which the public hated) and even after it was ratified as a Constitutional Amendment (1919), Wilson vetoed the Volstead Act (that September) that would have given the government the power to enforce the 18th Amendment.[62] After March 4, 1919, however, the Republicans controlled both the House of Representatives (240 Republicans to 190 Democrats) and the Senate (49 Republicans to 47 Democrats), and they simply overrode Wilson's veto a month later. Wilson appeared to be the only one looking out for the interests of the little guy. Wilson ranks with Washington, Jefferson, Jackson, Lincoln, and Teddy Roosevelt as one of the most beloved and respected presidents America ever had.

Wilson felt he was so popular that he could win a third term, despite the stroke; there was no outstanding rival candidate in either party. He was somewhat offended when he wasn't even nominated, and retaliated by refusing to endorse any candidate, including his son-in-law William G. McAdoo, who had become a protege (or puppet) of William Jennings Bryan and represented the dry (Prohibitionist) sentiment of the Democrat party. Wilson's endorsement might have influenced the election, but because he and the Democrats had paid very little attention to domestic issues, by the 1920 elections the country was again in the mood for a change.

THE ROARING TWENTIES

The early 1920s were a remarkable time. The end of the war brought about a profound change, catapulting America out of the Victorian Age and into the flamboyant Roaring Twenties.

Before the War, life in America was hard and bleak for most people. They lived in small, dank houses without modern conveniences and worked long hours at low-paying mundane jobs, which in itself had a detrimental effect on family life. Their mediocre lives were boring, devoid of intellectual stimulation or

---

62. Smith, p.112.

satisfaction, and they were desperate for some excitement. Alcohol was an occasional treat, it added a little spark, a little fun, to their otherwise lackluster lives. This is why, despite its illegal status, they continued using alcohol. When the dough-boys (young men) came home, they had a much different perspective on life and a more realistic understanding of what was important — being on the front lines of a war does that to people. Home now struck them as foreign and far too strait-laced — especially after France, where there is more emphasis on enjoying life. Our dough-boys quickly adapted to the more liberal French views on alcohol (mostly wine) and especially sex. Indeed, they'd had plenty of time to get acquainted with the French *demoiselles*, as Pershing's Expeditionary Forces spent their first six months behind the lines, in the French countryside, contemplating how and where US forces should be used. The lyrics, "How ya gonna keep'em down on the farm, after they've seen Paree?," by George M. Cohan, pretty much summed it up.

At the same time, America's young women were also feeling far freer and wanted to get out and enjoy life a little — the "flapper era" was born. It was a time for celebrating life and easing restraints; and everyone wanted a drink. The Victorian Era was over, it was now the Roaring Twenties, and virtually every night people, *particularly women*, filled the local speakeasies and night clubs looking for a good time, despite the Prohibition laws.

AMERICA EMERGES FROM WORLD WAR I AS AN ECONOMIC POWERHOUSE

With Europe in ruins, the United States emerged from World War I as the world's leading industrial and creditor nation. However, although the economy flourished during the war years, when the US was a weapons supplier, after the war industry had to re-tool and reorganize to meet the needs and wants of a consumer-based economy.

That, combined with the closing down of the liquor industry and the return of tens of thousands of ex-dough-boys (now ex-servicemen looking for work), caused a recession. War veterans found they had no job to come home to. In hard times, people do whatever they feel they must do to survive, legal or illegal — and many law-abiding veterans were enticed into a life of bootlegging and crime. They were opposed to alcohol prohibition anyway; they had risked their lives, as they thought and as Woodrow Wilson had proclaimed, "to make the world safe for democracy"; now, they returned home to find their lives in ruin and their civil liberties denied by their own government. Furthermore, bootleg-gers were not seen as criminals in the eyes of the public, who overwhelmingly opposed Prohibition. They had never voted for it, and hated having it imposed on them.

> The prestige of government has undoubtedly been lowered considerably by the Prohibition law. For nothing is more destructive of respect for the government and the law of the land than passing laws which cannot be enforced. It is an open secret that the dangerous increase of crime in this country is closely connected with this.
> — *Albert Einstein on Prohibition, 1921*

Because of the enormous profits associated with bootlegging, competing gangs resorted to violence to resolve their territorial disputes. Army training, as much as the ruthless influence of the Mafia, allowed many of the men involved in bootlegging to kill or be killed. The established whites were able to hide their involvement; the desperate ethnic minorities — young Irish, Italian, Germans, and Jewish refugee immigrants living in the slums — were especially susceptible to becoming criminal victims of Prohibition. They had grown up in families where the use of alcohol was a tradition — they knew both the danger and plea-sures associated with alcohol, and they thought Prohibition was absolute fool-ishness. Some of them were also somewhat desperate and disenchanted with America. They had come seeking freedom and a new start, but found a quite big-oted society that refused to accept them. They saw bootlegging simply as a job — supplying the public with the alcohol they wanted. It also provided their fam-ilies with food, shelter, and clothing — the government certainly wasn't helping them!

Another important change was in the way Americans learned about what was happening in the world. By the 1920s, people were better educated and newspapers were more widely circulated; even more important, radios and tele-phones were making inroads. Both were invented in the late 19th century, and were quickly replacing the saloons (now speakeasies) as the major source of news and information.

Prohibition was the law, but it was also still an experiment — "The Great Social Experiment." Prohibitionists maintained that the public would get used to it and grow to accept it, but they were soon proven wrong. The US govern-ment never made the consumption of alcohol illegal — they knew that would be going too far; it was only illegal to manufacture, import, transport or sell alcohol.

And the law was only halfheartedly enforced, for the first five years. For a while, it was a stand-off. The Prohibitionists were relatively happy: Alcohol was illegal, the saloons were closed and the police were arresting people for breaking the law. Those who opposed Prohibition were also relatively happy: alcohol was still readily available and drinking alcohol wasn't illegal — it just cost more.

Unfortunately, when the stockpiled liquor ran out, large numbers of people began dying from drinking "bathtub gin," even pure wood grain alcohol. New brands of home-brew were coming out every day. Innocent people were also being killed in "collateral damage" from gang fights. Actually, Prohibition served mainly to escalate the development of organized crime in America.

Also contributing to the lack of enforcement of the law was a lack of leadership from the White House. Wilson did not support Prohibition, but there wasn't much he could do about it.

Harding, the next president, had a sordid background including many affairs and was known generally as an "enthusiastic drinker." In fact, Harding was a full-fledged alcoholic as well as a hypocrite. Publicly, he was an ardent supporter of Prohibition — a team player, but behind closed doors Harding served bootlegged hooch at his weekly White House poker games[63] Harding also allegedly was initiated into the Ku Klux Klan in a private White House ceremony.[64]

In August 1920, Tennessee became the 36th state to ratify the 19th Amendment to the Constitution, giving women the right to vote. Ironically, although Suffrage became the law of the land during her tenure, Edith Wilson was very much opposed to women voting — often calling the Suffragettes picketing in front of the White House "detestable."[65] Reportedly having no interest in politics before marrying Woodrow, this was apparently the only political issue she was passionate about. Perhaps in part because of Edith's disdain, many of the women demonstrating for their rights were arrested and badly very treated.

---

63. Schlesinger, p. 444.

64. Kennedy, Stetson. *Jim Crow Guide to the U.S.A.* Florida Atlantic University Press, Boca Raton: 1990, p. 30

65. Dixon-Healey, Diana. *America's First Ladies, Private Lives of the Presidential Wives.* Simon & Schuster: 1988, p. 158.

THE REJUVENATED REPUBLICAN PARTY

Having reinvented itself under the prohibitionists' banner after the 1912 election disaster, the Republican Party successfully regained control of the House in 1916 and the Senate in 1918. Congressional Democrats were seen as too inept. It's not that the Republican Party rode the popular ripple of alcohol prohibition all the way back into the White House; there was no popular ripple. The people hated Prohibition, and they were frustrated by the almost impossible task of repealing a Constitutional Amendment. They detested the Republicans for having proposed it, and were even more disgusted with the Democrats for allowing it to pass into law. On the 44th ballot the Democrats were deadlocked between William McAdoo and John M. Palmer and compromised on Governor James M. Cox of Ohio. The Republicans were deadlocked between Leonard Wood and Frank O. Lowden. Harding's selection is described as taking place in a smoke filled hotel room at about two in the morning by a dozen or so Republican Party bosses. The Republicans won the 1920 election for three basic reasons. The liberal giants, Wilson and Roosevelt, were no longer on the political scene — Wilson suffered a stroke and Roosevelt died unexpectedly in January, 1919. There was apparently nobody capable of taking their places. Then, the people were angry about how little attention had been paid to domestic issues and about the economic recession that followed the war. And they were angry about income tax. Plus, neither Warren G. Harding (R) nor James M. Cox (D) had distinguished himself politically. They were both compromise candidates, the result of deadlocked nominating conventions, with no national recognition or following. Not a very appetizing choice for the voters. Franklin D. Roosevelt was Cox's vice-presidential running mate.

The Republican Party bosses liked Harding because he was "one of the boys," with no real political philosophy or agenda. He had never sponsored a single piece of significant legislation either as an Ohio State Senator or a US Senator. Harding was the "go-along, get-long" kind of politician; he was also the last presidential nominee obviously chosen by party bosses in a smoke-filled backroom: After the 1920 election, party nominees were chosen in primary elections.

Harding didn't particularly want to be President. He knew the job was beyond him. He was, however, a practiced liar. When asked by Republican Party bosses if there was anything in his past that might be politically embarrassing, Harding neglected to mention his weak heart, the several occasions he had checked himself into a sanitarium, and a 10-year affair with a friend's wife — for which he was later blackmailed. (He also may have fathered a child with a woman 30 years his junior.) Once nominated, Harding enthusiastically campaigned and the well-organized religious right wing, the prohibitionists, busied themselves getting out the vote.

Harding won by a huge margin. It must have been because of his good looks: he looked "presidential," as was often noted in accounts of that election. His ability to deliver a good speech also helped, but unfortunately, image and personality were all Harding had. Borrowing a phase from Winston Churchill, "There's a lot less there than meets the eye." The real power in Washington lay with Harding's Secretary of the Treasury Andrew Mellon, who made his fortune in oil and banking.

Harding was first noticed shortly after Wilson asked Congress to declare war on Germany — he absurdly co-sponsored a bill promoted by Roosevelt to establish and finance a volunteer army[66] to be led by Roosevelt, like the Rough Riders whom Roosevelt had commanded in Cuba. Apparently, Roosevelt wanted to recapture his youth. Wilson tried to convince him that World War I was a different kind of war, a war that had to be fought by younger men; when Roosevelt refused to withdraw the bill, Wilson directed its defeat — leaving Roosevelt somewhat embittered.[67] Harding's rise to prominence within the Republican Party ironically came about because Wayne B. Wheeler, the Washington lobbyist for the Anti-Saloon League of America selected Harding to guide the Volstead Act through the Senate — it was labeled as an attempt to show party unity, but more likely Wheeler chose Harding because he obviously had personality, which Wheeler lacked. Actually, Wheeler was the real author of the Volstead Act,[68] and he wrote it incorporating the strongest features of the various state laws. He then chose Rep. Andrew Volstead (R-Minn), a dedicated prohibitionist, to introduce it in Congress. Volstead served in Congress 1903 to 1922 when he was defeated, only three years after the Volstead Act was passed.

---

66. Schlesinger, p. 440.

67. *Information Please Almanac.* p. 629.

68. *Encyclopedia Americana*: 1989 Vol. 22, p. 647.

THE SCANDALOUS HARDING ADMINISTRATION

Warren G. Harding's victory meant the captains of industry, who actually controlled the Republican Party, also controlled of the government. Now they could do anything they wanted. Woodrow Wilson asked, "How does he expect to lead when he doesn't know where he is going?" Wilson's son-in-law William Gibbs McAdoo called Harding's speeches "an army of pompous phrases moving across the landscape in search of an idea."

Harding's cabinet, known as the "Poker Cabinet" or the "Ohio Gang," was made up primarily of his friends, relatives, and political cronies from Ohio, who were also filling their pockets. He even appointed his brother-in-law Superintendent of Prisons, and essentially made his personal physician Doctor Sawyer, of Sawyer's Sanitarium the Surgeon General. Harding's administration became known as the most corrupt and scandal ridden in US history. It included the notorious Teapot Dome scandal, in which drilling rights to three naval oil reserves (Wyoming's Teapot Dome along with California's Elk Hill and Buena Vista Hills reserves) were leased by Harding's Secretary of the Interior Albert Fall to two privately owned oil companies — the Mammoth Oil Company and the Pan-American Petroleum and Transportation Company. Fall was convicted of accepting a bribe of $400,000 in gifts and loans and was sentenced to one year in jail and a $100,000 fine; Secretary of the Navy Edwin N. Denby, who consented to the leases, resigned.

There were other scandals involving the Ohio Gang. Jesse Smith, assistant to Attorney General Harry M. Cramer, was exposed as a "bagman" who carried bribes to and from the Attorney General's office. After being banished from Washington, Cramer committed suicide. Charles Cramer, legal advisor to the Veterans Bureau, was also exposed for taking bribes, and he too committed suicide. Charles Forbes, head of the same bureau, was convicted of taking at least $250 million in kickbacks and bribes. Colonel Thomas W. Miller, head of the Office of Alien Property was convicted of fraud and taking bribes, having sold valuable German patents seized in the war for far below market value. Daugherty, Harding's Attorney General, was forced to resign after being charged with receiving payments from prohibition violators. Harding was quoted as saying, "My enemies are not a problem, it's my friends. . . they're the ones that keep me walking the floors nights!"

New York Repeals Enforcement of Prohibition

When Al Smith, New York's anti-Prohibitionist Governor, proposed to repeal the state's alcohol prohibition Enforcement Act, Harding warned against it. A stern warning was all Harding could really do — Prohibition was enormously unpopular, especially in New York City (a liberal stronghold), where people were marching in the streets demanding an end to Prohibition. Forcing the issue would simply have escalated the situation and created even more negative publicity about Prohibition — which the Harding administration could not afford. New York's Governor Al Smith, a Tammany Hall Democrat, ignored Harding's warning and repealed the New York Enforcement Act on May 4, 1923. That act of defiance is considered the beginning of the end of Prohibition — it meant that the State of New York was no longer arresting or prosecuting bootleggers, and if the federal government wanted to enforce the Prohibition law in New York, they were going to have to send in federal troops and declare martial law.

That, of course, didn't happen. News of the scandals was beginning to leak out, and the almost constant stream of reporters literally forced Harding to get out of town. In the summer of 1923, he embarked on a cross-country speaking tour including a visit to Alaska, still just a US territory — it was the first time a sitting president visited Alaska. While he was there, Harding reportedly received a distressing coded message from Washington indicating that the corruption within his administration was far worse than even he had thought. He decided to return to Washington, but he collapsed en route. Harding died unexpectedly in a San Francisco hotel room on August 2, 1923. The exact cause of death is unknown. One account claims the official cause of death was listed as a stroke, while others have suggested a heart attack possibly caused by an embolism, a brain tumor, apoplexy,[69] or even that he ate a batch of bad crabs and died of ptomaine poisoning. Rumors flew: Had Harding's wife Florence, fed up with his many affairs and to save him the embarrassment of the burgeoning scandals, intentionally poisoned him? She refused to allow an autopsy.

The Harding administration lasted only 28 months but set a standard for political graft and corruption that lasted long after Harding and his cronies were gone. Bootleggers found it easy to bribe local officials, particularly Republicans, which allowed them to operate openly. Although history has labeled Harding

---

69. Schlesinger, p. 444.

the worst president we ever had, there is nothing to indicate that he played a part in or personally profited from any of the scandals. Upon Harding's death, Vice President Calvin Coolidge became President, and spent most of his time trying to overcome the political damage; the Republican Party concentrated on reelecting him in 1924. The transition from Harding to Coolidge was almost seamless because Treasury Secretary Andrew Mellon, who had received most of the credit for the country's industrial growth in the early and mid-1920s, was still the power behind the throne.

The Coolidge Administration

Coolidge easily won reelection and had an easy time as President — there were no wars and the economy was prospering. He spent most of his time cleaning up the corruption that permeated the government and the Republican Party.

Coolidge saw his primary role as restoring a measure of respect to the office of President and prosecuting corrupt officials. Reducing the income tax rates probably accounted for most of his enormous popularity. On the surface, everything looked good; but appearances can be and usually are deceiving. Despite Coolidge's efforts, graft and corruption continued to run rampant, and alcohol prohibition was the principal cause.

Coolidge (Silent Cal) kept a low profile; he is perhaps best remembered for proclaiming that "the business of America is business" — which could be interpreted as meaning the US government was comfortably situated in the pockets of big business, a reaffirmation of big business's hold on government.

Mellon, formerly Chairman of the Board of the Mellon Bank of Pittsburgh, principal owner of the Gulf Oil Company, and DuPont's chief financial backer,[70] held the office of Secretary of the Treasury for an unprecedented eleven years — throughout the Harding and Coolidge administrations and well into the Hoover administration.

Mellon was touted as the greatest Treasury Secretary since Alexander Hamilton. And like Hamilton, Mellon was committed to the financial well-being of corporate America, not the average man, as demonstrated by his constant urging of Congress to keep taxes on the wealthy and corporations extremely low "so they could hire more people." Hearing one of the richest men in America espous-

---

70. Herer, p. 24.

ing the benefits of not taxing big business or the wealthy did not sit well with the working-class of either political party. However, neither the Democrats nor the progressive Republicans were in power; and the newspapers, particularly Hearst newspapers, were beneficiaries of Mellon's policies. They promoted Mellon's point of view, making it seem as if the public actually supported trickle-down economics.

AMERICA'S MOST PROSPEROUS DECADE

Actually, Mellon had little to do with the robust economy. In the early 1920s industry began mass producing a whole range of new consumer goods — automobiles, airplanes, washing machines, electric refrigerators, radios, telephones, electric lighting and a variety of major and small electrical appliances and more goods that households were eager to buy. The period between 1923 and October 1929 was perhaps the most prosperous in American history, and people were generally very optimistic about the future. (It probably would have been much more prosperous without alcohol prohibition.)

The economic upturn in approximately July 1921 marked a point when industry finished retooling and people were back on the job. Industry was far more sophisticated and efficient than before the war. Following Henry Ford's example, companies set up assembly lines to mass produce their products, which made them affordable to a wider group of consumers. And the war had created shortages, which everyone was keen to make up. By this time, also, most American cities provided electricity to the urban home. The future that everyone had dreamt about was here and it was making life brighter and easier. People had a few bucks in their pockets and the value of the US dollar was quite high (twice what it was in 1967, according to the Consumer Price Index), meaning that wholesale prices remained low. Everyone loved it, and the buying binge sparked a boom that catapulted the economy out of its depressed state.

Actually, Mellon had little to do with it. The economic upturn in approximately July 1921 marked a point when industry recovered and starting hiring larger work forces. Industry was far more sophisticated and efficient than before the war. Following Henry Ford's example, companies set up assembly lines to mass produce their products, which made them affordable to a wider group of consumers. By this time, most American cities provided electricity to every household. In the early 1920s, industry began mass producing a whole range of new consumer goods — automobiles, airplanes, washing machines, electric refrigerators, radios, telephones, electric lighting and a variety of major and small electrical appliances, and more goods that families were eager to buy. And the war had created shortages, which everyone was keen to make up.

The future that everyone had dreamt about was here and it was making life brighter and easier. People had a few bucks in their pockets and the buying power of the US dollar was quite high (twice what it was in 1967, according to the Consumer Price Index), meaning that wholesale prices remained low. Everyone loved it, and the buying binge sparked a boom that catapulted the economy out of its depressed state. People were generally very optimistic about the future. That is principally why Noble Prize-winning MIT Economist Paul A. Samuelson identified the "Roaring Twenties" as the most prosperous period in American history. It probably would have been even more prosperous without Alcohol Prohibition.

After 1927, when the economy began to falter and jobs became harder to find, as the negative economic effects of Alcohol Prohibition took hold, Mellon became the focus of attention. By then, people began to realize he was the one who was calling the shots. After the stock market crash, Mellon found himself under very heavy criticism and he was seen as the epitome of the wealthy robber baron industrialist looking out for his friends. By early 1932, Hoover was forced to replace him. For all damage he did, Mellon was quickly nominated and confirmed by the Republican-controlled Senate to the post of U.S. Ambassador to Great Britain, the most prestigious diplomatic position within the Department of State. Unfortunately, his real legacy is the tax laws he urged Congress to pass favoring corporations and the wealthy — many of which are still in effect.

> It is difficult to get a man to understand something
> when his salary depends on his not understanding it.
> — *Upton Sinclair, The Jungle*

Because people were simply not willing to go along with the Prohibition law, corruption and misuse of the law was inevitable. The bootleggers saw paying off police and public officials as part of the cost of doing business, and it was a drop in the bucket compared to the money they were making. However, with the Republicans securely in control, the federal government dramatically stepped up its enforcement of the Prohibition laws and that seriously elevated the street price of alcohol. The underground economy was draining $10 million a day out of the legal economy. That, in conjunction with the million dollars per day ($2 million, after Hoover became president) that the government was spending to enforce the Prohibition laws, began affecting the purchasing power of the consumer and the legal consumer-based economy softened, causing extensive layoffs.

LOOKING BAD IN THE EYES OF THE WORLD

Congress has a history of passing irrational laws or taking positions contrary to the general will of the people — Prohibition, the Marijuana Tax Act, and our failure to even join the League of Nations are examples; and the details are most always veiled in obscurity.

We're taught, for example, that the League of Nations failed because it proved unworkable. Why, indeed, did the Republican-controlled Congress resist America's involvement in the League of Nations? The primary reason may well have been that the Republicans were fanatically promoting Alcohol Prohibition, a concept our European allies considered sheer foolishness. The issue of joining the League came up at a point when the states were still deciding whether or not to ratify the 18th Amendment, and the Prohibitionists were on the verge of winning that contest. Joining the League of Nations would have entailed treaty obligations that would stand in the way of Alcohol Prohibition — the other League members certainly would not have agreed to it. The Republicans would have had to change their position on Prohibition. No wonder they fought so hard against the League. (In contrast, the United Nations was founded after World War II, there was no question about US participation — in part, because Alcohol Prohibition was no longer a divisive issue.

The League of Nations was growing in influence — even without the US, startling as that may seem; and it was emerging as the de facto mechanism for conducting the world's business. The Second Opium Conference (at Geneva in 1924) was held under the auspices of the League of Nations, who invited the United States to send a delegation because the US had participated in the 1911 conference. The League was still hoping the US would come and take a place in the general assembly and as part of the five great powers on the permanent council.

Reflecting the prohibitionist mentality of the Harding and Coolidge administrations, the US State Department sent a delegation headed by none other than Elizabeth Washburn Wright, who insisted on a heavy-handed approach to recreational intoxicants — she went as far as to admonish the British for passing what she considered to be extremely lax drug regulations.

Actually, the United States wasn't the only country to try alcohol prohibition: Iceland (1908-1933), Sweden (1909-1922), Canada (1918-1921), Greenland (1918) and Finland (1919-1932) also initiated alcohol prohibition, and, of course, the Moslem religion has always forbid the use of alcohol. But this time, the United States. was unquestionably the leading proponent. Interestingly, the chief ally of the United States delegation was the white South African delegation, who saw the use of marijuana by Africa's black population as a threat to their authority and wanted it outlawed worldwide.

It quickly became obvious that the rest of the League, especially the British, were diametrically opposed to America's strident approach to the use of recreational intoxicants and they were not going to be lectured to by the US representatives, their invited guests. The US delegation was practically laughed out of the conference when British Lord Robert Cecil attacked Mrs. Wright and her delegates, asking, "Who sent you, the people of the United States or the Almighty?"

How embarrassing. The convention went with Lord Cecil almost unanimously, at which point Mrs. Wright and her convention cohort Congressman Stephen Porter of Pittsburgh (home of the Mellon Bank), then chairman of the House Foreign Relations Committee, gathered their papers and left the floor, probably to a standing ovation. That pretty much ended Elizabeth Washburn Wright's diplomatic career, but she remained very active in Prohibition and women's issues. She and a small group of followers often stopped and lambasted congressman and senators in the Halls of Congress for not supporting even more stringent laws.

The confrontation between Lord Cecil and Mrs. Wright exemplified the ill feelings that still existed between the United States and Great Britain. The British were upset that in the early days of World War I the United States helped only the French — America's way of repaying them for their help during the Revolutionary War; no such help was offered to the British, who were fighting the same enemy. It wasn't until World War II, long after America had abandoned its infatuation with alcohol prohibition, that the US and Britain finally resolved their Revolutionary War differences.

The British and French were both still angry with the US for allowing Pershing's Expeditionary Force to sit on the sidelines for six months after arriving in

Europe while their countries were ravaged and destroyed. It was also somewhat insulting of President Wilson to come to the Paris Peace Conference and try to dictate the terms of surrender — Europe suffered the brunt of the War and the United States took most of the credit for ending it. Actually, the Europeans ignored all of Wilson's 14-point peace proposal except the proposal to create the League of Nations. In the US, however, the Republican-controlled congress, led by Henry Cabot Lodge (the Senate majority leader), fought against and finally denied US participation in the League of Nations, and America's Great Social Experiment (Prohibition) became the law of the land.

America's Prohibitionists were able to win a number of rural elections and take control in America, but most Europeans thought us foolish. The US government, at the time, was hardly in a position to dictate terms to the rest of the world, especially about alcohol.

The League of Nations continued successfully without the United States, until the mid-1930s. It failed to keep the peace, essentially because of the unreasonable World War I reparation demands inflicted on the Germans by the French and British. When Hitler came to power in Germany, he stopped paying the French and British and used the money to build an army that he used to attack his economic oppressors.

THE FOLLY OF PROHIBITION

It was naïve and simplistic to believe that criminalizing alcohol, prostitution and gambling would stop people from engaging in those activities. Human nature doesn't change that easily. Speakeasies, brothels, and casinos were profitable because someone (a lot of someones) was willing to sell, and someone was willing to buy, the products and services in question. Outlawing these activities simply forces them to operate illegally; it redirects enormous sums of money into the criminal underground economy. During Prohibition, the demand was so high that by the late 20s, the country had more illegal speakeasies than there were legal saloons before Prohibition started.[71]

Bootlegging was a very lucrative and highly competitive business, and because they were forced to operate outside the law, without the protection of the police and courts, they made their own rules to protect themselves and their

---

71. *Encyclopedia Americana*, 2003, Vol. 22, p. 647.

operations. Unfortunately, it didn't take long before things turned ugly, and gangland-style killings became commonplace, particularly in Chicago.

Prohibition redirected hundreds of millions of dollars into criminal hands. Al Capone's bootlegging operation was so successful that he reportedly set a record for the most wealth ever acquired in a single year (1927). Even when inflation is factored in, that achievement may still have not been surpassed. Capone was the best-known bootlegger but he was only one of thousands all across the country who made millions smuggling or manufacturing illegal alcohol. Most were never caught, but we do know about a few. In Cincinnati, George Remus, an attorney, reportedly earned $40 million from nine distilleries he operated in the Midwest. Out of Jacksonville Florida, Capt. Bill McCoy founded "Rum Row," a fleet of boats anchoring just outside the three-mile limit; they brought liquor from the Bahamas to New York. And, of course Joseph Kennedy, president John F. Kennedy's father, made his fortune smuggling whiskey into the US from Canada. It was a business, big business, highly organized, very competitive, and run by businessmen, not mere thugs.

Since the "liquor company executives" were forced to operate outside the law, they had to protect themselves and their operations and make their own rules. Disputes and competition naturally arise in a highly profitable market; this time, there could be no recourse to the police or the courts. Gangland-style killings began to seem commonplace, particularly in Chicago.

Contrary to popular belief, Al Capone was born and raised in America. He grew up in the Brooklyn slums with the children of Italian, Irish, Jewish, Germans Swedish, Black, and Chinese immigrants. Learning early on that friends and enemies came in all colors and from all ethnic backgrounds served Capone well as an adult, and his greatest attribute was that he was a nice guy who got along with virtually everyone. Capone found his way into organized crime as a runner for his friend and mentor, Johnny Torrio. Torrio wasn't a tough guy, he was a new breed of gangster — an organizer, unlike many of his friends and associates. Torrio actually thought he was doing the 18-year-old Capone a favor when he got him a job as bartender and waiter at his cousin Frankie Yale's new Coney Island restaurant, the Harvard Inn. Frankie, an associate of Lucky Luciano, had the reputation of a thug and a killer.

A few years later, Capone met Mae, a pretty Irish girl, whom he married after she gave birth to their son (Albert) Sonny. With a wife and child to support, Capone wanted to get into a legitimate business. He moved his family to Baltimore, and got an "honest" job as a bookkeeper.

Capone's bookkeeping career lasted until early 1921, about a year after alcohol prohibition went into effect. By then, Johnny Torrio was managing the prostitution and gambling empire of his uncle Giacomo "Big Jim" Colosimo and his wife Victoria Moresco, the biggest in the Chicago area. Colosimo was doing exactly what every saloon/restaurant owner around the world has been doing for centuries — trying to attract the city's leading citizens by providing their customers with good food, good wine, and good company. Colosimo and his wife were very good at it, and the influence they developed with their powerful clientele protected Colosimo from anyone trying to muscle in on his territory. That was important because Chicago was a tough town with a rising crime rate and was filled with crocked politicians, police, and so-called businessmen (gangsters in suits), long before Prohibition or Capone. Chicago was known as "the city built on the frontier, between civilization and the wilderness. It brought together urban corruption and Wild West lawlessness. A city steeped in blood, built around the slaughter houses, its business was butchery."[72] Prohibition simply exacerbated the city's political and police corruption problem, which lasted long after Prohibition ended and Capone was long dead.

Torrio did such a good job that Colosimo later made him a junior partner, which put him in a position to hire people he trusted. Capone moved his family to Chicago and became Torrio's right-hand man. Capone kept the customers happy and kept them coming back. The price of liquor was going up and Torrio quickly discovered that people willing paid seventy-five cents for a drink that had cost only fifteen cents before Prohibition.[73] Torrio saw an opportunity to make a great deal of money and wanted to get into bootlegging — but Colosimo, the boss — the restaurateur — didn't. He was satisfied with his very profitable gambling and prostitution business. Actually, gambling and prostitution accounted for less than a 20% of the profits of Capone's criminal empire,[74] in which bootlegging was 60%.

Colosimo hastened his own demise by playing around with Dale Winter, a pretty 19-year-old singer, whom he married immediately after divorcing Victoria. Colosimo's family trouble and conflict with his former wife and business partner Victoria over dividing their property probably created a considerable amount of turmoil within the Colosimo organization. According to some reports, Al

72. *Prohibition, Thirteen Years That Changed America.* Mirimax Films. A&E documentary.

73. *Ibid.*

74. *Ibid.*

Capone killed Colosimo; at least one historian, Laurence Bergreen,[75] suggests the real killer was Frankie Yale, Capone's former New York employer. Instigated or possibly ordered by Johnny Torrio, Frankie Yale got word of the situation in Chicago and decided to move in on Colosimo's operation. For Frankie, that simply meant eliminating Colosimo, and according to Bergreen, it was apparently Yale himself (not Capone) who assassinated Colosimo in his own nightclub. "A witness described the man he had seen enter the cafe shortly before Big Jim's murder — and his description fitted Yale. However, he failed to identify Yale when confronted with him in person. Although no one was ever convicted of Colosimo's murder, it is generally believed that Yale was the killer, hired by Torrio."[76] It is also believed that Frankie Yale was one of the hit men in the Dion O'Banion murder (known as the handshake murder).

Bergreen goes one to describe Colosimo's funeral as the first of Chicago's great gangster funerals: "the last rites became a gaudy demonstration more appropriate to... a powerful political figure or popular entertainer... an event that priests and police captains alike attended to pay their last respects to the sort of man they were supposed to condemn. Colosimo was universally recognized as Chicago's premier pimp, yet his honorary pallbearers included three judges, a congressman, an assistant state attorney, and no less than nine Chicago aldermen."

Frankie couldn't exactly take over the Colosimo operation as he was the prime suspect in the murder investigation. Both Torrio and Capone were questioned, but only Frankie was arrested. However, since nobody was willing to testify against him, he avoided prosecution. Meanwhile, Johnny Torrio consolidated his position and his control of Colosimo's former empire — now the Torrio Mob.

Torrio liked and trusted Capone, and soon made him a junior partner, because he was good at managing the restaurant and got along with virtually everyone, high-roller customers or lowly employees. Their "organization" employed people of all races and ethnic backgrounds, enabling many of them to escape from poverty. Capone introduced jazz to the people of Chicago and brought in performers like Louis Armstrong, Duke Ellington, and Cab Callaway to entice even more people into his speakeasies. Business was good. Capone's

---

75. Bergreen, Laurence, *Capone: The Man and the Era*. Simon & Schuster: 1996, p. 82.

76. Oak Woods, a historic cemetery of Chicago's South Side. Online at http://www.graveyards.com/oakwoods/colosimo.html: 1996

contribution to creating the "Chicago School of Jazz" was probably equal to or greater than that of the various artists who made the music. Jazz may not have been born in the speakeasies Capone built, but it grew to maturity there.

The Torrio/Capone Mob was probably the largest, politically best-connected, and best financed bootlegging gang in Chicago. They catered to some of Chicago's most elite clientele and controlled the most lucrative beer territory in the city, but they were not the only ones vying for control of Chicago and the surrounding area. Their chief opposition was Dion O'Banion's Northside Gang (O'Banion, Hymie Weiss, George "Bugs" Moran and the Genna brothers). Competition between the two gangs quickly escalated and included hijacking each others shipments of alcohol. Torrio, the organizer and businessman, tried to resolve their differences, offering O'Banion a deal that would make them partners, but leave both gangs in control or their own half of the city. He told O'Banion, "We can't kill each other, there's too much for us both to lose"; and Torrio said, "I offer you no interference in your territory, if you provoke none in mine."

They actually came to an agreement, but O'Banion was simply biding his time. Tensions between the parties did not subside, and pretty soon they were at war again. At this same time, the political atmosphere in the city of Chicago was changing. Big Bill Thompson, Torrio's mayor, lost the election and the Torrio/Capone Mob decided to move their headquarters into Cicero, a suburb outside the new Mayor's jurisdiction. (Big Bill Thompson is credited with the expression, "Vote early and vote often," reflecting the city's corrupt voting practices.)

After months of warfare, O'Banion came upon a plan to get rid of Torrio. He sent word that he would be willing to quit the rackets if Torrio would buy his Seiben Brewery on Larabee Street. Torrio jumped at the chance. A week after Torrio took possession of the brewery, it was raided by federal agents (probably Ness). Torrio realized he had been set up by O'Banion. That led to the infamous "handshake murder" of Dion O'Banion in his recently acquired Northside floral shop, across the street form a large Catholic church. O'Banion's funeral was the biggest in gangland history. Hymie Weiss took over the Northside gang and attempted to murder Torrio. Torrio wasn't killed but he was seriously injured, and forced into retirement. It was now the Capone Mob; Al Capone was only 26 years old. Hymie Weiss was soon to become the victim of a gangland killing and eventually Bugs Moran, by default, became head of the Northside Gang, until everyone except Moran was wiped out in the St. Valentines Day Massacre.

Prohibition was a catastrophic failure; it never effectively discouraged or stopped people from drinking. Instead, it created a situation in which people were drinking considerably more hard liquor than ever before. There had certainly been times and events when people drank excessively and got drunk, especially before the beginning of the 20th century, but that was always the exception — especially as the West was becoming more "civilized." People were more aware of the negative effects of regularly drinking hard liquor, and as purified water and homogenized milk became available, there was less need to drink alcoholic beverages, anyway. Most people weren't drinking to get drunk; they were drinking socially, and most seemed quite satisfied with beer or wine. Beer, or ale, has always been the most used alcoholic beverage, and that was true even during Prohibition. It was even reported that the majority of Al Capone's wealth came from producing and distributing beer, not hard liquor.

As beer became scarce (large breweries were easy targets for police and government prohibition agents, like Eliot Ness), people simply switched to hard liquor, which was more readily available. They began carrying flasks of whiskey, bourbon, or gin so they could have a shot whenever they wanted it. Hard liquor carried a higher profit margin. There are no accurate figures (since it was illegal), but we know that the consumption of hard liquor substantially increased during the Prohibition era, and women accounted for much of that increase. As social rules became more relaxed, it was only a matter of time before women became a regular part of the bar scene. The convoluted reality of Prohibition was that the more breweries the government closed, the more hard liquor people consumed.

Whenever there is demand for a commodity, there will always be someone willing to supply it, regardless of the legality. All that needs to be negotiated is the price. Widespread corruption of elected officials and police can be expected when there is a huge demand for an illegal commodity. Alcohol prohibition dramatically accelerated the level of corruption all across America. The political and police corruption that existed in Chicago during alcohol prohibition is legendary and lasted long after Prohibition ended, and the agency with the worst reputation was, in fact, the US Treasury Department's Prohibition Unit. During America's 13-year experience with alcohol prohibition, the Prohibition Unit trained and later dismissed (for cause) a far greater number of agents than any other branch of the federal government, at a substantial cost to the American taxpayer. Eliot Ness, who headed the Treasury's Prohibition Unit in the City of Chicago, known as the "Untouchables," may have found a few honest men — but he went through hundreds looking for them. The corruption that ran rampant in Chicago didn't end with Prohibition, it was simply institutionalized; on the federal level, too, primarily due to America's drug war.

The Need to Outlaw Marijuana

Well before the 1928 election, and despite skyrocketing stock prices, the economy was generally faltering. Jobs were becoming scarce and people were getting worried. Public opinion opposing alcohol prohibition was growing stronger and louder, especially in the cities. Andrew Mellon, Rockefeller, and the other robber barons were concerned. If alcohol became legal and readily available again, the automobile industry, still young and evolving, might reconsider the decision to use gasoline as the standard fuel.

Of even more concern was the need to capture the newly evolving plastics market, made possible by the discovery of plastic polymers in the mid 1920s. Hermann Staudinger first published his theory of polymers in 1922, followed in 1928 by German chemist Karl Ziegler, who explained the mechanism of polymerization. With the advent of this stunningly promising new industry, Mellon and his cohorts were getting firsthand information, just as Rockefeller had received inside information about the developing automobile and airplane industries thirty years earlier. And just like Rockefeller, they (Mellon — Gulf Oil, Rockefeller — Standard Oil, and the DuPont family — DuPont Chemical Co.) were willing to do anything necessary to ensure that the plastics industry used petroleum (which they controlled) as its base material. Considering the effort made to outlaw the cultivation and use of hemp, one has to suspect that petroleum wasn't the leading contender at the outset.

Although the utilization of hemp had severely declined after the Civil War, it was reemerging as a viable basic raw material because of the 1917 introduction of a machine designed by George Schlichten, known as the "Decorticator." The Decorticator separated the long hemp fibers from the pulpy celluloid (hurds) center of the hemp stalks, dramatically reducing the exorbitant labor costs associated with cleaning and preparing the hemp for further processing. The Decorticator promised to do for hemp what Eli Whitney's 1793 invention of the cotton gin did for cotton.

Schlichten had primarily intended to use his Decorticator to produce paper — spurred on, in part, by Bulletin 404, published on October 14, 1916, by the US Department of Agriculture, which stated that at the current rate of consumption, America would exhaust its forest resources by the year 2000. (Today, 90% of the virgin forests that existed in 1916 are gone.) The bulletin went on to say that we could produce all the paper we needed, from hemp, instead.

Schlichten and his partners were also trying to get E.W. Scripps, who owned a number of newspapers across the country, to invest in their endeavor. Scripps was interested in Schlichten's Decorticator because it represented an opportunity to dramatically reduce the cost of paper, which had been escalating as demand kept pace with the increasing levels of literacy and growing interest in world events since 1910. The Decorticator afforded Scripps an opportunity to enhance his profits and also get into the business of making paper. He did finance some preliminary trials of the Decorticator, but became disgruntled when the government imposed income taxes. Scripps was already rich and apparently decided that getting richer would only benefit the government. He decided instead simply to raise the price of his newspapers.

Bulletin 404 was ignored by the paper industry because it conflicted with the interests of William R. Hearst, America's leading paper maker. He, because of his political influence within the Republican Party, controlled most of the forests in the northwestern US. It also concerned the DuPont Chemical Company, which derived an estimated 80% of its profits[77] from supplying paper mills (many owned by Hearst) with their patented sulfuric acid process for breaking down wood fibers into pulp. And, it concerned the Mellon Bank, the DuPont Company's principal banker. These were the industrialists — Hamilton's old Federalists — who controlled the Republican Party and the US government, after the 1920 election.

The cultivation and use of hemp certainly did threaten the monopolies of Rockefeller, Mellon, Hearst, and the DuPont Chemical Company, in several markets (fuel, paper and plastics). The evidence indicates that, as indirectly and discreetly as possible, they set out to eliminate the competition. They had the motive, the opportunity, and the tool — the prohibition model that Rockefeller used to eliminate alcohol as competition to gasoline. The only problem was that farmers were aware of the industrial uses of hemp and they had no mind to support outlawing it. Hearst stopped lambasting Pancho Villa (since no one was listening) and concentrated instead on drawing attention to a plant material called marijuana — and demonizing it.

Mellon wanted the enforcement of US anti-narcotic laws under his control, and in 1927 he got the Republican-controlled Congress to pass legislation that took responsibility for enforcing the Harrison Anti-Narcotics Act from the Internal Revenue Service and gave it to the Treasury Department,[78] — but regulated

---

77. Herer, p. 24.

by the Federal Narcotics Control Board under the Justice Department. On March 10, 1934, congress abolished the Federal Narcotics Control Board and transferred its powers to the Commissioner of Narcotics, under the auspices of the Secretary of the Treasury. It was promoted as somewhat of a consolidation of responsibilities that included enforcement of both alcohol prohibition and the Harrison Anti-Narcotics Act. Initially, that responsibility fell to the Prohibition Unit of the Treasury Department but, in reality, there was very little enforcement of the anti-narcotic law during alcohol prohibition.

Because alcohol prohibition was so unpopular, the mood of the country was against further restrictions. Growing opposition to alcohol prohibition created some doubt about its future, especially with the Democrats nominee in the upcoming 1928 election, Al Smith, promising to repeal it. The Republicans had no rational argument for the virtues of alcohol prohibition, so they discredited Al Smith by attacking his allegiance to the Roman Catholic Pope. Smith was an Irish Catholic, and the thought of a Catholic president didn't sit well with the Protestant and Baptist majority.

While Hoover and the Republicans were able to win the 1928 election, they had very little time to enjoy their victory. Mellon and his cohorts were upset because the first Decorticators were already coming off the assembly lines. The popularization of hemp-based paper would have opened the floodgates to ideas for using hemp for many more applications. It is a very versatile and adaptable material, and could dramatically affect the profitability of the oil and lumber industries. Despite the defeat of the Democrats who promised to repeal alcohol Prohibition and despite Hoover's get-tough-on-bootleggers policies, opposition to Prohibition was growing — and conditions on Main Street were deteriorating even more.

In October 1929, the stock market crashed. It wasn't the crash that caused the American economy to nosedive, it was Prohibition — the Crash simply reflected the poor economic health caused by Prohibition.

Hoover did not cause the Depression; he had only been president for seven months. The public blamed Andrew Mellon, who had been Secretary of the Treasury and the power behind the throne for over a decade. In truth, Hoover

---

78. Section 163, act Mar. 3, 1927, ch. 348, Sec. 4(a), 44 Stat. 1382, provided for transfer of control of narcotic drugs to the Secretary of the Treasury from the Commissioner of Internal Revenue and his assistants, agents, and inspectors.

was little more than a puppet, just like Harding and Coolidge before him, incapable of putting forth any legislation or doing much without Mellon's blessing.

Mellon knew his time in government "service" was coming to an end and he needed to insure that his plans to outlaw the cultivation and use of hemp would go on, regardless of whether or not Alcohol Prohibition continued, which even then seemed doubtful. Opposition to prohibition continued growing and in June 1930, with America focused on the depression, the Treasury Department pushed through legislation creating the Federal Bureau of Narcotics (FBN) — separating narcotic enforcement from alcohol, just in case. Mellon then appointed his nephew-in-law[79] Harry J. Anslinger as the FBN's acting commissioner on July 15, 1930, and the appointment became permanent less than a month later — a position he held for 32 years.[80]

Anslinger is an important link because he picked up the Prohibitionist banner with gusto. He and Hearst were primarily responsible for vilifying "drug" use, particularly marijuana, and promoting legislation to criminalize it. Anslinger supposedly came to the Prohibition Division of the US Treasury Department in 1926 because of his zealous efforts as a member of the State Department to promote alcohol prohibition and the Harrison Anti-Narcotics Act internationally — he was the government's point man in its war against alcohol. In reality, Anslinger was a low-level employee of the State Department and his rapidly advancing career within the Treasury Department was due mostly to his marriage to Mellon's niece. Along with providing Anslinger an executive salary, it is also highly likely that Mellon bequeathed a good deal of Gulf Oil and other stocks to his niece, to insure that Anslinger had a financial interest in pursuing the outlawing of hemp. Within three short years, Anslinger was appointed (in 1929) Assistant Commissioner of the Prohibition Unit of the Treasury Department, probably Eliot Ness's immediate supervisor.

THE 1928 ELECTION

When Calvin Coolidge announced in 1927 that he did not choose to run for reelection, the nation began focusing on his successor. Maybe Coolidge realized where Prohibition was taking America and knew that Mellon (because of his

---

79. Herer, p. 22.

80. Boonie & Whitebread, p. 65-66.

financial interest in the petroleum industry) would not change policy just because the economic optimism of the early 20s was fading and the public was losing faith in the government. Large numbers of people were beginning to lose their jobs; that did not bother Mellon. Coolidge may well have known that Mellon and his cronies were planning to outlaw hemp for their own financial benefit. He probably could have easily won re-election, but he may not have wanted to be associated with Mellon or the Republican Party any longer. In any event, the voters focused on the primaries, hoping the forthcoming election would resolve the situation.

The Republicans nominated Herbert Hoover, Secretary of Commerce under Presidents Harding and Coolidge, and the Democrats nominated New York's Governor Alfred E. Smith — the same man who, in 1923, had led the fight to repeal New York's Prohibition enforcement law. Smith was now promising to end alcohol prohibition nationally. Smith was clearly the most qualified candidate for the job, based on experience. He had held numerous elective offices and headed several important commissions in his 25-year political career, including four terms as governor. Smith was the right man for New York, which had experienced a huge migration of people from war-torn Europe and Russia, but he was much too progressive (liberal) for the "American heartland." Smith was even admonished for appointing so many immigrants to political positions in New York, but he rebuffed his critics by saying, "The government should meet the needs of all the people."

Hoover, the Republican nominee, had never been elected to any office but he was seen as a strong administrator and a humanitarian. He had brilliantly directed the country's relief program after World War I, feeding and clothing millions; and so Harding appointed Hoover his Secretary of Commerce. He did not distinguish himself in that job but held the position through the Coolidge administrations.

As the Republican nominee, Hoover promised the workingman a bigger share of prosperity. He also promised to increase farm aid and to strengthen protective trade tariffs, which farmers wanted. Hoover employed the same already-tired rhetoric of being tough on crime, meaning stricter enforcement of the law and harsher penalties; but he avoided discussing the merits of Prohibition. Unfortunately, a rational debate between the candidates on alcohol prohibition never took place. It should have; that election was our last chance of avoiding the massive hardships caused by the Great Depression of the 1930s.

Instead, the election deteriorated into a discussion of Al Smith's religious orientation — Smith was the first Catholic presidential candidate in US history. Unfortunately rural America, particularly the Midwest (the center of the Prohibitionists' movement), was heavily influenced in 1928 by the Baptist and Protestant Churches. They didn't want Prohibition repealed, and they feared the prospect of having to answer to the edicts of the Pope — at least, that was the rhetoric being delivered every Sunday from church pulpits all across America. The Catholics and Jews lived primarily in the cities; they did not support alcohol prohibition. But rural America, most of America, saw alcoholism as an urban problem and saw the big cities as dens of sin (as they still do, to some extent). Church leaders vilified Al Smith, New York's Governor. Methodist Bishop James Cannon, Jr., one of the most powerful men in the Anti-Saloon League,[81] was Smith's most ardent critic. They also believed that electing Smith, a Democrat and a product of New York's corrupt Tammany Hall political machine, would send the wrong message and encourage widespread government corruption.

Although the mood of the country, especially in the urban areas, was increasingly against Prohibition and even the liberal Progressive Party (made up mostly of farmers and union workers) supported Smith, it was not enough to beat Hoover. Hoover's big victory came in the Electoral College, particularly from the Midwest states. These people supported Prohibition and thought it was working. The Republicans barely maintained their majority in that election, and their control of the house and senate. However, the election did send a message to millions of unemployed workers and independent family farmers facing depressed agricultural prices: nothing was going to change. At least, not for the better. Over the next few months, economic conditions deteriorated dramatically.

A month before Hoover's March 20, 1929 inauguration, the nation was shocked by the infamous St. Valentine's Day Massacre, perhaps the most brutal atrocity of the Prohibition era. This was a failed attempt by Al Capone to eliminate his chief rival, George "Bugs" Moran. Moran was not one of the six men killed but he fled Chicago, effectively leaving Capone in control of the entire Midwest. Capone's criminal empire not only controlled all the prostitution, gambling, and alcohol distribution, he essentially had all the local politicians and police in his pocket.

---

81. *Encyclopedia Americana*, 2003, Vol. 5, p. 554.

News of the Massacre enraged president-elect Herbert Hoover; or, at least, it presented an opportunity for Hoover to show himself as "presidential" — tough on crime, and firmly in control.

THE HOOVER ADMINISTRATION

Getting Capone became Hoover's prime objective. He requested that Congress increase funding for Prohibition enforcement to an estimated $2 million per day. That enabled the administration of hire and train even more federal prohibition agents, generating a sharp increase in the number of arrests, clogging the courts and overcrowding the prisons. However, the impact on consumption of alcohol was insignificant. It made things a little harder for the bootleggers, but they simply raised their prices and sucked even more money out of the legal economy. That also made things harder for ordinary people, who were facing crises left and right; now, they had to live with increased violence associated with bootlegging, too. Essentially, with the increased emphasis on enforcing the Prohibition law, Prohibition had a stronger impact on the economy.

The stock market crash followed by the massive Depression spread economic devastation worldwide. By early January 1930, an estimated 4 to 5 million Americans were unemployed. Support for Prohibition dropped and anti-Prohibition sentiment shot upward, with large numbers of people demonstrating in the streets demanding its repeal. On May 24, 1930, *The Literary Digest*, one of the nation's leading periodicals, stated the results of its nationwide poll showed a majority favored repealing Prohibition.[82] Hoover convened committees of "influential people" to study the problem, but nothing of substance was accomplished and economic conditions only got worse. Between the stock market crash on October 29, 1929 and December 11, 1930, 1300 banks reportedly closed, including one of New York's largest. The voters showed their displeasure in the November 1930 mid-term elections, by returning control of the House to the Democrats and drastically reducing the Republican control of the Senate.

It had to have been embarrassing for Hoover and the Republicans when Capone, a known bootlegger and believed murderer, opened "soup kitchens" in the Chicago area to feed thousands of unemployed people — 10,000 on Christmas Day (1930) alone. Capone became a national hero. There was no unemploy-

---

82. Schlesinger. p. 455-457.

ment insurance or welfare for working-class people to fall back on; Hoover and the Republican-controlled Congress were doing nothing to help. Everyone knew Capone ran numbers and a bookmaking operation in the back rooms of his soup kitchens, but the police never raided them for fear of being stoned to death by the people being fed there. Everyone knew he was breaking the law, even committing murder — but they considered that the fault of the Prohibition law, not his character flaws. If Capone had been seen as nothing but a crook, thug or murderer, someone would have killed him long before he attained the heights he did.

Capone was no fool and the government, despite a seemingly unlimited supply of money and resources, was quite unable to finding the evidence or witnesses needed to convict him of anything. Capone was one of the most beloved men in America, especially in Chicago. Newspapers constantly ran his picture and the government's latest accusations on the front page — news about Capone sold newspapers, more newspapers than any other public figure.

The public appreciated his providing what they wanted, and they enjoyed watching him openly defying laws they hated. They particularly liked Capone for not putting on any false airs, in sharp contrast with Hoover and the Republicans, who were claiming the moral high ground.

Abjectly failing to enforce the Prohibition laws or to convince the public to stop drinking, and faced with a drastic increase in violence, the Hoover administration was desperate to make an example of Capone. Hoover asked none other than Treasury Secretary Andrew Mellon to spearhead the government's attack. Actually, as the Prohibition Unit was part of the Dept. of the Treasury, that was already part of Mellon's responsibilities. But now, the Treasury Department mustered all of its resources against Capone, not just its Prohibition agents. Bring on the Internal Revenue Service!

Veteran organized crime reporter Hank Messick suggested that. Meyer Lansky's brother Jake suggested prosecuting Capone on tax evasion and even supplied IRS officials with at least some of the data necessary. Messick alleges that Lansky and others thought Capone was too public, too visible, and too notorious to be allowed to continue as a major organized crime figure. Arranging for him to be jailed was a far neater solution than having him killed.[83]

US Attorney E.Q. Johnson headed the government's assault. He planned a two-pronged attack, using a small task force, the Special Intelligence Unit, from the IRS and one from the Prohibition Unit — both part of the Treasury Depart-

---

83. Lyman, Michael & Potter, Gary W. *Organized Crime*, Prentice Hall: 1996, p. 24.

ment. The IRS agents got a warrant and seized Capone's records, looking for anything they could use against him. Eliot Ness, just 26 years old, was recommended by his brother-in-law to head the Prohibition Unit group (which consisted of nine agents, all under thirty years old). It was Ness's job to hurt Capone financially, closing down his stills and breweries so that he would not have the funds to bribe police and public officials. But, most important, the Prohibition Unit's activities were meant to divert Capone's attention from the tax case. And Johnson thought the tax case was actually his best bet to get Capone. He was right.

The government won its case and put Capone away on tax evasion charges. There is no record of who was Ness's counterpart at the IRS, and even Ness's mmediate boss E.Q. Johnson is a relative unknown.

With Hoover so fixated on Capone, there was no way Capone could have gotten a fair trial in a federal court. On October 17, 1931, Capone was convicted on tax evasion charges, sentenced to eleven years in prison and fined $50,000. Nobody had ever received so severe a sentence for tax evasion and the public found it outrageous. No one felt good about income taxes (which were promoted on the suggestion they would "soak the rich," but were instead hitting the rest, because the wealthy found loopholes and avoided paying). Using the tax laws to punish Capone was meant to intimidate the public and alert them to the powers of the Internal Revenue Service.

Their inability to convict Capone on anything but tax evasion made Hoover and Mellon seem even more inept and made them even more unpopular. After Capone's conviction, the public focused again on Mellon and he soon retired from his cabinet position.

There are a number of interesting ironies and myths about the Prohibition era. Eliot Ness, for example, had nothing to do with Capone's arrest or conviction. The story of the Untouchables is pulp-fiction, written as entertainment; it is not history. Ness was not a modest, low-profile government agent; he courted publicity. Ness never met Capone face to face until after his tax evasion conviction; and he did not kill Frank Nitti. Considering the Prohibition Unit's rogue reputation, chances are that Ness's men were not as pure as their "untouchable" name suggests.

Perhaps the only truth in the 1987 Brian DePalma film *The Untouchables* comes at the end when Ness is asked, "What are you going to do, now that Prohibition has ended?" "I'm going to get something to drink." In fact, Ness was known to have a proclivity for scotch — and he died an alcoholic

Like America's Civil War, Prohibition split families, even brothers, along ideological lines. The Capone family was no exception. In 1908, long before the start of Prohibition, Al Capone's older brother Vincenzo (later known as Richard "Two-Gun" Hart) left home at the age of 16, apparently changed his name, and joined the Army. He was the only Capone brother to fight in World War I. At one point he was a bodyguard for President Calvin Coolidge, but he really made a name for himself as a Prohibition enforcement officer in and around Homer, Nebraska. Hart was aggressive in fighting the bootleggers and busting up illegal stills, which brought him to the attention of the US Indian Service who hired him to keep alcohol off the Sioux and Cheyenne Indian reservations. When Prohibition ended, Hart became a town marshal in Homer.[84]

Hart kept his real name a secret even from his wife Kathleen and children, although occasionally he would ask his brother Ralph to send a check. After Al Capone was released from prison in November 1939, Hart quietly contacted and then met Ralph and John Capone in Sioux City, Iowa. In late 1940, Hart went to Chicago to see his mother, Theresa. Before leaving for Chicago, he told Kathleen and the boys that he was in fact Al Capone's brother.

Capone was a model prisoner and supposedly was released early because of his good behavior and work credits but in reality he was in terrible shape — he was suffering the effects of tertiary syphilis and no longer represented a threat to society. Mae, who stood by Al until the very end, took him to a hospital in Baltimore where he was treated until March of 1940. With few exceptions, Capone spent the rest of his life at his palace in Palm Island, Florida. One of those exceptions was in 1946, when Two-Gun took his son Harry to a Capone family cabin in Wisconsin, where he had a chance to meet his famous uncle. Al Capone by then was almost totally disoriented. Two-Gun told Harry not to get too close to Al during this family visit, probably not wanting his son unduly influenced by his gangster kingpin brother. Al Capone died on January 25, 1947 of cardiac arrest, a week before Andrew Volstead, author of the Volstead Act, died at the age of 87.

Another Prohibition irony was that Mabel Walker Willebrandt, who as the US Assistant Attorney General in charge of liquor law prosecutions sent

84.   Bardsley, Marilyn, *Al Capone biography*, accessed in 2002. Crime Library, online at http://www.crimelibrary.com/capone/caponechicago.htm

many bootleggers to prison, including Remus and McCoy, became a wine industry attorney after Prohibition.[85]

The Stock Market Crash

The bull market of the mid-1920s reflected the extraordinarily prosperous
economy and there was good reason for people to be optimistic — the world was
at peace, jobs were plentiful, consumers were buying, stock prices were soaring
and the Dow Jones Industrial Index was hitting new highs. Most important,
people were enjoying the Roaring Twenties, despite Prohibition. Life was good
and there was nothing in the foreseeable future that even suggested anything
other than an even better future. More and more people were dabbling in the
stock market. Stockbrokers and banks were encouraging people to enhance
their position and buy more stock on "margin."

If the banks hadn't been as optimistic as everyone else, they might not have
been so willing to finance so many stock purchases on credit. Buying stocks on
margin essentially meant an investor could control a large block of stock by coming up with a small percentage (10-20%) of the stock's actual value at the time of
purchase. The bank would put up the balance, keep the stock certificates for
security, and charge the investor interest. It was a good deal for everyone — if
the value of the stock went up. The investor knew he would lose his investment
if the value of the stock declined, and he also knew that the bank would protect
its principal by selling the stock before its value fell below the bank's investment; so losses theoretically would also be limited. Buying stock on margin was
considered a sound financial practice — and the only difference today is that the
investor has to put up more of his own money (50%) to buy stocks on margin.

By 1927, the prosperity was coming to an end — the effects of Prohibition
had drained many wallets and put a sudden halt to the booming consumer-based
economy. People may not have been selling apples on street corners yet, but the
economy stopped growing. Working-class people were caught between the
soaring prices for alcohol and higher taxes to pay for increased federal enforcement of the Prohibition laws. Alcohol Prohibition created an underground economy that competed with the legal economy for every available dollar.

---

85. *Encyclopedia Americana*, Vol. 22, 1989, p. 648.

People were still optimistic about the future and despite a serious dive in the stock market in mid-1927, they believed they could pull the economy out of its slump by investing more. An avalanche of cash-poor individual investors began buying stocks on margin. For the first time in the history of the stock market, small investors became the dominant factor in pushing up prices. The unrestrained speculation pushed the stock market to all time highs, but sales of the companies' underlying products did not improve; company profitability declined and so dividends dwindled.

Up to the very end, the consumer-based economy looked great on paper and inventors were making money hand-over-fist as stock prices rose. But what investors were seeing on Wall Street was quite different to what the businesses on Main Street were experiencing. By mid-1927, unemployment was up significantly, causing sales and profits to decline sharply; that caused even more unemployment. People understood this as a temporary downturn and were confident they could brave it out. Many investors, encouraged by rosy economic forecasts, saw the dip as an opportunity to purchase more stock at reduced prices — causing the Dow to again skyrocket. Of course, the Dow is a statistic that does not represent the health of the much broader market, where most investors were speculating. And, of course, those rosy economic forecasts were based on incomplete and misleading information. The robust black market did not send the government quarterly sales reports or pay taxes.

The imposition of an income tax was heartily resisted and by the mid-1920s the government had put in place more sophisticated methods of collecting those taxes. To thwart the government's ability to identify money obtained through illegal activities (primarily bootlegging), those involved sought ways to legitimize themselves. They took control of numerous mid-sized businesses, not for the income but to account for their illegal income. Indeed, many of these businesses were commercial laundries — thus the expression "laundered money." Money was pumped into these legal businesses; and their apparent success contributed to the publication of promising economic forecasts, making the economy look even better — on paper.

Most investors and economists did not see the crash coming. There certainly was no lack of demand for the small appliances, refrigerators, and automobiles that were being produced; but sales were not robust enough to support all the expanding industry. The scarcer jobs became, the less consumers spent. As profits plunged and companies failed to meet expected dividends or loan payments, the value of the stocks started to fall. Banks and big investors acted quickly to limit their losses. Months before the actual crash, those at the top of the food chain had pretty much pulled back, leaving the less informed and less educated to take the hit. The bubble did break, on "Black Tuesday," October 29, 1929. Billions of dollars worth of equity simply evaporated in a matter of a few days. Millions of people were bankrupted; companies and banks, too. Panic selling erupted into a full-scale decline; but the real collapse of the economy showed up in the months following, when many of the troubled companies were forced to close down, expanding the depression even further.

People did not have jobs, did not have money, and were not buying the products and services companies produced. Essentially, Wall Street collapsed because the illegal economy Prohibition created simply overwhelmed it.

The public's cry to repeal Prohibition grew louder and it became much harder for Hoover to ignore them. Still, the defeat of Al Smith and the Democrats in the 1928 election had given quite a boost to the prohibitionists. In early 1930, Senator Morris Shepard of Texas, coauthor of the Prohibition Amendment and a die-hard Prohibitionist, confidently asserted: "There is as much chance of repealing the Eighteenth Amendment as there is for a hummingbird to fly to the planet Mars with the Washington Monument tied to its tail."[86] However, as the effects of the massive economic depression, set in the anti-Prohibition voices got much louder.

The AmeriTrust Graph of Economic Activity on the next two pages, courtesy of the AmeriTrust Bank (now part of the Key Bank System), is a pictorial history of the US economy, charting from 1790 to present both the levels of business activity (the GNP, or Gross National Product) and the cost of goods and services (depicted by the Wholesale Cost of Goods, WC of G). The juxtaposition of the GNP and the WC of G determines whether or not the economy is prosperous. Paul Samuelson of MIT used the AmeriTrust graph to identify the 1920s as the most prosperous period in American history and to explain his "Stagflation" theory.

Using this definition of prosperity, the period between 1943 and 1945 seems even more prosperous; however, because that boom was created by World War II and the benefits ended with the end of the war, that was considered an artificial and unsustainable economy. Wars do not last forever.

---

86. Nadelmann, Ethan A. *American Heritage Magazine*. Feb/Mar 93. p. 48.

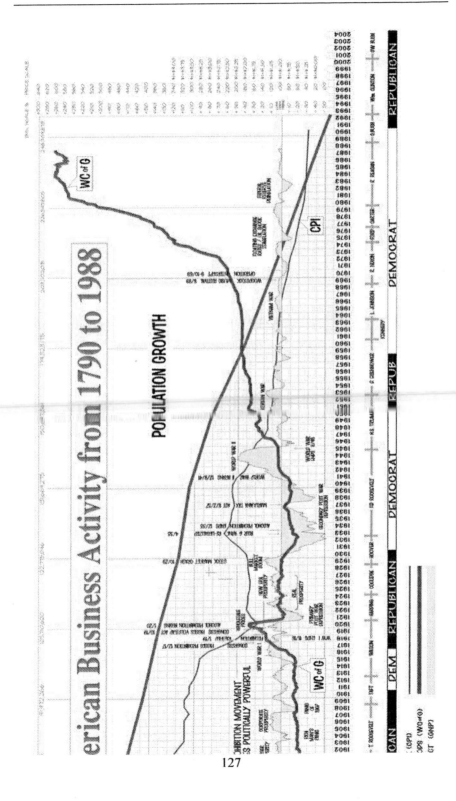

erican Business Activity from 1790 to 1988

POPULATION GROWTH

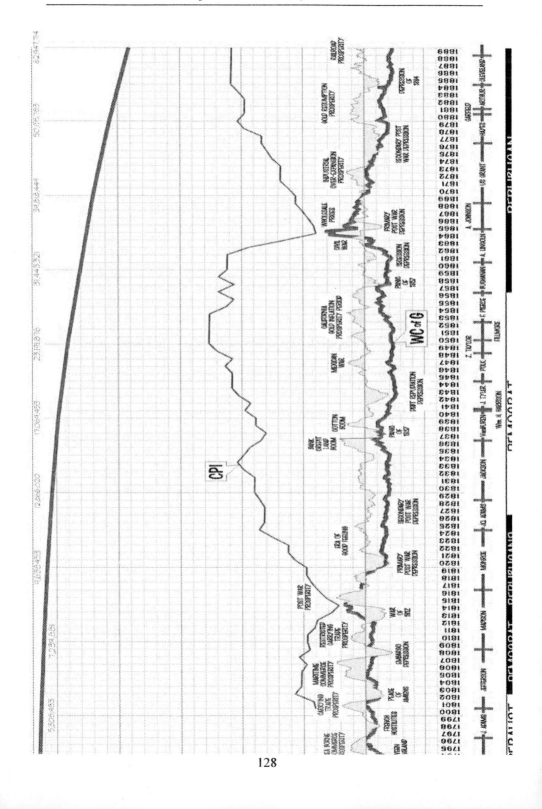

Here, I have added data on population growth, the Consumer Price Index (CPI) and the presidents and political parties that were in power during the period. This graph puts in perspective the economic impact, both positive and negative, of wars, embargoes, the discovery of gold, maritime and railroad commerce, financial panic, the effects of monetary restraints and even our optimistic or pessimistic perception of the future. It shows the severity of the Great Depression in comparison to previous economic depressions, and also the immensity of the war machine built during World War II and how suddenly the economic benefits ended at the conclusion of the war. It even almost pinpoints the October 1929 stock market crash.

Everything we do affects the economy, and our standard of living. Historical references cannot be recognized, quantified or factored in completely, but it's tempting to try — they remain the best explanation economists have for the fluctuations in the economy. The various factors contributing to every rise or drop in the economy may involve chains of events that take place over time. Thanks to the AmeriTrust Graph, we can pretty clearly identify the economic effects of Prohibition, all of which were negative.

Five economic dips or depressions can be attributed to Prohibition almost entirely, starting in 1917 and ending with the Great Depression.

1) The recession starting in approximately September 1917. This was a reaction to the Lever Food and Fuel Control Act, a wartime bill to control food distribution under Herbert Hoover's supervision. It prohibited the production of whiskey between September 1917 and the end of World War I in November 1918. The loss of the production, distribution, and sales of whiskey (which had been part of the economic statistics the government uses to chart economic progress) helped drag down the numbers. This recession reversed a two-year-long economic boom that had been caused predominately by America's production and sale of weapons to France. The recession was short-lived because the government was pouring money into the war effort.

2) Christmas 1917 was not a happy time in America. Troops were risking their lives in Europe and with a shortage of whiskey, the holiday celebrations lacked spirit in every sense. The US Congress passed the Webb Resolution in December 1917, calling for the 18th Amendment, Alcohol Prohibition. Ratification came two years later, and the economy took another serious dip.

3) By September 1918, a slow down in war spending preceded the expected peace settlement and an even sharper decline came two months after the end of the war, in January 1919; that can be seen in part as an acknowledgment of the

ratification of the 18th Amendment by the states. Once people recovered from their shock, they hurried to buy whatever reserves were still available, driving up alcohol prices and virtually wiped out existing stocks. That spending spree was more than offset by the number of alcohol-related businesses that shut down.

There was also a slight recession on or about October 28, 1919, when Congress overrode Wilson's veto and passed the Volstead Act, which attached criminal penalties to the Prohibition Amendment and demonstrated the government's intention to enforce the Prohibition law.

4) The stockpiling of alcohol stopped immediately after January 20, 1920, when Prohibition went into effect and the economy dramatically plummeted into a state of severe depression reflecting the closing of breweries, distilleries and saloons. For lack of a better explanation, academic economists refer to the economic depression of 1920-22 as the Primary Post War Depression. After every war, there is an economic recession or depression because of the time it takes to convert from a wartime economy to a consumer-based economy. But in this case, the war had ended over a year earlier and could not have been the sole or even main factor. Prohibition shut down the legal liquor industry and put tens of thousands of people out of work.

5) Labeling the Great Economic Depression of 1929-1941 as a Secondary Post War Depression is unrealistic and quite unfounded. Half way through the eleven years between the end of World War I and the beginning of the Great Depression, we experienced the most prosperous period in American history. But it is highly inconvenient to officialdom to acknowledge the negative economic effects of Prohibition.

The fundamental flaw with economic information about the Prohibition Era, like the AmeriTrust Graph, is that it is compiled from incomplete data and cannot give an accurate picture of the economy. Prohibition may have stopped the legal manufacture and sales of alcohol, but the illegal manufacture and sales continued throughout the Prohibition Era; it simply was not reported and no longer included in the statistics the federal government used to determine the health of the economy.

The graph also shows us, thanks in large part to passage of the Marijuana Tax Act, that changing from a basically agrarian society (before the stock market crash) to an industrial society (after it) dramatically and permanently reversed the traditional relationship between the Wholesale Cost of Goods and the CPI, which refers to inflation and rises or declines in the purchasing power of the dollar. The transition occurred after the war because wage and price controls imposed during the war years had kept prices artificially low, and after that, from the early 1950s to the late 60s, the economy was struggling despite high levels of production (particularly of consumer goods), an abundance of jobs, and a relatively low cost of living. MIT economist Paul Samuelson coined the term "stagflation" to describe the lackluster economy of that period; previously, stagnation and inflation were not expected to occur simultaneously. Admittedly, interest payments on the national debt, which substantially increased after the stock market crash and because of the extraordinary cost of World War II, were a drag on the economy, but probably were not enough to put such a damper on the long term growth of the economy.

But after 1937, virtually all of the everyday consumer products — paint, lubricants, clothing, paper, and practically everything that was previously produced from low-cost hemp were now being produced from petroleum (oil). That pushed up the demand for and the price of oil, gas, and petroleum by-products both domestic and imported. It meant that manufacturers were paying more for raw materials and absorbing the increased costs to keep their products competitive — resulting in lower profits. Oil was replacing hemp, and we began using more plastics, also made from oil. The increase in the Wholesale Cost of Goods after the war, and particularly after the mid 1950s, reflects that increased use of oil and the increased cost of finding, drilling, and transporting oil. The 1973 OPEC oil embargo also sharply increased prices, which have remained high ever after.

No major study has been published showing academic or government analysis of the enormous growth of the underground economy beginning in the late 1950s when white Americans, starting with the Beatniks, started using a wider range of illegal recreational intoxicants, particularly marijuana. By the mid-1960s, the use of marijuana, particularly, and cocaine was widespread. There is no way to determine how much people were spending on illegal goods, since they do not report their activity to the government; but it has been estimated that in the late 1960s, there were 40 or 50 million Americans spending $10 or $20 a week for an ounce of marijuana every week or two, along with millions more spending $100 or so every once in a while on a gram of cocaine. Rough calculations make that into a figure as high as $300 billion per year. If that were true, it would mean the illegal drug industry was the top industry in America — bigger than AT&T, General Motors, General Electric, and a dozen other major corporations combined. Overlooking the economic effects of $300 billion annually makes a mockery of economic studies, just as ignoring the black market in liquor made senseless the economic projections of the 1920s.

PROOF OF PROHIBITION'S DESTRUCTIVE NATURE

Alcohol Prohibition, the "Great Social Experiment," lasted an excruciating thirteen years from January 1920 to December 1933 and ended only after it destroyed the US economy. Unfortunately, it is rare to find a historical reference even suggesting a possible cause and effect between Alcohol Prohibition and the Great Depression. The federal government (and other institutions who played a role) refuses to admit its mistakes.

The worst three and a half years of the depression came right in the wake of the stock market crash (see AmeriTrust Graph, 10/29–4/33). For 32 consecutive months the economy plummeted, and then floundered for an additional ten months. The robust improvement in the economy in approximately April 1933 came precisely when the Beer and Wine Revenue Act went into effect. It was another tax, but at least it exempted beer and wine from the Volstead Act and essentially re-legalized the manufacture and sale of beer and wine. Congress passed the Beer and Wine Revenue Act on March 22, 1933 just two days after Roosevelt's inauguration. It became effective on April 7, 1933, allowing manufacture and distribution of 3.2% beer and wine. The almost instantaneous improvement in the economy reflected the re-opening of vineyards and breweries, distributorships, liquor stores and saloons.

Hard alcohol was still illegal and the Volstead Act was still in effect until ratification of the 21st Amendment, which actually repealed Prohibition. Congress passed the Blaine Resolution, proposing the 21st Amendment to repeal the 18th Amendment, on February 20, 1933. Although Roosevelt and the Democrats were enacting all sorts of legislation to stimulate the economy and get people back to work, it is likely that without the repeal of Prohibition economic recovery would not have been possible.

Despite the gloom and doom of the Great Depression, the end of Prohibition was celebrated by singing, dancing, and drinking in the streets. Now, those who opposed Prohibition were no longer criminals. People break laws for many reasons; but when the majority recognizes a law as unreasonable, it saps the credibility of the legal system and government in general. It weakens people's respect for authority. Frequently, laws reflect only the interests and desires of a small segment of the population, a particular industry, or the government itself. What is good for one group may inflict loathsome hardships on others, and often does not represent society's best interests. Laws are not handed down from an unquestionable source of wisdom; they must pass a validity test.

In essence, ending Prohibition ended the need for a criminal subculture and ended the justification of their exorbitant profits. It enabled the economic components of manufacturing and distributing alcohol to again bolster the legal economy instead of competing with it. This sparked an economic explosion that created thousands of new businesses, new investment, new plants, new equipment and new jobs. The repeal of Prohibition, starting with beer and wine, caused a dramatic improvement in the health of the economy. The economic effect was somewhat less striking in December 1933 (when Prohibition was actually repealed), because much of the planning and investment had already begun eight months earlier. The 21st Amendment to the US Constitution, repealing Prohibition, was ratified extraordinarily quickly — in only nine and a half months.

Prohibition officially ended on December 5, 1933. The economy continued to improve, in part because once again the economic impact of the liquor industry was being included in the statistical calculations which now reflected a more realistic picture of the economy. Roosevelt's New Deal policies put even more people back to work, and the economy was well on the road to recovery. The positive economic effects of repealing Prohibition were far less dramatic than the negative effects of implementing it, because the effects of destroying an industry are immediate whereas rebuilding takes time. It would have been difficult, perhaps impossible, for the people living through that experience to identify Prohibition as the cause of their economic problems; nor did they have the luxury we have today of almost immediate economic feedback.

THE "EXPERTS" EXPLAIN THE GREAT DEPRESSION

Soon after the crash, academic economists posited three main reasons for it and for the collapse of the US economy. Those claims are still believed in the world of academia, even today. They are (1) Overproduction — thought to be caused by automation, (2) The unequal distribution of wealth, and (3) Banks financing stock purchases on margin. Let's examine them one by one.

Overproduction Due to Automation — Blaming automation for causing an over-production problem ("too many products") is off base, considering the primitive nature of automation in the late 1920s. Automation is simply an efficient means of production, enabling manufacturers to be even more competitive and profit-able. Automation helped improve the quality of the products being produced; it made it possible to come out with a greater variety of products; and reduced the production cost so that they could be sold at lower prices. More goods at lower prices means that more people can afford to buy them (unless people are out of work and deprived of income).

The stock market did not crash because we were producing too much. It crashed because Prohibition destroyed the economy. It killed whole categories of jobs and increased the cost of certain goods that people were not willing to do without, thus preventing them from buying other goods with their very tight budgets. It is highly unlikely that automation had anything to do with the Great Depression.

Consolidated Wealth — The inequitable distribution of wealth is capitalism's primary weakness, and we have unfortunately failed to address it rationally. Wealth itself is not inherently bad; it is the incentive for people to develop and use their intelligence, knowledge, and skills; and without incentive we would not have the variety of products and services we enjoy today. But taken to the extreme, wealth accumulated only in the hands of a few can be counterproduc-tive. Wealth means power, and America's late 19th and early 20th century indus-trialists, exemplified by Rockefeller, blatantly abused that power by serving only their own needs with no regard for society as a whole. (By the way, income dis-parities between the top percentiles and the average American have never been higher than today. It will be interesting to see what happens next.)

Wealth can nullify the principle that "all men are created equal"; the ineq-uitable distribution of wealth inherently makes men unequal. America's found-ing fathers knew that under most preceding systems, society functioned at the will, whim, and intellectual limits of those who controlled the wealth. They sought to create a far more diverse society, with a smaller gap between the haves and have-nots. In effect, this means having a vibrant and economically stable middle class. Yet America's industrialists were the first to amass such enormous fortunes; they were followed by multimillionaire bootleggers like Al Capone and Joseph P. Kennedy. There was not much left for the working middle class, who suffered the brunt of the Great Depression.

A great many people have used their wealth to benefit mankind and pre-serve our heritage. It is simply a question of whose interest is being served and at whose expense. Every society takes a crack at this puzzle, and it remains very much an open question today. How much is enough? Is it possible to place a limit on individual or family wealth, without destroying the incentive to strive for success? Is it possible to control wealth at all, given mankind's inventiveness in finding ways to avoid taxation, mask income, and derive benefit from resources that are held in someone else's (or a corporation's) name?

Buying Stocks on Margin — Could buying on margin have caused the crash? It must have played into the dynamic, but in fact the Federal Reserve Board for-bade member banks to make such loans on February 2, 1929 a full nine months before the crash, saying that such loans are highly speculative, causing stock prices to rise, but adding no real value.[87] Extending credit to enable people and institutions to buy stock is a recognized way to encourage investment and it cre-ates the capital needed for new factories, equipment, and salaries. If the underly-ing situation is sound, buying on credit makes sense.

In the late 1920s, the problem was an unhealthy economy combined with runaway speculation. No matter what you are paying with, if you buy something that is worthless, you are likely to lose money. Prohibition had sucked the life-blood out of the legal economy and many many companies were in bad shape — yet people kept buying stock. The problem of overextended credit would have been absorbed and stock prices would have recovered if the overall situation had been more solid.

Blaming margin buys was a convenient ploy to divert attention from the real problems of stock price manipulation by brokers, large investors and specu-lators, which was not addressed until the creation of the Securities and Exchange Commission enacted a series of more stringent banking laws, rules, and regulations that set some limits on what those players can do.

---

87. Schlesinger p. 542.

CHAPTER 4

THE BONUS ARMY

The stock market crash may well have been the equivalent of a release-valve on a pressure cooker that prevented an even larger disaster — a bloody revolution. Of course, after the crash, people had far less patience with Prohibition and the call to repeal it grew louder. Some people began equating Prohibition with the chaotic economic predicament.

Unfortunately, the Hoover administration and the Republican Party, still heavily influenced by sanctimonious Prohibitionists, failed to resolve the economic problems and left the nation to wallow in despair for three and a half long years. However, because of budget constraints, the government was forced to back off on enforcing the Prohibition laws. Had the government continued to step up the Prohibition pressure, the situation may well have escalated from simply ignoring the law to outright civil disobedience. That is not simply hyperbole — the Bonus Army that descended on Washington in the summer of 1932 illustrated the desperation festering in the country. It was the closest America had ever come to the brink of anarchy.

The bonus army incident was the final straw for Hoover and the Republicans. Destitute World War I veterans, many with their wives and some with children, converged on Washington to demand the government make good on its promise to grant loans against the bonuses they were given for fighting in the war. Congress passed the Soldiers' Bonus Bill in April 1924, over Coolidge's veto, and bonus certificates were mailed out. Unfortunately, the government does not always do what it promises to do and Congress never appropriated the money necessary to pay thos bonuses. The certificates were worthless.

Because of the Depression, in February 1931 Congress passed the Bonus Loan Bill authorizing 50% cash loans against the face value of those certificates. Hoover vetoed the bill and Congress again overrode his veto; however, again no money was appropriated.

Veterans were furious and they started organizing. By May 1932, they began arriving in Washington, DC, demanding full payment of their certificates. By June, there were 17,000 veterans encamped in makeshift shantytowns all around the capital known as Hoovervilles. They called themselves the Bonus Army. The Republican Congress listened to the Bonus Army's grievances and the House even responded by passing the Patman Bonus Bill, which supported the veterans' demand; but the Senate rejected it, claiming the cupboard was bare.

The Bonus Army had pressed its case and lost; most, although disgruntled, accepted defeat and went home. The remaining 2000 veterans vowed to continue their protest. The police tried to evict the protesters, resulting in the death of two officers and two protesters. The Army was called in. Just after sunrise on the morning of July 28, 1932, a company commanded by MacArthur, with Eisenhower as his aide, marched on the encampments and opened fire without warning, killing unarmed men and women. The events of that morning sent shock waves across the land. The popular outrage was channeled into the upcoming presidential election; and the reverberations added to a sense of instability that brought America closer to the brink of anarchy.

THE 1932 PRESIDENTIAL ELECTION

The public blamed the Republicans for Prohibition and for the depression. They were frustrated by Hoover's lack of leadership and inability to revive the economy, and they were revolted by the way the Republican Congress and Hoover handled the Bonus Army affair. The Republicans faced almost certain defeat.[88] They made the best of the situation by promising to repeal the 18th Amendment, but the public no longer trusted the Republican Party. In fact, the Democratic Party won a 20-year-long control of the White House and even longer control of Congress — Republicans did not regain control of the House or

---

88.   Boller, Paul F. Jr. *Presidential Campaigns*, Oxford University Press, New York: 1984, p. 232.

Senate until 1996. It really did not matter who the Democrats nominated in 1932; all the Democrats had to do was to reassert their 1928 platform calling for the repeal of Prohibition. Al Smith saw the public's hatred of Prohibition as vindicating his 1928 Presidential campaign, and he wanted the Party's nomination again, but the Democrats, wanting to avoid another religious debate, chose Franklin Roosevelt — Smith's friend and successor as New York's Governor.

Hoover and the Republicans suffered a catastrophic defeat, losing the presidency and control of the House and Senate by large majorities. But that election was not a resounding endorsement of the Democrats, either — it was simply the most expedient way of getting rid of Hoover and the Republicans. The voters were disgusted with politics as usual and with both political parties.

In fact, it was during the Depression that the Communist and Socialist Parties gained broad acceptance. Many of those who were thrown out on the streets were given money to get back into their apartments by Communist Party members, who stood on the streets begging passers-by to be charitable. The stated goals of Socialism and Communism offered the common man protection from exploitation by the wealthy and a guarantee of a minimally decent standard of living — in stark contrast to capitalism. The possibility that Communism would win the hearts and minds of American voters was real.

Then came Franklin Roosevelt. He, too, was promoted as someone looking out for their interests. Americans are very patriotic but when people feel the government is working against them instead of for them, it puts a real strain on that relationship. If the rules under which the society operates prevent the overwhelming majority of its people from prospering, a rupture occurs.

Under Franklin Roosevelt, the then Democrat-controlled Congress ended Prohibition and initiated programs like Welfare, Social Security and Unemployment Insurance to help people through the bad times. These programs have more to do with socialism than free market competition, and were indeed enacted to counteract the rising Communist and Socialist sentiment. They also reflected the growing understanding that it takes widespread wealth to keep an economy thriving. A handful of millionaires do not buy a lot of toasters and washing machines. A thriving middle class creates demand for all sorts of goods and services; and that requires that wealth be distributed somewhat throughout the society — preferably through jobs but, in a pinch, through temporary aid.

Roosevelt's social programs were never meant to support the population for an extended period of time, nor were they put forth as a solution to the long-term economic problems. The social support programs reassured the populace that the government once again had at its helm a man of the people, not a puppet of big business. Ever optimistic, they believed that prosperity was just around the corner; at least, they felt the obstacle to prosperity, Prohibition, was no longer in the way.

In 1936, there was a short-lived revival of liberal power within the Republican Party and they nominated Alf Landon to run against the beloved incumbent Franklin Roosevelt. Landon represented a massive ideological shift away from Prohibition in the Republican Party, but as a Republican candidate he never had a chance of winning —the country still blamed the Republicans for Prohibition and the stock market crash.

Roosevelt and his men knew Prohibition had caused the Depression, but they also realized they could not wait for the economy to recover on its own. The first hundred days of the Roosevelt Administration were so productive that they set a standard by which to judge the progress of succeeding administrations. The cornerstone of Roosevelt's economic recovery plan was the National Industrial Recovery Act of 1932 (NRA), which empowered the President to establish fair competition for business and industry. However, despite its enthusiastic support by the man on the street, the Supreme Court unfortunately declared unconstitutional. In Schechter Poultry Corp v. United States, the Court found the NRA unconstitutional because it excessively delegated legislative power to the President, because it involved the federal government in regulating intrastate commerce (trade wholly within a state) That left Roosevelt and the country with little more than a band-aid plan for economic recovery. Roosevelt put people to work with programs like the CCC (Civilian Conservation Corps) and WPA (Works Progress Administration), which were used to improve public lands and public buildings. However, these programs were not directed at getting the consumer-based economy back on its feet as the NRA was meant to do.

Roosevelt became embroiled in a major battle with the Supreme Court, hoping public pressure would force it to reverse its decision, but his efforts were futile — most of the justices had been appointed by the three preceding Republican presidents. Roosevelt even proposed legislation to increase the number of justices on the Supreme Court so he could appoint justices that would support his proposals — a common enough tactic. But Congress rejected this effort to "pack" the court and the NRA decision was allowed to stand.

THE GREAT SOCIAL EXPERIMENT ENDS IN FAILURE

The 1932 presidential election, which took place during the worst days of the Great Economic Depression with millions of Americans suffering severe hardships, really marked the end of the Prohibition era. Any public sentiment for Prohibition and its lofty goals had soured and most believed it was tearing the country apart. The election was the opportunity the people had been waiting for to make a change.

The "Great Social Experiment" ended as a miserable failure for a number of reasons. It never proved itself an effective deterrent to the use or abuse of alcohol. Prohibition fostered the creation of organized crime by making a popular commodity illegal and extremely profitable. Instead of uplifting everyone's moral fiber, as it professed to do, it destroyed moral and ethical values, created disdain for the authorities, and wrecked the economy. Prohibition failed to resolve the problem it was meant to address and was probably the most unpopular law ever enacted in America.

Prohibition proved that we cannot resolve our problems without rationally understanding and addressing them. Using the law to impose unrealistic moral standards is an irresponsible and inappropriate use of the law, and the resulting hardships the people suffered were much too high a price to pay to promote one group's sense of morality. It is costly to allow moral extremists and militant zealots to acquire influence. Their biased views prevent a reasonable understanding of a problem and cannot present reasonable solutions.

Prohibition was not instituted because the society decided it would be better than allowing continued alcohol use; it was an abuse of the law to impose a particular philosophy on the society — an imposition that was rejected by the public on numerous occasions. But the desire to impose one's moral convictions on others runs deep, in some sectors. We are still heavily influenced by Prohibition mentality — today, it is called the "war on drugs."

GOING OFF THE GOLD STANDARD

The stock market crash not only bankrupted millions of people and business, it dramatically reduced government revenues. And that meant the government would have to borrow a huge amount of money to pay for Roosevelt's plans to rejuvenate the economy. This was money the government would have to repay, with interest; and because the dollar was tied to the price of gold, the government could not simply print more dollars to repay the loan. Borrowing money would have created many of the disastrous economic conditions that existed in Germany after World War I.

Roosevelt needed a way to pay for steady jobs and long-term investments in infrastructure — schools, bridges, dams, power plants, and parks. Here's a basic truth of economics: Precious metals (gold and silver) and currency have no value in themselves; they are accepted as a common denominator, used to determine value in the exchange of products and services — they work, as long as everybody agrees. Real wealth comes from the production of goods and services. So, instead of borrowing money, Roosevelt took America off the gold standard in 1933, and since then the value of the US dollar, its purchasing power internationally, has been tied to the perceived strength of the US economy. It also meant the government could print as many dollars as it needed to buy materials and pay workers. It was a risky move; good thing it worked.

ON THE BRINK OF ANNIHILATION

When Roosevelt and the Democrats took up the reins of government during the "Great Depression," the tax base had shrunk and government revenues had severely declined. The federal bureaucracy faced austere budgetary cuts. However, the bureaucracy, the "career government employees," especially management, mostly appointees who owed their allegiance to the Republican Party, had their own agenda. That was particularly true in the US Treasury Department, which Andrew Mellon had headed through three Republican administrations. The people he appointed were still very much in charge — like Mellon's nephew-in-law, Harry J. Anslinger, Director of the Federal Bureau of Narcotics.

Anslinger quickly realized he faced more than a severely reduced operating budget; he faced the possible dismantlement of the FBN, his new agency. The Harrison Anti-Narcotics Act (which did not include marijuana) was the only directive Anslinger had, and although he used it to move against illegal drug traffickers, there really was not enough of a social problem to justify the expenditure. The Pure Food and Drug Act of 1906 had resolved the real problem with opiates and cocaine, so that the Harrison Anti-Narcotics Act was irrelevant when it was first enacted and it was still irrelevant in the 1930s. There was no "drug problem" to speak of. Anslinger knew the only way of insuring the continued existence and financing of his department was to exaggerate the "threat" narcotics use posed.

He set about to revive the Uniform State Narcotics Drug Act, which had been proposed but failed to pass into law four years before he was appointed Director of the Federal Bureau of Narcotics. Now, Anslinger declared its passage would be the Bureau's first major project and zealously fought to include marijuana. To help convince Congress to pass the Uniform State Narcotics Drug Act, Mellon enlisted Elizabeth Washburn Wright. Mrs. Wright had the reputation of being so influential that she was able to pick up the telephone and talk to any member of Congress, any cabinet officer, even President Hoover.[89] *But that was probably only true when the Republicans were in power.* In his book, *The Protectors*, Anslinger idolizes Mrs. Wright. When asked to get her to go a little easier, Anslinger's typical response was to align himself, and his bureau, with Mrs. Wright's cause. Anslinger, in fact, was very much indebted to Mrs. Wright, whose lobbying efforts helped to create the Bureau of Narcotics. Apparently, Harry Anslinger was not Mrs. Wright's first choice to head the newly formed Federal Bureau of Narcotics, but it was not her choice to make; it was Mellon's.

To save his agency and his job, Anslinger immediately embarked on a public relations campaign intended to heighten an unwitting public's fear of "drugs." The "press releases" Anslinger issued were nothing more than horror stories pandering to the protective instincts of parents, lumping together various intoxicants under umbrella catchwords like "drugs" and "dope." The newspapers, particularly the Hearst papers, published these fabrications as real news without investigating the facts. Of course, Hearst put more emphasis on marijuana. Anslinger even publicly commended Hearst for "pioneering the national fight against dope," but many other newspapers (including *The Washington Post, Denver News, Cleveland Plain Dealer*, the *St. Louis Star Times* and the *New York Times*) also exploited the sensational appeal of Anslinger's tales.

Anslinger was also adept at using political cartoon. Drugs were depicted as a growing menace, dealers as vicious reprobates lurking on every street, and law enforcement, especially, his bureau, as the good guys. These cartoons were extremely effective, even with those of little education, the semi-literate.

Such propaganda turned particularly vicious in the mid-1950s, when McCarthyism sparked a fear of communism that went well beyond anything founded in reality. Anslinger used the growing anti-communist sentiment to

---

89. Anslinger, Harry J. *The Protectors.* Farrar, Straus & Co., New York: 1964, p. 20

instigate another round of newspaper horror stories, which very well may have influenced the US government's decision to support Chiang Kai-Shek (who supported a prohibition against opiates — morphine and heroin) instead of Mao Tse Tung (who was financing his army through the drug trade). It did not matter whether there was any truth to Anslinger's horror stories or not; sensational stories sold newspapers.

And people believed what they read. The City was still seen as a center of crime and misconduct. By the mid-1930s Anslinger's efforts were clearly elevating the public's awareness of "drugs," but even that did not bring forth the massive public outcry he needed to get marijuana outlawed at the federal level. And only that would justify the kind of budget he wanted. He had enough success that, while other government agencies had their budgets cut, the FBN's annual budget steadily increased — at the expense of many more important social programs.

The Treasury Department supported passage of the Uniform State Narcotics Drug Act, but after investigating Anslinger's proposed inclusion of marijuana, they rejected it. They found that the drug abuse problem was being exaggerated, that marijuana use did not constitute a threat to America, and that the mood of the country after the failure of Alcohol Prohibition was set against any new prohibitions. Unable to get any satisfaction from his superiors at the Treasury Department, and with Congressional hearings (1935) on the Uniform State Narcotics Drug Act approaching, Anslinger began employing Mrs. Wright's tactics. He paced the halls of the capitol, armed with copies of Hearst's newspapers filled with marijuana horror stories.

Before the creation of the Federal Bureau of Narcotics, there was nothing to suggest that this country ever considered recreational "drug" use anything more than a very minor social problem. Anslinger exploited the issue for his own benefit. Those testifying against including marijuana in the Uniform State Narcotics Drug Act quoted the 1925 Canal Zone study, which found prohibition unwarranted. None reported any knowledge of abusive use. They almost unanimously challenged the implication that marijuana was "habit-forming" and considered it a far-fetched assertion. They concluded that the recreational use of marijuana was not enough of a problem to justify the red tape that such a law would impose on the pharmaceutical industry. That was also the position held by an overwhelming majority of pharmacists and pharmaceutical companies, according to a survey[90] conducted and reported at those hearings by Dr. William C. Woodward, director of the AMA's Bureau of Legal Medicine.

Congress passed the Uniform State Narcotics Drug Act as per the Treasury Department's recommendations but included marijuana as an optional clause, which the states were not obligated to adopt. Anslinger responded by mounting a campaign to get cities and states on board.

Anslinger slung around such terminology as "lethal weed," warping reality beyond recognition in order to scare people into supporting his position. Marijuana use in and of itself has never been shown to have caused the death of a single human being. Anslinger also lied when he insinuated that the Treasury Department urged adoption of this optional text. His superiors at the Treasury Department were the very people who rejected Anslinger's proposal to include marijuana in the first place.

Anslinger's only real ally in the fight to outlaw marijuana was Hearst. In the months following those Congressional hearings Anslinger stepped up his vilification of marijuana, knowing that if enough states adapted the optional clause, it would be easier to get marijuana criminalized on a federal level in the future. Thirty-five states adopted the optional text. Many in the South and West, with large Hispanic and black populations, included draconian penalties (20- to 50-year sentences) as a combination of bigotry and an overreaction. As a result, a Texas woman was sentenced to 110 years in prison for possession of a single marijuana cigarette — about like being caught with a six-pack of beer.

Anslinger also probably realized that he would gain the full support of his Treasury Department superiors if he managed to justify increased budget allocations. He knew the bigger the perceived problem, the more money Congress would spend, every year. That's called job security.

The federal bureaucracy pecking order is based on the importance of cabinet departments (State, Defense, Treasury, etc.) as measured exclusively by their annual budgetary allocations. Big budgets mean more jobs, more promotions and more political influence for the cabinet member in charge. The Treasury Department had lost a good deal of its prestige because of the stock market crash and the Depression, and the loss of the Prohibition Unit and its large annual budget diminished its influence even more. A new and credible expense category would be very welcome.

Of course, Anslinger did not emphasize to his superiors at the Treasury Department that a considerable amount of the Prohibition Unit's annual budget had gone into training new agents to replace the enormous number of corrupted

90. Bonnie & Whitebread. p. 65.

agents who had to be fired. Then again, Treasury officials may have concluded that effectiveness was less important than budget allocations. Corruption became an endemic problem at the FBN and all the subsequent alphabet government departments and agencies that replaced it, including today's Drug Enforcement Administration (DEA).

PASSAGE OF THE MARIJUANA TAX ACT

After seven years of resisting Anslinger's attempts to criminalize marijuana, suddenly and without explanation the Treasury Department reversed its position and supported his proposal in the form of H.R. 6385, which came to be known as the Marijuana Tax Act. The reversal officially came on April 14, 1937, while Congress was involved in preparing and debating the budget; it was presented as a revenue-enhancing proposal. It required manufacturers, importers, dealers and users of marijuana to register with the federal government and pay an occupational tax. It also required a considerable amount of paperwork (designed to discourage people) and imposed a $1-an-ounce tax on transfers to registered persons, and $100-per-ounce tax on transfers to non-registered persons. That was exorbitant, considering that at the time a marijuana cigarettes could be bought for twenty-five cents at one of New York City's many tea houses or an ounce of marijuana could be bought on the streets for a couple of dollars.

The Treasury Department had a difficult time finding a way to criminalize marijuana without abrogating the US Constitution. They came up with the Marijuana Tax Act, which did not criminalize marijuana but did impose prohibitive taxes and red tape on its use. According to one description,[91] the Treasury Department set out to "find a way to criminalize marijuana." Herman Oliphant, the Treasury Department's Chief Counsel, modeled the Marijuana Tax Act after the National Firearms Act (recently upheld by the Supreme Court), which prohibited conduct and imposed penalties. (Wasn't one of Elizabeth Washburn Wright's relatives a Treasury Department lawyer?)

The prevalent use of machine guns during and after the Prohibition era caused the federal government to seek ways of outlawing their possession and distribution. In response, Congress passed the National Firearms Act, which was challenged on the bases that the law imposed a tax on unregistered illegal

---

91.   Bonnie & Whitebread. p. 123.

weapons. Non-payment of that tax was what offenders were prosecuted for, and that was perceived as unconstitutional., On March 29, 1937, the Supreme Court decided machine guns did propose a threat to society and upheld the law.

It may never have been the Treasury Department's intent to collect taxes from the Marijuana Tax Act; and little or no tax ever was collected. They did get their budget increased, however; and they did it by taking advantage of the "drug" hysteria Hearst and Anslinger created. And they did it in the midst of the Great Depression, when so many real and important causes went unfunded.

The manner in which Anslinger and the Treasury Department presented their proposed legislation can only be described as deceitful. They suppressed the truth and misrepresented facts, keeping the Congress and public unaware of what they were really up to: outlawing hemp.

Anslinger and Oliphant kept the Marijuana Tax Act a complete secret until the day it was presented to the House Ways and Means Committee so that no one could muster any opposition. There was no notification or mention of the predictable effect this legislation would have on the hemp industry or medical profession before the Congressional hearings took place, and the committee members were not alerted to the connection between marijuana and hemp; that knowledge would have killed the Marijuana Tax Act dead in its tracks.

Although their deceit proved extremely effective, it was not an example of what we would like to expect in a democracy. Even the name, the Marijuana Tax Act, was misleading and the House Ways and Means Committee that deliberated on and later recommended passage to the full House was hardly the appropriate legislative body to address this issue. Jack Herer suggests that Anslinger and Oliphant selected the Ways and Means Committee for two reasons: (1) It is the only Committee able to send bills directly to the House floor without having other committees debate them, and (2) the Chairman, Robert L. Doughton, was a known Dupont Company ally that would rubber-stamp the legislation and allow it to sail through Congress and onto the Presidents desk.[92]

It is highly unlikely that Anslinger and Oliphant could have maintained the secrecy of what they were doing after April 14, 1937 when it was presented to the Ways and Means Committee, without Doughton's complete cooperation. Essentially, Doughton sped the Marijuana Tax Act through the Ways and Means Committee; he then helped push it through Congress.

---

92.   Herer, p. 28.

Only a few people were present to voice any opposition when it came up. Anslinger and Oliphant, however, were prepared, and they had packed the hearing with their supporters. Anslinger appeared as the chief "medical" witness, testifying under oath that marijuana addicts go crazy and that it could drive people to insanity. Anslinger was not qualified to testify as a medical expert and his unfounded and unsubstantiated assertions were in no way scientific fact. According to Jack Herer, testimony at the hearings consisted almost entirely of Anslinger, reading aloud excerpts from articles published in "Hearst's and other sensational and racist newspapers."

Anslinger's outrageous statements did not go completely unchallenged. Dr. William Woodward of the American Medical Association's (AMA) Legislative Counsel (a doctor and a lawyer) testified that:

> We are told that the use of marijuana causes crime. But as yet no one has been produced from the Bureau of Prisons to show the number of persons addicted to marijuana. An informal inquiry shows that the Bureau of Prisons has no information to this point. You have been told that school children are great users of marijuana cigarettes. No one has been summoned from the Children's Bureau to show the nature and extent of the habit among children. Inquiry into the Office of Education, and they certainly should know something of the prevalence of the habit among school children of this country, if this is a prevalent habit, indicates that they had not occasion to investigate it and know nothing of it.

Woodward further stated that there was "no evidence proving the recreational use of marijuana posed any danger to the country" and decried the newspaper reports as "nothing but heresy." He also strongly objected to the secretive methods employed, claiming that with more time he could have produced expert witnesses to disprove the government's (specifically Anslinger's) allegations. Apparently, the AMA had discovered only two days earlier[93] that the "drug" (marijuana) Congress was considering outlawing was known by the medical profession as Cannabis, a medicine that they had safely prescribed for numerous ailments for more than a hundred years.

Dr. Woodward was well versed on the subject. In May 1937 an article by Woodward appeared in the Journal of the American Medical Association vigorously opposing any legislation that would criminalize marijuana, which he described as "providing mankind with enormous medical benefits." Woodward

---

93. *Ibid.*, p.28

had written that article in response to the hysteria Hearst and Anslinger were promoting, and it reflected a general consensus among doctors that laws like the Harrison Anti-Narcotics Act and the (failed, then revived) Uniform State Narcotics Drug Act represented unwarranted interference that hindered the physician's ability to treat patients. Woodward's article went on to say,

> After more than 20 years of federal effort and the expenditure of millions of dollars, the opium and cocaine habits are still widespread. The best efforts of an efficient Bureau of Narcotics, supplemented by the efforts of an equally efficient Bureau of Customs have failed to stop the unlawful flow of opium and coca leaves and the components and derivatives, on which the continuance and spread of narcotic addiction depends.

At the Atlantic City Convention of the American Medical Association in June of that year, Woodward reported that,

> There is positively no evidence to indicate the abuse of Cannabis as a medicinal agent or to show that its medical use is leading to the development of Cannabis addiction. Cannabis at the present time is slightly used for medical purposes, but it would seem worthwhile to maintain its status as a medicinal agent for such purposes as it now has. There is a possibility that a restudy of the drug by modern means may show other advantages to be derived from its medical use.

Unfortunately, the merits of the AMA's opposition to the Marijuana Tax Act were undermined by the AMA's opposition to including health insurance coverage as part of the Social Security Act of 1935. That had infuriated Roosevelt and his Democrat colleagues, many of whom sat on the Ways and Means Committee conducting the hearings.

Woodward was correct in his assumption that investigating marijuana's modern medical application would prove advantageous. Despite the federal government's imposed research ban since 1937, marijuana has proven effective in reducing the nausea associated with chemotherapy treatment, in countering the blinding effects glaucoma, and in countering the effects of AIDS, where it may be among the most effective palliatives we have.

In addition, the National Oil Seed Institute sent its General Counsel, Ralph Loziers, who commented that hemp seeds had been used for food and oil in China for centuries without any observable deleterious effect.

The birdseed industry sent a representative who testified that "they had just come to realize that marijuana and hemp came from the same plant." He urged the committee to consider the importance of hemp seeds as bird-feed, claiming that pet birds would molt and die without it, and went as far as to put in a good word for the Army's carrier pigeons. Nonetheless, after passage of the Marijuana Tax Act most bird-feed manufacturers simply eliminated the Cannabis seeds because they could no longer be produced domestically and had to be imported and sterilized — too expensive. Ironically, August 2, 1937, the day the Marijuana Tax Act was signed into law, is also known as the day the birds stopped singing. Americans had discovered the pleasure of keeping songbirds in their homes in the early 1830s, when American merchants first established trade with China, and it had become quite popular. But, after the Cannabis seeds were removed from the feed, the birds stopped singing and the popularity of keeping songbirds declined.

It is hard to believe the US Congress understood the implications of what they were doing when they passed the Marijuana Tax Act, which exorbitantly taxed the transfer of marijuana but did not actually outlaw it. The Congressional hearings were an unequivocal shame; no scientific evidence was presented supporting the need for such legislation and no real public outcry existed to criminalize marijuana. Passage of the bill on the floor of the House of Representatives was almost automatic; there was virtually no discussion, and voting on the bill was halted only long enough for the Speaker to respond to a Congressman's question asking what the bill was all about. Sam Rayburn replied, "It has to do with something called marijuana. I believe it is a narcotic of some kind," whereupon the bill was quickly passed.[94] It passed with similar expediency in the Senate, and President Franklin Roosevelt signed the bill into law on August 2, 1937; it went into effect four months later. Like most Americans, Roosevelt realized Alcohol Prohibition had torn the country apart, but he knew nothing about narcotics and he, too, apparently, became caught up in the "drug" hysteria Anslinger and Hearst created. And so marijuana, a relatively unknown commodity, was outlawed less than four years after Alcohol Prohibition was repealed.

By passing the Marijuana Tax Act, Congress failed to meet its responsibility to the American people. Thanks to Anslinger, Congress was ill-advised and

---

94. 81st Congressional Record (1937) Pg. 5575. An in-depth overview of the situation can be found in Chapter 8 of Bonnie & Whitebread book *The Marijuana Conviction, A history of Marihuana Prohibition in the United States.*

ill-informed. Congress did not understand the issue and did not diligently investigate the ramifications of what they were doing and its effect on the health and well-being of the general population. The Marijuana Tax Act caused needless economic hardship and imposed an unnecessary limitation on people — just like Alcohol Prohibition.

Congress passed the Marijuana Tax Act and Roosevelt signed it, not knowing that they were actually outlawing the cultivation and utilization of hemp, a well-known commodity.

There is no evidence to indicate that it was ever the intent of Congress to destroy the hemp industry. Unfortunately, Congress and the President leave the details of interpreting and enforcing the laws to the discretion of the various branches of government, in particular the department heads. In Anslinger's case, he dictated rather than directed bureau policy; his power rivaled that of J. Edgar Hoover at the FBI. Ironically, Mellon died on August 27, 1937, 25 days after Roosevelt signed the Marijuana Tax Act into law. Almost 32 years later (May 1969) the US Supreme Court declared the Marijuana Tax Act unconstitutional, in Leary vs. US — that's Dr. Timothy Leary, a former of Harvard University professor.

The Effects of Outlawing the Use of Hemp

The initial effects of Marijuana Tax Act of August 1937 were both immediate and dramatic. Another severe decline in the economy was touched off just then, and it is no mere accident that these two events corresponded precisely. Although it was not in Congress's plan to destroy the hemp industry (which was already at a historic low), the new law was the final blow that ended this country's cultivation and use of that plant. At the time, America was still producing many products from hemp and hemp oil — including paints and varnishes, lubricants, linoleum, soap and others. America imported large quantities of hemp seed every year to meet that demand. Anslinger immediately warned every manufacture using hemp or hemp oil in their products, other than the bird feed manufactures, that the new law prohibited the use of any form of Cannabis. When asked what they could use instead, Anslinger would suggest they look to the emerging petrochemical industry.

The negative spike in the economy indicates that even as late a 1937 America was still using an enormous amount of hemp — and with the cultivation and use of hemp outlawed, an economic decline was inevitable. Unable to find suitable, affordable substitutes or unwilling to conform, many manufactures were forced out of business. Millions more factory workers were laid off and farmers were devastated. The depression was so severe in 1938-39 that several states felt obliged to enact legislation providing unemployment insurance — long after the worst years of the "Great Depression" were over. Of course, benevolence had little to do with initiating the economic safety net. Rather, another round of accelerated crime rates was too frightening to even consider.

A New Billion Dollar Crop

Passage of the Marijuana Tax Act came at a time when the cultivation and utilization of hemp had reached its lowest ebb in over three centuries. However, because of the introduction of the Decorticator, the industry was also poised for a dramatic resurgence in the use of hemp. The Decorticator had dramatically reduced the labor involved in cleaning raw hemp. *Mechanical Engineering Magazine*[95] talked about the introduction of the Decorticator and the bright future for hemp, saying:

> 1) Hemp, the strongest of the vegetable fibers, gives the greatest production per acre and requires the least attention. It not only requires no weeding, but also kills off all the weeds and leaves the soil in splendid condition. This, irrespective of its own monetary value, makes it a desirable crop to grow.

> 2) Hemp yields a beautiful fiber so closely resembling flax that a high-power microscope is needed to tell the difference.

> 3) 15-20% of this is fiber, and 80-85% is woody material. The rapidly growing market for cellulose and wood flour for plastics gives good reason to believe that this hitherto wasted material may prove sufficiently profitable to pay for the crop, leaving the cost of the fiber sufficiently low to compete with the 500,000 tons of hard fiber now imported annually.

> 4) Hemp is two to three times as strong as any of the hard fibers, so that much less weight is required to give the same yardage.

---

95. *Mechanical Engineering*, February 1937.

5) Hemp is not subject to many of the kinds of deterioration that beset tropical fibers, and none of them lasts as long in either fresh or salt water. 6) Paint and lacquer manufacturers can use hempseed oil, which is a good drying agent. When markets have been developed for the products now being wasted, seed and hurds, hemp will prove a highly profitable and desirable crop, and one that will make American mills independent of importations.

Popular Mechanics Magazine also hailed the anticipated resurgence in the use of hemp with an article[96] entitled "New Billion Dollar Crop," the first time any American agricultural crop was referred to as being worth so much. The article specifically mentioned the energy, paper, clothing, and plastics industries, in which hemp fibers and hemp oil could be substituted for petroleum and wood-based products, noting:

1) Hemp is the standard fiber of the world. It has great tensile strength and durability. It is used to produce more than 5,000 textile products, ranging from rope to fine laces, and the woody "hurds" remaining after the fiber has been removed contain more than 77% cellulose, which can be used to produce more than 25,000 products ranging from dynamite to Cellophane.

2) From the farmer's point of view, hemp is an easy crop to grow and will yield from three to six tons per acre on any land that will grow corn, wheat or oats.

3) It can be grown in any state of the Union.

4) It has a short growing season, so that it can be planted after other crops are in.

5) The long roots penetrate and break the soil to leave it in good shape for next the year's crop.

6) The dense shock of leaves, eight to twelve feet above the ground, chokes out weeds.

7) Two successive crops are enough to reclaim land that has been abandoned because of Canadian thistles or quack grass.

---

96. Complete article available online at http://www.cannabis.com/untoldstory/pmpage1.shtml

But the Marijuana Tax Act was passed, and this promise remained unfulfilled.

Ordinary Cannabis, as grown for hemp, contains only a minuscule amount of THC. But by manipulating information and craftily equating the industrial raw material with the intoxicant, Anslinger was able to squelch the notion of cultivating hemp for industrial uses.

But what was good for Rockefeller, Mellon, and DuPont was good for Hearst and Anslinger. The petrochemical companies took over hemp's former markets, starting us all on the road to petroleum dependency.

The Marijuana Tax Act also allowed Anslinger to use other government agencies like the Dept. of Agriculture and programs like the Works Progress Administration to help eradicate Cannabis. Under Roosevelt's "New Deal" WPA program, Anslinger was able to pay unemployed American workers and even got Boy Scout volunteers to pull up cannabis wherever they found it — along the banks of the Potomac, for instance, where it had been growing wild since colonial days.

All that kept the American economy from falling back into the depths of Depression after the 1937 economic decline was the enormous build up of the war machine, which actually started in 1938. Growth of the petrochemical industry also strengthened the economy as it moved into all the markets where hemp-based products were traditionally used. Perhaps the most important factor was that Alcohol Prohibition had been repealed and was no longer a drag on the economy.

The enormous investment necessary to build and equip an army for war, especially one as immense as the one we mobilized for World War II, stimulates the economy, of course — but only temporarily, and when the war ends, the economic stimulus stops and the economy quickly declines (See AmeriTrust Graph, 1945). Preparing for war, even maintaining a standing army for defensive purposes, is actually an expense. Bullets and bombs do not stabilize or grow the economy like selling washing machines and automobiles does.

America's domestic manufacturing capability and consumer-based economy grew dramatically after the Civil War and kept growing, sputtering only slightly after World War I, until just before the stock market crash and the Great Depression began. After World War I, the US economy looked extraordinarily strong compared to war-torn Europe and for the first time America was considered a real world power and an equal among the leading nations. When World War II began, the "free world" looked to America for help.

154

World War I ended with England and the United States still adversaries, not friends; less than a quarter century later, the need for friendship quickly developed. At the beginning of World War II the Germans demonstrated their technological advances in the weapons of war by jumping the "moat" of the English Channel and bombing London with rockets. The French, having not even the water to keep the Germans at bay, were easily invaded in both world wars. America by contrast stood as a fortress, protected by the Atlantic and Pacific Oceans and friendly neighbors both to the North and South. And America was able to keep its economy going — although the economy was not as robust as it seemed.

CHAPTER 5

RACE RELATIONS IN AMERICA

From the mid-1940s to the early 70s, racial barriers were beginning to fall and the racial balance of power was starting to change. Minorities were no longer confined to specific sections of cities (ghettoes) or certain areas of the country. In short, the Anglo-Saxon dominance was being seriously threatened. Although white America was pretty much unaware of any recreational intoxicants beyond alcohol, tobacco and caffeine, some of the minorities were familiar with marijuana and other substances. As the different ethnic and racial factions began intermingling, in the military, on college campuses, and on the job, the knowledge and use of these illegal intoxicants, particularly marijuana, began to spread.

America had started out as a predominantly white Protestant Anglo-Saxon culture, and that is the ethnic group that retained the most power in shaping the culture going forward. Ethnic enclaves such as Chinatown, Little Tokyo, Little Havana, Little Italy, and the Borscht Belt kept the unfamiliar cultures at a comfortable distance while providing a sense of community for the "outsiders." The majority group used its legal system to limit behaviors it decided was unpalatable. White Protestant Anglo-Saxon America preferred drinking; if Caribbean immigrants liked to smoke marijuana, they learned early to keep it to themselves. Alcohol prohibition could not last, but when it comes to other drugs, those associated with minorities, more laws come into play; and obviously, the people most likely to break those laws and suffer punishment are those minorities who are caught messing around with the illegal "drugs."

That is one reason why blacks and Hispanics make up a disproportional share of the prison population. That adds to the distrust between the races; and given the distrust, it is no wonder much of white America has little knowledge about the intoxicants other groups use. Morphine addiction dramatically increased after every war since the Civil War, proving how little Americans understood the effects of opium. Chinese immigrants could have told them a thing or two. The Chinese opium dens that were opened in the US during the late 19th century began to impart some of that knowledge. They were providing a relatively safe, controlled environment and experienced supervision for both new and experienced users.

Marijuana is perhaps the most widely used recreational intoxicant other than alcohol. It was traditionally known as a poor man's intoxicant. Marijuana was always available at low cost, or no cost; whereas alcohol is harder to produce at home. Not surprisingly, the first anti-marijuana laws coincided with the massive migration of Hispanics into the United States because of the Mexican Revolutionary War.

Before Alcohol Prohibition, marijuana was only illegal in a few Southern and Western states; that was purely intended to discourage settlement of black or Latino populations. During the Depression many people of every color could not afford the price of a drink and they sought alternatives — mostly marijuana; but they also experimented with several drugs including morphine and heroin, and cocaine. For most people, opiates were too dangerous and cocaine, "the rich man's drug," was too expensive. Marijuana began to become a more popular intoxicant in the white community — particularly in the large urban centers of the Northeast and Midwest, where racial integration and assimilation were more advanced.

Since knowledge of (and initial access to) marijuana spread only as racial intermingling took place, large parts of the US did not even know what marijuana was — beyond some vague evil highlighted in Anslinger's constant racially-biased "news" stories. However, in the bigger cities, artists, writers, and musicians and young people in general were more open to racial integration, and to new ideas.

After World War II, more mingling began to take place. A barrier in sports was broken when Jackie Robinson was admitted to major league baseball in April 1947. In January 1948, President Truman issued an executive order desegregating the civil service and the military. As it became more possible and more likely for people of different backgrounds to share work and recreation, they shared their knowledge and positive experiences with each other — one of which was Marijuana.

"THE MEZZ"

Milton "Mezz" Mezzrow, often called the "Johnny Appleseed of Marijuana," the "White Mayor of Harlem," or "The Man that Hipped the World," grew up on the streets of Chicago. Mezz was a white guy who learned to play jazz in reform school and in prison, from black musicians who were in there with him. They also familiarized him with marijuana. After prison, Mezzrow earned his living as a jazz musician and moved around the country playing with many of America's best bands, including Louis Armstrong's. Mezz supplemented his musical career by dealing marijuana, and had a reputation for selling good quality.

Mezzrow's importance is not that he was either a musician or a marijuana dealer. His experience proves that friendliness and open-mindedness breeds acceptance and eradicates racial prejudice. Mezzrow was a white man living in the black world. He learned from them and they learned from him, and he was not only accepted, he was loved. Examples of this were happening in communities all across the country. Americans with different cultural backgrounds, traditions and experiences were learning from each other — including learning about their preferred intoxicant, marijuana. The use and knowledge of marijuana spread quickly, moving into the awareness of America's white middle and upper classes, despite all the propaganda against it. In Manhattan alone, the LaGuardia Commission Report noted some 500 known marijuana tea houses, the equivalent of a saloon or speakeasy, during the Prohibition era. Marijuana was legal at the time and these establishments were not causing a disturbance or any problems, so the police simply ignored them. The seven states that had laws outlawing the use of marijuana on their books before the beginning of Prohibition had enacted them in reaction to the massive influx of Mexican nationals, and used the laws as an excuse for controlling that population. In 1950, the United Nations reported that 10% of the world's population was using marijuana in one form or another — and that may be a gross underestimation.

After passage of the Marijuana Tax Act, America had to import all its hemp rope, canvas, and burlap from the Philippines, which at the time was a territory of the United States. It was labeled "Manila" so that Cannabis (hemp) would not be identified as the raw material. Hemp was slowly being erased from view as a useful and positive industrial product.

Then the Japanese invaded the Philippines and cut off the hemp supply. Since hemp-based products were vital to the war effort, the US had to reverse itself. After essentially criminalizing the cultivation and utilization of hemp just a few years earlier, the government began encouraging farmers to grow it. The 4H Club encouraged members to grow hemp seeds and the Department of Agriculture even produced a fourteen-minute film, "Hemp for Victory," espousing the benefits of cultivating and utilizing hemp. Unfortunately, after the war ended, the US government reverted to its earlier position and the USDA buried "Hemp for Victory," denied the film's existence, and prevented future Americans from learning from that experience. (That denial ended only after the USDA was confronted with a copy of the film.)

With the exception of that brief interlude after Japan invaded the Philippines, no hemp cultivation has been permitted in the US since August 1937 when the Marijuana Tax Act was passed. Yet we still need hemp, even today. Because of this absurd law, we have become overtly dependent on petroleum that is used as a replacement for hemp in many products, including rope and durable fabrics. That simply equates to fewer American jobs and more of money leaving the country.

THE LAGUARDIA COMMITTEE REPORT

Anslinger's heavy-handed approach did not go unnoticed or unchallenged. Despite the hysteria Anslinger created, vast numbers of Americans, including whites, particularly in the Northeast, saw the implementation of the Marijuana Tax Act as a return to the fanaticism of Prohibition and they did not like it. For many, the ideological question of right or wrong in recreational intoxicants was settled with the repeal of Alcohol Prohibition. Many simply ignored the new law — as was pointed out in the LaGuardia Committee Report of 1944.

The LaGuardia Committee Report was the culmination of a five-year study (1939–1944) concentrating on the scope and effect of marijuana use within the City of New York. New York City's Mayor Fiorello LaGuardia initiated the investigation into the drug hysteria by enlisting the New York Academy of Med-icine to study the situation. They concluded, over a year after the passage of the Marijuana Tax Act, that their knowledge of marijuana was inadequate. LaGuardia agreed and appointed 31 scientists (not politicians and bureaucrats) to do a much more sophisticated sociological and clinical study than Congress had done. The City of New York was doing what the US government should have done before it acted on the Marijuana Tax Act.

The LaGuardia Commission conducted the most comprehensive investiga-tion of marijuana to date and unlike the Congressional hearings, it included sci-entific evidence and testimony from marijuana users. The committee's final report was published as the book *Marijuana Problems*, and concluded that mari-juana use proposed no real threat to America.

The report repudiated Anslinger's vilification of marijuana, found no truth to his claims of marijuana use being a determining factor leading to major crimes, nothing to substantiate the claim that marijuana use caused insanity, nothing to support the notion that marijuana use caused juvenile delinquency, and nothing to confirm allegations that marijuana use leads to the use of hard core drugs. Nor did they find anything to indicate that it was either addictive or lethal.

Anslinger's reaction, as always, was to attack anything and anybody that opposed his perspective. He mustered his own army of experts to repudiate the findings of the LaGuardia Commission and berated the publication, groups, and institutions that supported it. That effectively drove a wedge between the medi-cal and scientific communities and left the public confused. The release of the LaGuardia Commission's report, in 1944, was badly timed, coinciding with some of the heaviest fighting of the war. The report made the daily news but was quickly forgotten as the focus of the newspapers and radio news turned back to the war. The LaGuardia report was essentially ignored.

The LaGuardia Report concluded that marijuana is not addictive and acts as a fairly mild intoxicant. Like beer, it isn't likely to increase a person's ambi-tion, drive, and focus; but the LaGuardia Report did not produce any evidence that it could cause physical dependency or other long-term effects, either. The Report found that marijuana causes "[no] significant alterations of the personal-ity," although while under the influence, the subjects tended to be less judgmen-tal and less inhibited, and more talkative; men showed a bit more self-confidence, and women tended to lose interest in participating in anything that required effort.[97]

The drug hysteria enabled Anslinger to carry out a campaign of terror on those who used or distributed substances categorized as illegal drugs. Anslinger ran the Federal Bureau of Narcotics the way J. Edgar Hoover ran the FBI. In fact, the reputation of the FBN had gotten so bad that Hoover would not let his FBI agents get involved in drug-related matters. Anslinger was also very busy legislatively. It served his interests to suggest that it was a communist plot to addict America's young people to drugs. That notion, combined with his lobbying skills, enabled him to get two bills introduced in the House in the 1940s, one calling for the death penalty and the other calling for a 100-year prison sentence for "dope peddlers." At least, these excessive penalties were rejected by the liberals who were in control of the House at the time.

Then Anslinger convinced Congressman Hale Boggs to introduce a bill (probably written by Anslinger) that, for the first time, identified marijuana as a narcotic and substantially increased the penalties for narcotics trafficking, mandating a minimum two-year prison sentence.

Because marijuana was now listed as a narcotic, anyone deemed to be addicted to marijuana immediately became eligible for already existing government-sponsored narcotics treatment programs in Lexington, Kentucky. The Lexington hospital facility, at least when it came to its "drug rehabilitation programs," was little more than outright taxpayer fraud. There was no meaningful program in place, but the "patients" sure were kept off the streets.

With the Boggs Act passed by Congress in November 1951, Anslinger had the stringent law he needed to persecute drug users as well as dealers. He immediately embarked on a state-by-state campaign to pressure local legislatures to act "as responsibly as the federal government" — at that time, "state's rights" apparently were more respected than they are today. He urged enactment of similar legislation known as "little Boggs Acts" which would also identify marijuana as a narcotic and stiffened the penalties for narcotics distribution. Anslinger then went after the individual users. He intentionally went after people in the entertainment industry — celebrities like Billie Holiday, Lenny Bruce, Louis Armstrong, and Gene Krupa, and William Holden. Arresting celebrities made front-page news, and Anslinger was giving notice that "drug use" would not be tolerated. In 1956, Anslinger was instrumental in pushing the Narcotics Control Act through Congress, which increased the criminal penalties for possession of

---

97. Full text of The La Guardia Committee Report is available online at the Schaffer Library of Drug Policy, http://www.druglibrary.org/schaffer/Library/studies/lag/lagmenu.htm

narcotics to five years. Until this point, sentencing was at the discretion of the judge and jury.

What puzzles many people is why the penalties should be so stiff for a victimless crime. After all, in many people's view, smoking marijuana hurts no one else: like sleeping late, it is a choice to be made by the individual.

THE BEATNIK GENERATION

The Bohemian culture known as the "Beatnik" generation developed in the late 1940s and early 50s, attracting a wide range of people, mostly artist, writers, musician and scholars. These people did not fit the mold — they lived in a world of cultural innovation. They challenged white America's stuffy moral values. The "Establishment" felt threatened by the Beatnik's unconventional ideals, appearance, and particularly by their conspicuous use of marijuana. It was the first time the white middle class was openly using marijuana and, because of the lingering hysteria, mainstream men and women were afraid it would contaminate their children. Congress reacted in 1951 by passing the Boggs Act.

Progressive change is not easy to accomplish. Since those in a comfortable position have no incentive to change the status quo, such change is often driven by people outside the mainstream. Lack of change means stagnation. The Beatniks were stretching the envelope of acceptability with their advocacy of new music, abstract art, unconventional poetry, and broadminded intellectual ideas. Undoubtedly, in their acceptance of minority cultures, especially blacks, they were far ahead of the suburbs. As the tidy domesticity of the postwar Fifties gave way to the rebellious and nonconformist trends of the Sixties, racism, sexism, and other attitudes that were adopted without consideration began to be questioned and rejected. Martin Luther King, Jr. began articulating his dream of a free and racially equal America, and many other social changes were in the offing.

THE EISENHOWER-KENNEDY ERA

This was a period of social revolution, and better race relations topped the list of demands. The US (like Europe and, for that matter, Russia) was in the mood for change. The "liberal" Democrats gained an even larger majority in the Congressional elections of 1958, 1960, and 1962. John F. Kennedy, America's first

Roman Catholic president, won the presidency by just 0.2% of the popular vote (some 118,000 votes) but won a resounding victory in the electoral college (303 votes vs. 219 for Richard Nixon).

Disillusioned by the Vietnam War and the drug war that set authorities to hunting down individuals who appeared to be doing no harm to anyone but themselves (if that), a generation of hippies grew out of the contradictions of the times. Some of them were politically astute and militant; they were willing to demonstrate to challenge racist bigotry, the war, and other national policy issues. The injustices of segregation inspired many young whites as well as blacks to take to the streets in protest. As educated, middle-class whites they were better able to stand up to the "Establishment."

The hippie generation, born in the 1940s, was the best-educated generation America ever experienced (and it was the last generation of Americans to receive a better education, generally, than their parents did). They found the society to be too straight-laced, artificial, bigoted, and war-mongering. This was a society, after 1964, that demanded their young men go to fight for freedom and democracy by slaughtering villagers in the jungles of Vietnam. Not surprisingly, the hippies adopted Timothy Leary's "turn on, drop out" philosophy and boldly flaunted their use of illegal intoxicants, particularly marijuana.

Middle-class parents did not like having their children use marijuana; but they did not want them to go to jail for it, either. With Kennedy in the White House and the more liberal Democrats in control of Congress, there was not much threat of that. Kennedy allegedly smoked marijuana in the Oval Office (never mind more serious things), and must have had reservations about the anti-drug laws, especially those directed against marijuana — especially considering that Anslinger and the FBN were under scrutiny for misconduct.

The Federal Bureau of Narcotics had developed a reputation as a rogue agency of corrupt agents and inappropriate policies and practices, such as paying informants with illegal drugs. Not wanting to be tainted by association, the FBI and CIA kept their agents away from the drug arena and the FBN, other than providing information. Anslinger's heavy-handed approach was no longer appreciated and by 1962, President Kennedy essentially forced him into retirement. Soon afterward, the FBN was scrapped altogether. The Bureau of Narcotics and Dangerous Drugs (BNDD) was created to take its place, with a new director, a much-reduced budget, and orders to go slow.

But before that, under the prodding of Anslinger, the United Nations outlawed marijuana in 1961. Anslinger had had eight years under the Eisenhower

(Republican) administration to institutionalize the drug war within the US Department of State, which initiated and spearheaded the UN's adoption of the Single Convention on Narcotic Drugs. Anslinger managed to drag the rest of the world into America's drug war. It took time: the United Nations adopted the treaty on March 25, 1961, but it still had to be agreed upon by the UN member nations. The United States, for example, did not become a signatory until late 1968.

The fact that Congress did not immediately sign onto the 1961 UN Single Convention treaty suggests that, at least in 1961, more rational heads prevailed. The Democrats were not interested in Anslinger's drug war. The country had plenty of serious things to worry about. The Cold War was heating up, culminating in the Cuban Missile Crisis. Then, of course, the assassination of John F. Kennedy shocked and devastated the nation; that was followed by an escalation of the Vietnam War.

Although long retired, on April 27, 1967 Anslinger testified before the Senate Foreign Relations Committee pleading for the United States to comply with the United Nations Single Convention of 1961. Anslinger argued that signing onto the Single Convention treaty would enable the US "to use our treaty obligations to resist legalized use of marijuana." Anslinger, a deputy assistant Secretary of State and a special assistant to the Secretary of Treasury were the only witnesses before the Committee. No witnesses testified in opposition to the treaty.[98]

Anslinger's testimony could not have been better timed. The Johnson Administration was busy defending its Vietnam policy, the presidential primary elections were in full swing, and the newspapers and TV news were busy covering both. Neither Anslinger's testimony nor the United States signing the UN Single Convention got much media coverage — Anslinger snuck it in.

ANSLINGER'S CAREER

Harry Anslinger did a lot of harm in his bureaucratic career, but apparently could not keep his own facts straight. Testifying at a 1937 Congressional hearing, he was specifically asked if marijuana addicts graduated into heroin, opium or cocaine users. His reply:

---

98. Sloman, Larry. *Reefer Madness, Marijuana in America.* Grove Press, New York: 1979, p. 226 & 227.

"No sir; I have not heard of a case of that kind. The marijuana addict does not go in that direction."

That position has been upheld by every scientific study, including the LaGuardia Committee Report of 1944, which spoke directly to this question. Eighteen years later, with no new medical or investigative research supporting his conclusions, Anslinger testified before a senate committee that,

"Eventually, if used over a long period, marijuana does lead to heroin addiction."

This statement was unfounded and remains unsubstantiated, but it succeeded in getting marijuana labeled as a "gateway drug." That lie has been perpetuated by those with a financial interest in keeping marijuana illegal.

Those who end up as heroin and cocaine addicts usually do start down the road to addiction using something milder. They usually start with legal drugs, like alcohol, tobacco, caffeine and even prescription medications. But not everyone who takes up smoking or drinking heads toward hard drugs.

Commenting on Anslinger's career in testimony before a Senate sub-committee in July 29, 1975, John E. Ingersoll, Director of the Bureau of Narcotics and Dangerous Drugs (1968-73) noted that under Anslinger's commissionership of the Bureau of Narcotics, "corruption reached high levels, especially in the New York office. . . . Key Informants were killed. Other law enforcement organizations did not trust the FBN. Someone was selling out. . . . Because of arrest quotas and poor controls over the use of informants, informants had to much freedom and too much influence in determining who would be arrested . . .there was no particular security over the files that revealed the identities of informants . . . some [agents] resorted to bartering narcotics for information."[99] Goldman goes on to say, "Anslinger is said to have known nothing of this dirty work. Hoover knew it all."

In their unreasonable campaign against recreational drug users, Anslinger and Elizabeth Washburn Wright misrepresented the truth and created laws that undermined the US Constitution and the American economy, corrupted the society, created international strife and, in the process, caused millions of people

---

99. Goldman, p.127.

to needlessly suffer. Perhaps even Anslinger finally realized that his approach was wrong. He closed his book *The Protectors* by saying,

> Prohibition, conceived as a moral attempt to improve the American way of life, would ultimately cast the nation into a turmoil. One cannot help but think in retrospect that prohibition, by depriving Americans of their "vices," only created the avenues through which organized crime gained its firm foothold.

Anslinger was talking about Alcohol Prohibition, but what he said is true of today's "war on drugs" or any other moralistically unrealistic prohibition.

Vanguard of Social Change

The Beatniks and Hippies of the 1950s and 1960s were not a lost generation; they played a leading roll in the developing social consciousness. Because they were less prejudiced and more open to people of different races, different religious beliefs and different cultural backgrounds, they were able to learn for each other; one of the things they learned about was marijuana. They were not ignorant of the dangers; but they discovered that marijuana was not the social treat the government said it was. Neither is there any evidence of a communist-inspired plot to get the youth of America addicted to drugs.

Meanwhile, the hippies enjoyed stepping on toes and poking the staid, conformist generation in the ribs by wearing their hair "too long," their jeans too scruffy, and their shorts and skirts too short. By sharing some of the risqué behaviors of the underclass, they also went some distance in taking race out of the equation when it came to certain laws the establishment had traditionally used to keep down the minorities. They forced a confrontation and set the stage for social change.

The "establishment" was ideologically opposed to everything the hippies were known for — unkempt appearance, loud music, free-spirited lifestyles, the use of illegal recreational intoxicants (particularly marijuana), and especially their anti-Vietnam War stance which was viewed as unpatriotic and pro-Communist. Anti-war demonstrations at the 1968 Democratic Convention in Chicago and in the Century City in Los Angeles in the early 1970s were met by heavily armed police and soldiers from the National Guard with billy-clubs and tear gas. Then four students were shot and killed during a protest at Kent State University. That effectively put a stop to anti-war demonstrations all across the

United States, but it did nothing to warm relations between the government and the young protesters and those adults who agreed with them. Alarmed at the degree of rebellion, the authorities stepped up the drug war.

The "drug war" is, if anything, a civil war pitting the US government with all its resources against its own people. It is the religious conservative right waging an ideological war against the more moderate elements of society, and vindictively using the law (victimless crime laws) to persecute, punish and destroy the people they perceive as their enemies; people who do not agree and would not conform to their convoluted perception of reality and morality. This policy is in stark contradiction to America's much-proclaimed tradition of liberty and individualism, tolerance, and a live-and-let-live attitude. It is those attitudes that made America a safe harbor for the oppressed people of the world, including the religious cults of the colonial era.

In a free society, the claim of moral propriety does not justify imposing laws on all groups to make them adhere to one group's moral standards. Historically, the most despicable despots and dictators have used the law to oppress their fellow man and justify committing horrendous atrocities against him. If we obeyed laws just because they are laws we would be living in a dictatorship, not a democracy; we'd be little more than sheep. (And if we had obeyed the laws the British imposed on colonial America, we'd be British sheep.) Lawmakers are not infallible. Attitudes change (often, much faster than the laws do). And laws are not always rational, just, or even practical.

History shows that the quality of laws affects the ability of the society to succeed and progress; when the laws are too oppressive or restrictive the society declines economically because the people with skills, knowledge, and financial resources hold back or simply leave. In fact, we have an obligation to ourselves, our loved ones, our friends and neighbors, and our fellow citizens to fight the injustice of oppressive and unreasonable laws, and force the government to act rationally and responsibly.

Three hundred years ago, anyone who did not like the society he found himself in could, theoretically, head for virgin territory and start over. Now, it is hard to find a frontier with free land for the taking, and there is not an inch of earth that is not under the mandate of one government or another. Now, we have no choice but to focus on improving government policy instead of dreaming of making a fresh start. Although it is not officially acknowledged, Americans are telling their government — at the ballot box, on the Internet, and in print — that they want an end to the war on drugs.

RIOT AT CHICAGO'S 1968 DEMOCRATIC CONVENTION

By late 1967, anti-Vietnam War sentiment had escalated dramatically. Even Democrat loyalists were unhappy with Johnson's handling of the war effort. After almost being defeated in the New Hampshire primary election by fellow Democrat Senator Eugene McCarthy, an early opponent of the Vietnam War, Johnson decided not to run for reelection. Hubert Humphrey, Johnson's vice president and a long-time Democratic senator from Minnesota, quickly became the leading contender for the Democrats.

On the campaign trail Humphrey espoused a continuation of Johnson's Vietnam War policies, which did not sit well with the young men and women demonstrating their objection to the war in the city streets and on college campuses. After the Tet Offensive in January 1968, in which General Vo Nguyen Giap of North Vietnam won a major psychological and media victory by simultaneously capturing several important cities and attacking garrisons and, most stunningly, the U.S. Embassy in Saigon, public opinion substantially shifted against the war. The ideological clash came at the 1968 Democratic National Convention in Chicago. Outside the convention hall an estimated 10,000 people were marching in opposition to the war. The tragic assassinations of Martin Luther King, Jr. and Bobby Kennedy earlier that year, combined with the Republican Party's nomination of Richard Nixon, three weeks earlier, heightened tensions considerably. For most of the demonstrators, the Democratic Party's convention represented the last chance to turn the nation away from war.

Earlier that year, dozens of cities had experienced large anti-war and civil rights demonstrations, and even riots that left many neighborhoods in flames. The establishment Democrats, particularly Chicago Mayor Richard Daley (the first), a well-established political boss, were determined to not permit the "peaceniks" and their revolutionary "Yippie" pals to disrupt a convention. But they underestimated the determination of the demonstrators, who refused police orders to disperse. The situation devolved into a full-scale riot after police brutally attacked the crowd. The demonstration at the 1968 Democratic National Convention was more than just one in a series of antiwar protests, and it was more than the Vietnam War that people were demonstrating against. The Chicago Seven, consisting of Abbie Hoffman, Jerry Rubin, David Dellinger, Rennie Davis, Tom Hayden, John Froines, Lee Weiner, and Bobby Seale, were arrested and prosecuted for instigating a riot. However, they were found not guilty when it was revealed that the police, not the demonstrators, had initiated the conflict.

(The Seven were also all "hippie types," many of who were known marijuana users, even advocates.)

In fact, the Democratic National Convention became a focal point of the decade because it represented a culmination of the social conflicts of the Sixties. It represented a time when more and more people began to disagree with the official direction, and in the end the dissent did accomplish its objective. Yes, Hubert Humphrey went on to win the nomination but he changed his position on the war dramatically — which enabled him, despite being the underdog, to secure the support he needed to become a serious contender in the November election. Nixon's lead vanished, and he won by a slim half million popular votes and by 290 to 203 votes in the Electoral College.

Although very much apart of the anti-war protests, the issue of legalizing marijuana took somewhat of a backseat to the question of ending the Vietnam War. Parents were far more concerned about the weekly body counts announced by the Defense Department than they were about their almost-adult children smoking marijuana. In fact, most participants had a strong and urgent incentive to keep the focus of the demonstrations and the public discourse on ending the Vietnam War. Legalizing marijuana would have to wait until that life and death problem had been resolved. Many people decided they would have to bide their time and work within the system to change the law. It was safe, but not necessarily effective.

THE CATASTROPHIC NIXON YEARS

By the middle to late 1960s marijuana, the mildest intoxicant, legal or illegal, had firmly established itself as the intoxicant of choice. Of course, the drug subculture experimented with LSD, cocaine and many other drugs, but most people were not interested in trying anything like that. The demographics of those who used illegal intoxicants now included American's white middle-class youth, and the drug war began to affect a much broader segment of the population. Now white America was beginning to experience the economic oppression and devastation they had been inflicting on the minorities. Once middle class kids started getting "busted" for using marijuana, the anti-drug laws began to be reconsidered. When only a small number of people used banned intoxicants, the negative effects were minimal; but not even parents and local police, in many cases, felt that it was appropriate to impose such penalties for marijuana. On their own kids.

The pervasive use of illegal intoxicants during the Sixties dramatically redirected the flow of money, as during Alcohol Prohibition, out of the legal economy and into an underground economy. This helped cause a recession that forced Nixon to impose wage and price controls in August 1971.

Fortunately Nixon (who barely beat Humphrey — a New Deal liberal Democrat) was too busy escalating the Vietnam War and dealing with a faltering economy to spend much time on the drug issue. Nixon also knew he was not very popular (he lost to Kennedy in 1960 and even lost in his attempt to become Governor of California), and like all newly-elected presidents he wanted to show himself as representing the people and uniting them behind his policies.

MARIJUANA TAX ACT RULED UNCONSTITUTIONAL

The US Supreme Court brought some sanity to the situation in Leary vs. US, May 1969, by declaring the Marijuana Tax Act unconstitutional. That nullified the Boggs Act.

The Supreme Court's ruling added credibility to what the "pre- and baby boomers" were telling their parents about marijuana, and at least temporarily marijuana was legal on a federal level. The Nixon Administration was not about to leave it that way, though.

Having the US Supreme Court find a law unconstitutional after thirty years is encouraging, in a sense, but it certainly raises questions about how the Congressional or judicial branches of government are meeting their responsibilities to the people. It is perhaps even more disheartening to find that the government failed to address the constitutionality of the law until forced to do so by Timothy Leary. Dr. Leary was only one of the millions (yes, millions!) of people who suffered needless legal persecution for ignoring this inappropriate law.

WOODSTOCK AND OPERATION INTERCEPT

While the Kennedy and Johnson administrations concentrated on the war in Vietnam rather than putting young adults in jail for smoking marijuana, Nixon saw the situation quite differently. He most particularly did not like seeing "marijuana-smoking hippies" marching in the streets to protest his approach to the Vietnam War. Nixon's stated position was to "end the war with honor," by which he meant no retreat and no admission of, or appearance of, losing. In other words, in Nixon's mind, it meant continuing the war until the North Vietnamese submitted to his terms. President Nixon vigorously stepped up the war effort and expanded the hostilities into Cambodia and Laos, which led to stepped-up and expanded anti-war demonstrations.

One of the watershed cultural events of the decade was the three-day-long Woodstock Music Festival held in upstate New York in August of 1969. It was a combination of a celebration of the demise of the Marijuana Tax Act three months earlier and an enormous peace rally. Woodstock was unique for a number of reasons. It was the first super concert featuring dozens of Rock & Roll's most popular bands; half-a-million people attended, creating a thirty-mile long traffic jam getting there. Despite all the people and all the "loose" behavior, including drugs both legal and illegal, there were no riots or fights, and nobody was seriously injured. At Woodstock, apparently one person died, non-violently, and a baby was born. Even the police considered the crowd well behaved. Actually, those three days of "debauchery" revealed America's worst fears about drugs and sexual freedom to be a lie. The young people attending the festival were espousing peace and love instead of violence and oppression. Woodstock was more than just a party; it was a political statement that included an almost constant stream of anti-war, anti-establishment and anti-Nixon speeches and songs. Woodstock established the anti-war "pot"-smoking hippie subculture as the most visible and vocal opposition to Nixon and the Vietnam War.

The Woodstock experience is still a fond memory for members of the baby boom generation (whether they attended or not), but it horrified the "establishment" — especially the finale, featuring Jimmy Hendrix's stylized electric guitar rendition of the Star Spangled Banner. That must have offended conservative sensitivities — especially Nixon's. Actually, everything about the Woodstock Music Festival: the anti-war sentiment, the blatant use of illegal drugs, the nudity and sex — infuriated Nixon. Hendrix was simply the last straw. There wasn't much he could do to stop it, though — sending in the National Guard would have caused a riot and outraged the public.

However, Nixon's disdain hardened and he saw the hippie drug subculture as his political enemy. He retaliated a month later, in September, by initiating Operation Intercept along the Mexican/US border, with the stated intent of stopping the flow of drugs by physically searching every car, truck, plane, and boat entering the United States. It was the largest operation of its kind, covering the entire 2,500-mile border and involving the military, Customs, border patrol and local police. Operation Intercept was planned by Gordon Liddy, of Watergate fame.

In fact, Operation Intercept was specifically intended to severely reduce the availability of marijuana on the street and it was timed to intercept the Mexican marijuana crop that is usually harvested in late September and early October. Even the drug-sniffing dogs the government had just started using were only trained to sniff out marijuana. Marijuana was unquestionably the most popular "recreational drug" and government agents were hoping to intercept bulk shipments, which carry an unmistakable odor and are easily detected, coming from Mexico, Colombia; they were also on the lookout for imports from South East Asia. Marijuana was commonly shipped in bulk because of the huge demand and marginal profits, kept low because of the competition of illegal domestic cultivation. Besides, most of the small-time marijuana smugglers, mostly hippies, were not doing it primarily for the money; they were providing marijuana for themselves and their friends.

Quite the opposite was true of the more dangerous illegal drugs being smuggled into the US — odorless powder drugs like cocaine and heroin could be packaged in much smaller containers and more easily concealed. There was no domestic competition for those products, which meant they were highly profitable — encouraging even more importation. The inability of the government to stop the importation of these more dangerous drugs was noted in a 1994 *Rolling Stone* article,[100] which stated that, "Law enforcement authorities readily admit that cocaine imports appear to be as high as ever. Heroin exports to the United States, meanwhile, are rising to unprecedented levels." It would have taken much more time to search every vehicle for cocaine or heroin, and there were already three- to five-hour delays in crossing the border, which was reported on every radio and TV newscast. Although they did catch a few hippies trying to smuggle in a couple of kilograms of marijuana, the big-time smugglers stayed away. They knew about Operation Intercept well in advance, because corrupt local officials on both sides of the border were themselves involved in and profiting from the drug traffic.

---

100. Nadelmann, Ethan & Wenner, Jann S.. "Toward a Sane National Drug Policy," *Rolling Stone*, Issue #681 May 5, 1994.

Once the news about Operation Intercept got out there was less traffic at the border, causing local merchants to lose sales; that drew criticism and complaints from newspapers and politicians on both sides of the border.

Operation Intercept lasted only twenty days and was considered a catastrophic failure, even by government standards; however, the long-term effects were profound, permanent and devastating. Operation Intercept did not stop the flow of illegal drugs but it did raise the level of risk and the costs associated with smuggling illegal drugs. That forced smugglers to become more sophisticated. This was no longer a job for amateurs. In the months and years that followed, America experienced a tremendous increase in the theft of private boats and planes. Few of these vehicles were ever recovered; many, overloaded, sank or crashed attempting to cross the border and many more were confiscated by the Mexican government. According to the US government's own estimates, small planes laden with marijuana were crossing the border from Mexico at the rate of 13 per hour and between 1975 and 1977, 165 planes crashed, killing at least 31. With all of those planes and boats being stolen, insurance rates went up; and that contributed to pushing up the already soaring inflation rate. Operation Intercept drove the hippies out of the drug smuggling business: Stealing boats and planes or getting into a shoot out with the police was not for them. That left the market to the hard-core, primarily Central American, heroin and cocaine dealers; and because marijuana was scarce their business was booming. Because of the huge profits associated with smuggling heroin and cocaine and "professional" quantities of marijuana, the drug kingpins ruthlessly protected their investments and territories. Many people, including police officers, ended up dead. Here again, it was the "war on drugs" and the huge profits associated with intoxicants that were made illegal (not the drugs, themselves) that caused the problem.

WAR IS HELL AND PEOPLE DIE

The goal of war is to force the enemy, by whatever means necessary, to surrender. The "drug war" has been one of the longest, deadliest and most destructive wars in history. Operation Intercept substantially reduced the availability and increased the price of marijuana. Since it was hard to get, expensive, and more convincingly branded as "criminal," people started to think it would make little difference if they moved up to more dangerous drugs — whatever was available, legal or illegal. During Alcohol Prohibition, when beer and wine disappeared people shifted to hard liquor. The same thing happened in "drugs." Operation Intercept ignited a drastic increase in the use of far more dangerous substances — particularly alcohol, but also cocaine, heroin, LSD, PCP, tranquilizers, barbiturates, and amphetamines (speed).

This acceleration of drug usage showed up in a rash of alcohol-related traffic deaths and a vast increase in the number of drug overdoses and deaths. During that period, 50% of all traffic related fatalities nationwide involved alcohol. Many of the victims were poisoned by unknown substances that unscrupulous street dealers added to increase their profits. The wave of drug-related deaths started in October 1969 (almost immediately after Operation Intercept went into effect) with the highly publicized death of Diane Linkletter, the daughter of TV personality Art Linkletter. Diane reportedly walked out of a high rise building window while under the influence of LSD. Angry at her needless death, Linkletter quickly became the leading proponent for stronger anti-drug laws; but a few years later he realized that anti-drug laws were not the answer. Operation Intercept also started the country off on an almost two-decade-long cocaine and crack epidemic.

Canadians suffered similar tragedies. Canada's LeDain Commission commented in 1970:

> We have been told repeatedly that LSD use increased rapidly during periods when cannabis [marijuana] was in short supply. Drug users and non-users alike have suggested that the effectiveness of Operation Intercept in the United States in reducing the supply of marijuana available in Canada was a major cause of the increase in the demand for acid."[101]

Unfortunately, the causal connection between Operation Intercept and the carnage was never acknowledged, in part because of all the other atrocities in the news — the Vietnam War, the killing of four student protesters at Kent State University on May 4, 1970, and a myriad of stories about the evils of narcotics trafficking — depicted as "narco-terrorism." In addition, the economy was faltering and people were worried. In the early 1970s, the stock market fell dramatically; that was followed by massive unemployment and rising inflation rates.

The carnage on the nation's highways continued and the federal government (Nixon) imposed a 55-mph speed limit in March, 1974. The Organization

---

101. Le Dain Commission Interim Report, p. 139

of Petroleum Exporting Countries (OPEC) voted in October 1973 to cut exports to the US and its European allies and to sharply raise prices, in response to President Nixon's shipment of arms to help Israel in its Yom Kippur War against Egypt and Syria. This handily allowed the focus to be quickly shifted from alcohol-related traffic deaths to the cost of gasoline. The administration claimed that the reduced speed limit was made necessary because of the OPEC oil embargo and was meant to conserve gasoline; but the need for the 55-mph speed limit was also rationalized by the extraordinary increase in alcohol-related traffic deaths. The real problem there was not excessive driving speed; it was the inappropriate drinking habits of young adults. A more rational assessment of the situation indicates that the use of alcohol dramatically increased because Operation Intercept created a marijuana shortage; and because 18-year-olds could drink legally in some states and not others, they would travel out of state, drink, and then drive home. The reduced speed limit did not bring down the number of alcohol-related traffic deaths. That number went down only when states began raising their legal drinking age to 21, across the board, so that "road trips" were no longer an option for young adults looking for a buzz.

Before Nixon escalated enforcement of the drug laws, marijuana was by far the most widely-used illegal recreational intoxicant among college-aged kids — and it was the least dangerous recreational intoxicant, legal or illegal. After Operation Intercept, marijuana was always scarce. People started regularly using much harsher and more dangerous drugs. The liquor and pharmaceutical companies enjoyed huge sales. They were allowed to laugh all the way to the bank, and no one held them to account for the deaths and destruction their products were causing. The use of heroin and especially cocaine also dramatically increased. With the supply of cocaine and heroin growing, the price dropped substantially — so more people got enmeshed. The fact that the price of marijuana skyrocketed while the street price of cocaine dropped is a reflection of supply and demand, and it shows that people prefer the softer "drug," marijuana.

CHAPTER 6

THE LAW PREVENTS KNOWLEDGEABLE USE

Many substances, drugs included, can be dangerous when misused but are not inherently dangerous in themselves. Driving a car, using various chemicals and pesticides, working with fire or guns, can be dangerous. The key to taking any drug is knowledgeable use. None of the illegal recreational intoxicants is inherently poisonous; they are only *potentially* dangerous, and of course, the more ignorant we are, the more dangerous they are.

Outlawing intoxicants does not prevent people from using them; it only prevents people from being well informed about what they are using. By proliferating the myth that illegal recreational intoxicants are dangerous, even deadly, and by preventing people from getting straight information about them, government helps create the dangerous situation.

There are some 8,000 deaths annually associated with the use of illegal drugs. Because they are illegal, it is a totally unregulated industry with no quality control standards. At least, when doctors prescribe a legal FDA- approved prescription or over-the-counter medication, or when they give a patient an injection, they are reasonably sure the drugs were manufactured in a clean, germ-free facility. They are assured of the quality and quantity of the drug they are using and they know that the hypodermic syringes they use are sterile. None of that is true of street drugs — only because they are illegal.

Many "drug-induced deaths" may be the result of impurities or add-ins that the victim never knew were there. Autopsies usually end when preliminary tests show indicate that illegal drugs are in the bloodstream.

THE 1972 PRESIDENTIAL COMMISSION ON MARIJUANA

The 1970s began with the knowledge and widespread use of marijuana as an intoxicant. It was a time of social turmoil, and the two major points of contention were the Vietnam War and Nixon's drug war — primarily focused on marijuana. Nixon's unyielding pursuit of victory on both fronts caused a great deal of dissension. After the slaughter at Kent State, the US Congress voted to start a dramatic reduction in funding for the war; that forced Nixon to end hostilities and begin negotiating peace with the Vietnamese.

To replace the defunct Marijuana Tax Act, the Nixon administration proposed in 1970 and Congress passed the Federal Controlled Substances Act, again criminalizing marijuana at the federal level. The Controlled Substances Act reduced simple possession from a felony to a misdemeanor and set a maximum prison sentence of one year. The individual states followed suit, starting with Oregon in 1973.

Actually, the Controlled Substances Act is no more constitutionally correct than the Marijuana Tax Act. The Controlled Substances Act also labeled marijuana a "Schedule I" substance — meaning an illegal drug with no approved medical purposes. This was supposedly a temporary classification, as the Congress was aware that they did not know enough about marijuana to make a permanent judgment.

Over the fervent objections of the Nixon administration, Congress also enacted the Marijuana and Health Reporting Act of 1970, which directed the Department of Health, Education and Welfare (HEW) to study the marijuana issue and produce an annual fact-finding report. The Act also established and funded a two-year-long nationwide bipartisan commission, known as the Presidential Commission on Marijuana and Drug Abuse (a.k.a. the Shafer Commission or the National Commission on Marihuana and Drug Abuse) to investigate and make recommendations to the president for a long-term strategy. The commission was loaded with staunch anti-drug conservative Republicans, and former prosecutor and former Pennsylvania Governor Raymond Shafer was appointed Chairman. Nixon's commission appointments were widely criticized as extremely biased against the idea of legalizing marijuana. Still, the commission went about its task and the nation patiently awaited its report, which even today is considered the most comprehensive review of marijuana ever conducted by the federal government.

Pro-marijuana activists were not waiting idly by. They were organizing to defeat Nixon in the 1972 election and to give the people a chance to legalize marijuana at the ballot box. Petition drives were run in a number of states to qualify marijuana legalization or decriminalization measures for the November 1972 elections. Groups were springing up all over, like Amorphia, launched in California by Blair Newman, which included James White, Ed Sanders, John Sinclair, Allen Ginsberg and Mike Aldrich, and other members of earlier pro-marijuana groups. Amorphia financed their pro-marijuana activities by manufacturing and marketing Acapulco Gold rolling paper. The "Yippies," a post-hippie group, was founded by Abbie Hoffman and Jerry Rubin and later directed by Tom Forcade (who went on to create *High Times* magazine). CMI, the California Marijuana Initiative, was led by Robert Ashford. Of course, pre-eminent among those groups was NORML (The National Organization to Reform Marijuana Laws), founded in 1970 by Keith Stroup, a young lawyer from Washington, DC

The news media focused on NORML, primarily because it was a nationwide organization but also because it was initially funded by the Playboy Foundation. Stroup spoke eloquently and compassionately to the inhumane persecution of marijuana users, who could be subjected to 20+ years in prison in some states for possession of even a small amount of marijuana. Unfortunately, the Nixon administration was not listening.

LEGALIZATION VS DECRIMINALIZATION

Considering the political climate, Stroup concluded that marijuana legalization was not an attainable goal at that time; he decided instead to push for marijuana "decriminalization" — by which he essentially meant reducing the "crime" of marijuana possession from a felony to a misdemeanor and eliminating the harshest penalties. Stroup believed it was important to avoid a loss at the polls, which would be interpreted as "the people having spoken." That would effectively take the pressure off legislators to change the law.

He promoted "decriminalization" as the legislative approach, believing that numerous state legislators would embrace it as more politically palatable. Many

of the groups working to legalize marijuana rejected decriminalization as settling for too little; they were not about to give an inch to the Nixon Administration. The Yippies organized Fourth of July "Smoke-ins" all across the country,
particularly in front of the White House. They also organized conferences; and
when they did not like what the opposition said, a pie or two would materialize
on the face of the offending speaker. These people were not interested in trying
to appease the establishment, which they saw as the enemy; and they were not
asking for the government's permission to smoke something that was arguably
not more harmful than tobacco. They were demanding their rights and utilizing
the initiative process to change the law. They wanted people to vote, insisting
that, "if you do not vote, you do not count." They opposed decriminalization,
declaring they would not support any initiative that did not permit personal cultivation — free backyard "grass."

All the state initiatives attempting to qualify for the 1972 ballot called for
full legalization, and although those campaigns were all under-funded and
under-manned, the people involved were very dedicated. Many put their own
lives on hold and went out every day collecting signatures. Several of the initiative efforts — California (where the initiative was identified as Proposition 9),
Colorado, and Oregon, did successfully qualify for the ballot. Many of the people
involved in these pro-marijuana initiative efforts went on to become very active
in the presidential campaign of George McGovern, who advocated during the
primary campaign both an immediate end to the Vietnam War and the legalization of marijuana.

However, the marijuana legalization initiatives were unanimously defeated
and Nixon was reelected. Most of the young activists considered it a temporary
set back; they went on with their lives, while continuing to use marijuana illegally. Keith Stroup became the leading marijuana activist and NORML remained
as the movement's largest organization almost by default; everyone else needed
to get back to work or to school.

THE PRESIDENT'S COMMISSION ON MARIJUANA REPORT

Long before either the Department of Health, Education and Welfare
(HEW) or the Commission could conduct their investigations and issue their
reports, President Nixon made his opinion known. In a televised news confer-

ence on May 1, 1971, responding to a question about the White House Conference on Youth, which had voted to legalize marijuana, Nixon said,

> As you know, there is a Commission that is supposed to make recommen-
> dations to me about this subject; in this instance, however, I have such strong
> views that I will express them. I am against legalizing marijuana. Even if the
> Commission does recommend that it be legalized, I will not follow that
> recommendation. [Several weeks later he also said] I can see no social or moral
> justification whatever for legalizing marijuana. I think it would be exactly the
> wrong step. It would simply encourage more and more of our young people to
> start down the long, dismal road that leads to hard drugs and eventually
> self-destruction.[102]

Whatever Nixon's expressed "strong views," the office of President of the
United States does not convey dictatorial powers. The United States Government is supposed to represent the will of the people, not special interest groups
or individual opinion — even the president's. Mr. Nixon was the product of a
very conservative Quaker background and was nominated by the Republican
Party. Nixon's position clearly did not represent the will of the average people. It
represented the will of corporate America, the oil, petrochemical, liquor,
tobacco, pharmaceutical companies and large defense contractors, all of whom
had a financial interest in either continuing the Vietnam War or escalating the
drug war (or both), and all of whom contributed substantially to Nixon's reelection campaign.

In early 1972, HEW issued its second annual report, quickly followed by
the report from the President's Commission on Marijuana and Drug Abuse, entitled "Marijuana: A Signal of Misunderstanding." The findings of both these
reports were essentially the same and can be summed up in the Commission's
own words:

> With regard to the law, the commission urges that the criminal sanction be
> withdrawn from all private consumption related activity, including possession
> for personal use and casual nonprofit distribution.

This has essentially been the basic conclusion of every major study on marijuana — including the 1894 Indian Hemp Drug Commission Study, the 1925

---

102. *New York Times*, May 2, 1971, p. 14.

Canal Zone Study, the 1944 LaGuardia Commission Report, and the 1975 Jamaican Study of Ganja (marijuana).[103]

Brecher *(Licit and Illicit Drugs,* a comprehensive study of recreational drugs), fell short of declaring marijuana harmless, saying "no drug is safe or harmless to all people at all dosage levels or under all conditions of use," but, unquestionably, they did not support the use of criminal sanctions.[104] In fact, the editors noted that: "1) the Consumers Union recommends the immediate repeal of all federal laws governing the growing, processing, transportation, sale, possession, and use of marijuana, and 2) the Consumers Union recommends that each of the fifty states similarly repeal its existing marijuana laws and pass new laws legalizing the cultivation, processing, and orderly marketing of marijuana – subject to appropriate regulations."[105] The editors went on to say, "Our recommendations arises out of the conviction that an orderly system of legal distribution and licit use will have notable advantages for both users and nonusers over the present marijuana black market. In particular it will separate the channels of marijuana distribution from heroin channels and from the channels of distribution of other illicit drugs – and will thereby limit the exposure of marijuana smokers to other illicit drugs. Even more important it will end the criminalization and alienation of young people and the damage done to them by arrest, conviction, and imprison."[106]

Three years later, in March 1975, after reviewing the scientific research since the publication of *Licit and Illicit Drugs,* Consumers Union issued a follow-up report, stating that, "We see no need to withdraw or modify that conclusion."

The 1980 Drug Abuse Council's Report found no basis for concern over the recreational use of marijuana, and a 1982 report by the National Academy of Sciences raised doubts over marijuana's potential danger. Nixon ignored the recommendations. Thirty years after the fact, declassified tapes from the Nixon Oval Office showed the President knew well in advance that the commission was about to recommend legalizing marijuana. Months before the report was issued, he publicly denounced the commission. Nixon even met with Raymond Shafer, warning him to get control of his commission and avoid looking like a "bunch of

---

103. Comitas, Lambros *The Social Nexus of Ganja in Jamaica,* p. 131, in Rubin, Vera. *Cannabis and Culture.* Mouton and Company, Chicago: 1975.

104. Brecher, p. 536.

105. *Ibid.,* p. 535.

106. *Ibid.,* p. 536.

do-gooders" who are "soft on marijuana." He also warned Shafer that the Commission would "look bad as hell" if it came out with recommendations contrary to the direction of Congress and the President. Shafer essentially told Nixon he would not support legalization, even though there were some on the commission who did. They went on to discuss Shafer's potential appointment to a federal judgeship (which never happened).

In the end, the commission did not recommend legalization; they recommended decriminalization. That essentially meant no serious punishment, criminal or civil, under state or federal law. Nixon was a sore loser. Discussing the situation with his advisors, Nixon said, "We need, and I use the word 'all out war,' on all fronts . . . we have to attack on all fronts." Nixon wanted a "Goddamn strong statement about marijuana . . . that just tears the ass out of them."

Remarking on the tapes, Kevin Zeese adds,

Nixon's private comments about marijuana showed that he was the epitome of misinformation and prejudice. He believed marijuana led to hard drugs, despite the evidence to the contrary. He saw marijuana as tied to "radical demonstrators." He believed "the Jews," especially "Jewish psychiatrists," were behind advocacy for legalization, and asked his advisor Bob Haldeman, "What the Christ is the matter with the Jews, Bob?" He made a bizarre distinction between marijuana and alcohol, saying people use marijuana "to get high" while "a person drinks to have fun." He also saw marijuana as part of the culture war that was destroying the United States, and claimed that Communists were using it as a weapon. "Homosexuality, dope, immorality in general," Nixon fumed. "These are the enemies of strong societies. That's why the Communists and the left-wingers are pushing the stuff, they're trying to destroy us." His approach to drug education was just a simplistic: "Enforce the law. You've got to scare them."

Unfortunately, Nixon did more than just "scare them," whoever they were. One year into his "all out war," marijuana arrests jumped to 420,700 a year — a full 128,000 more than the year before. Since then, nearly 15 million people have been arrested for marijuana offenses.

NIXON OFFICIALLY DECLARES GOVERNMENT'S "WAR ON DRUGS"

The commission basically declared marijuana innocent, but that news was buried under reports about the fumbling efforts toward a peace treaty with the

Vietnamese and the primaries leading up to the 1972 presidential election. With the Shafer Commission Report almost a distant memory, Nixon officially declared America's "war on drugs." Calling the "drug scourge" the nation's Number One social problem, he announced plans to revamp and escalate the federal government's drug enforcement efforts. That included reorganizing the BNDD into the Drug Enforcement Administration (DEA) and elevating it to the status of a super agency. The annual budget went from $69 million in 1969, to $719 million in 1974. Perhaps the major difference between the DEA and its predecessors was that its operations were being directed by the Oval Office and it was no longer confined to the domestic enforcement of drug laws — it was now operating internationally. Nixon also authorized the payment of $3 billion to Turkish farmers for not cultivating poppies (the source of heroin); that only lasted one year, because the farmers found it more profitable to grow poppies.

With Nixon's resignation in August 1974, the Drug Enforcement Administration was on its own and its blatant incompetence soon became apparent. Its critics described the DEA as a scandal-ridden agency that vindictively engaged in cruel, violent and murderous activities. Washington had created its own Gestapo and, under the cloak of morality, the "war on drugs" became a reincarnation of the Inquisition.

In mid-1975, DEA Director John Bartels was censured for administrative blunders by a Congressional Committee chaired by Senator Henry M. Jackson, and shortly afterward he was dismissed by Attorney General Edward Levi.

The following year, the same Committee concluded that the DEA's procedures were a travesty and had completely failed to deal with the drug problem, saying:

> The DEA has relied upon undercover work to an inordinate degree. The risks in this indiscriminate use of undercover agents outweighs hoped for advantages. The danger to the agent is great. Conversely, the results have proven to be minimal. Major traffickers do not sell narcotics; they have other people to do that. The notion that it is possible to reach the highest rungs of the drug traffic by buying at the low level and advancing progressively to the highest stages is questionable. . . . DEA inherited many personnel-integrity-related problems from predecessor agencies. . . top management has been at a disadvantage in dealing with personnel integrity problems because Federal narcotics enforcement personnel, unlike FBI agents, work under the rules and regulations of the Civil Service Commission. Adverse actions under Civil Service require stringent elements of proof in the transfer of suspected

employees. Because of this, the DEA has not been able to exercise the degree of discipline. . . which the FBI enjoys.[107]

The DEA admitted they were unable to stop the enormous flow of drugs into the United States and although they were actively pursuing that goal, budget restraints were forcing curtailment of their international activities. Essentially, they were telling Congress they needed more money to do the job (the same ploy every agency or office uses to get its budget increased), but interest rates were rising and neither Congress or the Administration (under Ford or Carter) wanted to increase the DEA's already humongous budget. Besides, several states had already lowered penalties for possession of marijuana, and politicians do not like to find themselves on the wrong side of public opinion.

1972 PRESIDENTIAL ELECTION

Marijuana's impact on presidential politics began in earnest with the 1972 election. The policies Nixon initiated during his first term inspired a whole generation, estimated at 25% of the population, to become politically active. While the Republican Party was again firmly behind Nixon and his policies, the Democrats were in turmoil. Their more moderate-to-conservative leadership had lost credibility with the majority of Democrats, particularly the more liberal and politically astute "baby boomers," many of whom were now adults. The demonstrators outside the 1968 Democratic Convention in Chicago had moved inside, in 1972, and as representatives of the party's liberal wing they were fighting ideologically with the conservatives for control of the party. They did not appreciate having their objections to the Vietnam War ignored by establishment Democrats nor did they like the way the Democrat-controlled Congress had rubber stamped all the budget requests for both the Vietnam War and the drug war. They were particularly outraged by the blatant abuse of civil liberties inherent in Nixon's newly declared "war on drugs."

Presidential politics is a cutthroat business, and that was especially true of the 1972 Democratic nominating process. McGovern was the only candidate to publicly support marijuana legalization. McCarthy, who had beaten Lyndon

---

107. Goldman, p. 133.

Johnson in the 1968 New Hampshire primary, was not a factor (nor did he support marijuana legalization). The field included former vice president and Senator Hubert Humphrey (who had lost to Nixon by a very narrow margin in 1968); Maine's senior Senator Ed Muskie (Humphrey's vice presidential candidate in 1968); Washington State's senior senator Henry "Skip" Jackson (a high-profile and influential committee chairman); and, with much less national recognition, South Dakota's senior Senator George McGovern, and a long-shot candidate Congresswoman Shirley Chisholm (a black woman) from New York. They were all liberal Democrats with the exception of Skip Jackson, who represented the conservative right wing of the Democratic Party.

Jackson, who supported the Vietnam War and vehemently opposed amnesty for "draft dodgers," even after the war, was also steadfastly against legitimizing any "drugs." He was clearly losing to both Humphrey (who tried to position himself as a middle-of-the-roader) and McGovern (who represented the most liberal wing of the Party). Like Nixon, Jackson completely disregarded the public's growing acceptance of marijuana. Jackson could not attack Nixon for policies he personally supported, so he took potshots at McGovern, calling him a "triple-A candidate," insinuating that McGovern advocated "Acid [LSD], amnesty and abortion." That was quite an unfair characterization of McGovern's position, and it failed miserably — as did his presidential aspirations.

McGovern's success was due primarily to a large, well-organized grassroots (mostly volunteer) organization, staffed by Nixon's most ardent opponents. These were the (mostly young) people who protested the war and supported reforming the marijuana laws. They catapulted McGovern into the lead for the Democrat nomination.

It was no secret that many or most of the people working on McGovern's campaign staff smoked marijuana, and news reporters covering the Democratic convention even noted the pungent odor of marijuana coming from McGovern's campaign headquarters trailer just outside the convention hall. The stage was clearly set for a confrontation and a major shift in policy. People like Gary Hart, McGovern's campaign manager, had come of age and were confident about winning the election because such a large segment of the population was dismayed with Nixon. Unfortunately, all that changed in a matter of a few minutes.

The 1972 Democratic Party convention in Miami was more of a coronation. McGovern had won enough primaries to assure his nomination — his job at the convention was to unite the Party, which politically meant taking a step to the right. The middle-of-the-roaders and conservatives, a substantial portion of the delegates, did not use marijuana, did not understand it, and did not feel comfortable supporting legalization. How could they give confidence to those constituents without losing the more liberally inclined? An incident at a McGovern rally late in the primary campaign illustrates the difficulty. In introducing McGovern to the crowd at the rally, Governor Frank Morrison felt compelled to try to limit the damage he perceived Jackson had done to the campaign with his "triple-A" remarks. He completely misread the crowd and tried to reassure them that McGovern did not advocate radical positions like legalizing marijuana and providing abortion on demand. The crowd was noticeably stunned and disappointed. After the rally, Morrison told McGovern, "Maybe I'm too old to understand this new generation. I'll get the oldsters for you, and you take care of the young ones as you think best."[108]

McGovern knew a number of states had propositions on their ballots calling for the legalization or decriminalization of marijuana, but the pollsters were correctly telling him in July that they would all be defeated in November. In addition, New York's Republican Governor Nelson Rockefeller (who was expected to win reelection) was calling for even more punitive anti-drug laws. McGovern may have decided pragmatically that "the people" had not yet made up their minds and that supporting marijuana reform was not an issue capable of carrying him into the White House. He believed that without the enthusiastic support of the mainstream Democrats he could not beat Nixon in the November election — besides, his liberal supporters would never vote for Nixon, even if he backed off on the issues closest to their hearts.

McGovern made the biggest mistake of his political career within an hour of officially capturing the Democratic Party's nomination. On his way into the convention center to thank the delegates, he stopped to answer some reporters' questions — and one of those questions was about his plans concerning marijuana. Not realizing that his remarks were being televised nationwide, McGovern replied: "I'm not ready to call for the legalization or decriminalization of marijuana."

Every politically astute marijuana smoker in the country heard him break what they considered a promise. McGovern lost the election that night because he lost credibility with the voters and with his campaign staff. The advice McGovern received about the marijuana issue was absolutely wrong, and the

---

108. McGovern, George. *Grassroots: The Autobiography of George McGovern*, Random House, New York: 1977, p. 162.

error destroyed both his chance of being elected and marijuana's chance of becoming legal again.

Nixon had lost his 1960 bid for the presidency specifically because he did not present well in the televised debates with John Kennedy; understandably, he refused to publicly debate either Humphrey in 1968 or McGovern in 1972. While conjecture is always hazardous, it is easy to imagine that if McGovern had not backed away from supporting marijuana legalization, he quite possibly could have sparked a nationwide debate (by whatever media weapon his opponent might choose!). That would have forced Nixon into a position of defending his anti-marijuana stance, which probably would not have held up under public scrutiny. If nothing else, it would have shown McGovern as someone willing to deal openly and rationally with the issues facing the nation, which would have contrasted favorably to Nixon's unpopular secretive methods. Forcing the issue might easily have affected the outcome of the election.

A month after the Democratic convention, the Republicans held their nominating convention. Although there was no thought of Republicans supporting legalized marijuana, the news media did question the delegates for their opinions. In a nationally televised interview and in a *National Observer* article, senior US Senator Pete Domonic of Colorado made public his personal opinion about the marijuana question, saying, "Coming out for legalized pot is like putting your head right on the chopping block." He also said, "Marijuana is not an issue for Presidential politics." He was wrong. In 1973, the Oregon state legislature decriminalized marijuana, and in November 1974 the senator paid for his remarks, soundly losing his reelection bid to, ironically, Gary Hart — McGovern's former campaign manager. Less than a year later Colorado also relaxed the penalties for marijuana possession, but did not decriminalize.

Unfortunately, the vote on marijuana in 1972 did not amount to much. There was very little discussion about marijuana between the nominating conventions and the elections, because the nation's attention was riveted to a number of other issues — the Watergate break-in, McGovern's political ineptness, and inflation — and particularly a substantial increase in the price of gasoline and heating oil. The gas price wars of the late 1950s and early 60s kept the price of a gallon of gasoline at under $0.30. The price skyrocketed to a $1.50 per gallon as of the result of the 1973 OPEC oil embargo.

The expected debate over marijuana never materialized. There was certainly no consensus either for or against marijuana and the lack of discussion erroneously suggested there was little interest in changing marijuana's illegal status. That distraction or misperception hurt efforts in many states to qualify marijuana legalization initiatives for the ballot. The few state initiatives that were able to get on the ballot all lost, but in California Proposition 9 (calling for legalization) lost only by 6 points.

Even before the dust settled over that election, OPEC initiated its oil embargo against the United States and the media's attention quickly narrowed in on the energy crisis. High prices, mile-long lines and serious shortages at the pump distracted everyone. That allowed Nixon, newly reelected and denying his involvement with Watergate, to go forward with his draconian war against marijuana. And that set the tone for succeeding administrations.

As revelations about the Watergate break-in conspiracy restricted what Nixon was able to do, several states began once again to consider lowering the penalties for marijuana use.

New York Takes a Step Backwards

In early 1973, New York (at the behest of Governor Nelson Rockefeller, a "liberal Republican" — if such an animal exists) severely increased the penalties for both drug use and trafficking. The so-called Rockefeller anti-drug law was the harshest in the nation. It was legislated, not voted, into existence; and it devastated the state's economy.

An economic recession was already in full swing, brought on by rising oil prices. Every city in the country felt the pinch but none experienced the dire financial hardships of New York City. In early 1975, the city was broke. Why did not Los Angeles, for example — with a larger population and many more gas guzzling automobiles, suffer the same or worse fate? Why were Boston, Chicago, Dallas, and San Francisco not equally devastated? One answer is that New York's stringent anti-drug law caused a severe increase in the street price of illegal drugs, which in turn fed an inflationary spiral within the state's economy and negatively affecting virtually every business, large and small. This contributed to the growing unemployment and crime rates as well — which hurt real estate prices, etc. It was not long before a number of major corporations announced plans to relocate, depleting the city's tax base and annual revenue. The city ran out of money and the state could not help. The situation was not as dire in other major cities because only New York had enacted such hard anti-drug laws; most other states were actually considering lowering the penalties.

Acting tough may have helped Governor Rockefeller's public image, but the people of New York paid a very high price for several years, and it was all for nought. Rockefeller's tough laws did not resolve the drug problem; quite to the contrary — they worsened it. And many of the convictions were appealed and overturned — the courts found many aspects of the law unconstitutional.

Economic conditions in New York did not start to improve until after June 1977, when the State of New York reversed itself and even decriminalized marijuana. Some remnants of Rockefeller's draconian drug laws still remain, but the shift was enough to allow New York to recover from its economic problems.

STATES BEGIN ADOPTING DECRIMINALIZATION

Nixon declared his war on drugs in 1972, but after the *Washington Post* broke the story of Nixon's "plumbers" breaking in at the Watergate office of the Democratic National Committee that June, the administration was too busy defending itself to bother fighting drugs. The enforcement policy was not officially relaxed but in practice the heat was off and stayed off through the ensuing Ford and Carter administrations. Even before Nixon was forced to resign, people all across the country were working on ways to end marijuana's illegal status.

In May–June 1973, a bill proposing the legalization of marijuana was introduced in Oregon's Legislature that would allow cultivation of two marijuana plants and eliminate all criminal penalties for possession of less than 8 oz. of marijuana. The bill was soundly defeated, but the very notion of such a bill stirred up so much controversy that another bill was immediately introduced to reduce possession of less than an ounce of marijuana to a non-criminal violation and a maximum $100 fine. That bill essentially called for the decriminalization of marijuana, which was what NORML's Keith Stroup was promoting.

Hearing that this new bill was likely to pass, Stroup flew to Oregon to lend his support. Oregon was the first state to decriminalize marijuana. Even more convinced that "decriminalization" offered the only real hope for reducing the unwarranted punishments being inflicted on marijuana users, Stroup redoubled his lobbing efforts in Maine, Maryland, Massachusetts, Rhode Island, Montana, Hawaii, California, Texas and Connecticut. But, instead of following Oregon's lead, the states decided on a wait-and-see approach. The Texas legislature did lower possession of under an ounce from a felony to a misdemeanor, but none of the state adopted decriminalization after Oregon.

Most likely, the other states did not act because all attention was focused on Washington. The then vice president Spiro Agnew was indicted for fraud and tax evasion and was forced to resign; Gerald Ford replaced him; and Congress was gearing up to impeach Richard Nixon for covering up his involvement in the Watergate conspiracy.

ALASKA UPHOLDS PERSONAL RIGHTS

In early 1975, the Alaskan State Supreme Court, the youngest and most liberal in the nation, was about to decide a case that could essentially legalize marijuana. Even more important, the Alaskan court was deciding the legal question of whether a citizen's right of privacy should prevail over the state's existing anti-marijuana laws.

Even before the Court could act, a bill calling for marijuana decriminalization was introduced and passed by the Alaska state legislature and became law, without the governor's signature or veto, making Alaska the second state to decriminalize marijuana. When the Alaskan Supreme Court did render its decision, it came down in favor of the right of privacy, automatically revoking the state's existing anti-marijuana laws in regards to personal possession and use of marijuana. The Court's decision did not address the issue of cultivation, but the State's Attorney General ruled that the right of privacy did include cultivation.

The distribution and sale of marijuana remained illegal in every state, but Alaska decreed that the personal use of marijuana was covered by the right to privacy. Alaska's fifteen-year blemish-free history serves as proof that resistance to legalized marijuana is ill-founded and based more on fear and ignorance than on a rational informed decision.

Yet, allowing marijuana to be legal anywhere in United States, even in Alaska, was contrary to the Reagan Administration's rejuvenated "war on drugs." In the late 1980s the Reagan Administration took the initiative to change the Alaskan law, and led by US Drug Czar William Bennett, a group of anti-marijuana Alaskans gathered enough signatures to qualify as a statewide ballot measure calling for the re-outlawing of marijuana, and it passed.

Later that year four other states, California, Maine, Colorado and Ohio, passed decriminalization legislation. In 1976, Minnesota became the seventh state to decriminalize marijuana and South Dakota lowered the fine for personal possession to $20. In 1977, Mississippi, New York and North Carolina all passed marijuana decriminalization laws and in 1978 Nebraska followed suit.

THE 1976 PRESIDENTIAL ELECTION

In 1976, the nation again focused on presidential politics. Gerald Ford, the incumbent, carried the political baggage of pardoning Richard Nixon — thereby preventing a trial and possible imprisonment. The country considered Ford an interim president, and with him as the Republican nominee, it did not much matter whom the Democrats nominated. Answering that mild challenge was the unknown conservative governor of Georgia, Jimmy Carter (affectionately known as "Jimmy Who?"). Carter emerged from the pack of would-be Democrat nominees almost entirely because he was the only candidate advocating the decriminalization of marijuana.

Carter may even have known about the industrial uses of Cannabis (hemp) because of his family's long hemp farming heritage — apparently the Carters were hemp farmers before they were peanut farmers. It is believed that Jimmy Carter is a direct decedent of Robert "King" Carter, a wealthy colonial era hemp farmer and spinner of hemp fabric.

With no national following, Carter desperately needed the grassroots support of the party's liberal wing to win the nomination and ultimately the presidential election. Since several states had already relaxed their penalties for possession of marijuana, and because it was clearly a liberal cause, Carter embraced the concept of marijuana decriminalization early in his campaign. It was no secret that many of the people on Carter's campaign staff, including his son Chip, and members of the press covering Carter's Presidential campaign, smoked marijuana and snorted cocaine on a fairly regular basis. Patrick Anderson, a Carter campaign speech writer, revealed that, "some of us on the Carter staff occasionally smoked, not only among ourselves but with friends in the media." Smoking marijuana was almost commonplace and, as part of the Carter campaign team, they weren't likely to get busted — especially since Carter endorsed decriminalization early in his campaign.[109] Peter Bourne, director of the White House Office of Drug Abuse Policy, upon leaving told the press that

---

109. Anderson, Patrick. *High in America, The True Story Behind NORML and the Politics of Marijuana.* Viking Press, New York: 1981, p. 5-6.

there was a high incident of marijuana use... [and] occasional use of cocaine" by staff members.[110]

Unfortunately, once the nomination was assured, Carter like McGovern backed away from decriminalization, believing it more important to unite the party. That meant Carter was depending on the party machine rather than his liberal grassroots organization to win. He had an enormous lead over Ford, but that decision almost cost Carter the election — the actual vote was much closer than the polls had previously indicated. Carter gave away his core constituency — the disenchanted liberals who supported marijuana reform. They abandoned Carter, just as they had abandoned McGovern. It was the biggest mistake of Carter's political career; it severely affected his presidency and split the party. In his bid for reelection he faced a serious challenge from US Senator Ted Kennedy, the de facto leader of the liberal wing of the Democratic Party.

Carter and the Democrats, in control of Congress, had an opportunity to bring about the social changes the people were demanding — particularly ending the drug war; but Carter thought he had a greater chance of being reelected if he could straddle the liberal/conservative fence. That attempt angered his liberal supporters and left him open to Republican (conservative) criticism.

New Mexico's Medical Marijuana Trial

Even though he had backed away from decriminalization, having Carter in the White House was far better than Nixon. At least Carter had once supported decriminalization and there was still a chance he might be convinced to support it again. Keith Stroup (of NORML) had become friendly with both Chip Carter and Peter Bourne (Carter's Drug Policy advisor) during the campaign, and on several occasions Bourne invited Stroup to the White House to discuss the administration's drug policy. That relationship later soured, for several reasons.

In late 1977, Stroup asked Chip to testify at a hearing before the New Mexico State Legislature that was considering a bill to legalize the use of marijuana for medicinal purposes. That hearing included the testimony of two medical marijuana patients — Lynn Pierson, a lung cancer patient undergoing chemotherapy treatments, and Bob Randall, who had glaucoma and was going blind.

---

110. Robinson, Rowan. *The Great Book of Hemp*. Park Street Press, Rochester, Vermont: 1996, p. 170.

Unfortunately, First Lady Rosalyn Carter vetoed Chip's plans to testify. She did not want the Carter family involved in the controversy over marijuana.

In fact, the family was already linked to the controversy, as Chip's use of marijuana in the White House and around Washington was well known by the reporters and became an issue with the Secret Service — the agents assigned to protect Chip were constantly having to look the other way or leave the room to avoid witnessing a "crime" when Chip, his wife Caron, and their friends started to light up (apparently, they also managed not to smell the distinctive aroma of marijuana through the door). Chip was eventually asked to stop smoking marijuana or move out of the White House; he moved out. It was a hollow victory for the Secret Service, as Chip and Caron still came regularly to spend the night at the White House and their use of marijuana continued to embarrass the Secret Service agents at concerts, parties, and on one occasion a visit to the NORML offices.

The eventual outcome of the New Mexico hearings, announced on February 21, 1978, was a recommendation to pass the bill, and subsequently the State of New Mexico did legalize the medical use of marijuana. Over the next eighteen months, twenty other states passed similar medical marijuana legislation, putting enormous pressure on the FDA to legalize the cultivation and distribution of marijuana for medicinal purposes.

Instead, probably thanks to the efforts of then vice president George Bush, in early 1980 Eli Lilly's Marinol (a synthetic form of THC) was put on the FDA's fast-track approval list. FDA officials begrudgingly granted approval of Marinol with the condition that it could only be prescribed after all other known medical remedies, including chemotherapy, had been tried and failed (which was seen as a pathetically small act of humanity on the part of the FDA).

The quality of advice Jimmy Carter got on drug issues is questionable. Dr. Peter Bourne, a psychiatrist who helped establish drug policy in both the Nixon and Carter administrations, was scarcely qualified to comment; his only real experience with "drugs" was administering a methadone program in Georgia, established at the request of then Governor Jimmy Carter. But that experience, plus a push from his college friend Robert DuPont (a big Republican party contributor), led to a position with the Nixon Administration — whose perspective on "drugs" was obviously skewed.

In 1974, Bourne's comments included his assessment of cocaine, which he called "the most benign of illicit drugs currently in widespread use."[III]

That is not, in fact, a very rational or realistic view. In reality, keeping the cost of illegal drugs high only encourages the establishment of organized cartels for the distribution and sale of drugs. The black, Hispanic, and Asian dealers of today are no different than the Irish, Italian, Jewish, and German immigrant poor of the Prohibition era. The police concentrate on the drug problems of the inner-city poor because of the violence associated with them. But the only rational approach to ending the violence associated with illegal drugs and the inner city is to eliminate the huge profits, and that can only be accomplished by ending the drug war.

Stroup got into some trouble with NORML's Board of Directors and was forced to resign as National Director. Before leaving, he agreed with the NORML Board to abandon decriminalization in favor of full legalization. Despite the successful campaigns for decriminalization in Oregon and a few other states, it was decided that reducing the penalties for possession rather than legalizing it altogether would only prolong the problem, not resolve it.

THE MEXICAN DRUG WAR

The Carter administration's immature understanding of illegal drugs, probably fostered by Bourne's ineptness, led to a new controversy in the war against marijuana, in late 1977, with the spraying of a chemical defoliant known as Paraquat on Mexico growing fields. The importation of Mexican marijuana was so pervasive that America's marijuana-smoking youth were learning the names of the various Mexican states because the quality (and price) of the marijuana they were buying was determined by the reputation of the area where it was grown — Michoacan, Oaxaca, Acapulco (Gold), even Panama (Red).

The Nixon Administration first tried to convince the Mexican government to use Paraquat in 1971, but they flatly refused. America's family farmers were hit particularly hard in the recession of the early 1970s and many were forced into bankruptcy. America was importing more and more of its fruits and vegetable from Central and South America, and Mexico finally had an opportunity to export agricultural products to its rich neighbor. Mexico could hardly start spraying Paraquat around. US consumers were unlikely to eat vegetables that they thought were grown anywhere near a known poison.

---

111. McWilliams, Peter. *Ain't Nobody's Business If You Do.* Prelude Press, Los Angeles, CA: 1993, p.81.

Use of marijuana, known as *mota* in Mexico, was not perceived as a serious social problem. They were primarily growing it for export and for them to engage in a US-style drug war would have been economically counterproductive. Mexican officials took the position that "illegal drugs" were a US problem, not a Mexican problem.

By 1977, however, the political situation within Mexico had changed considerably and the PRI (Institutional Revolutionary Party), which had been in power since 1929, was being seriously challenged. The PRI represented the country's elite industrialists, bankers, and large ranchers. For most of Mexico's poor, the Revolution did not end in 1920 — it was still going on, especially in those parts of rural Mexico where marijuana was grown. Even the Army knew to stay out of many places. The PRI only controlled the cities; the Mexican country-side was controlled by others. Social and health services, education, roads, and jobs were still in short supply, there; the PRI felt no obligatin to provide services for their rivals.

The US threatened to cut off foreign aid payments if Mexico did not stop the flow of marijuana. Knowing that the opposition party was financed by the marijuana trade, the PRI decided to go ahead and escalate the drug war. The US supplied weapons, helicopters, and Paraquat to help them crush their political enemies. This time around, however, the Paraquat spraying was not made public. NORML developed that knowledge by requesting information from the State Department, DEA and the National Institute for Drug Abuse (NIDA), under the Freedom of Information Act. Also discovered was a report written by John Ford, the man who set up Mexico's Paraquat program, which documented the government's involvement and contradicted DEA claims that it was entirely a Mexican program. The report also emphasized destroying marijuana fields, not poppy fields (which produce heroin). Mexico's agricultural export business was not affected, in part because the fruits and vegetables were never tested, thanks to the US government complicity.

The US-instigated Mexican drug war was a life-or-death struggle for the PRI, and the PRI pursued the drug war with a vengeance. This had severe consequences for both the US and Mexico. Escalating the drug war is only effective at reducing the availability of the least dangerous drugs — in this case, marijuana. The Mexican campaign did not stop the drug trade; it simply shifted the focus from supplying marijuana to supplying heroin and cocaine. Mexico became more of a drug distribution hub than ever.

And again, the marijuana shortage induced thousands of Americans to start growing marijuana themselves. In some cases, that meant a plant or two tucked in the back of Mom's nice suburban garden or a little patch at the edge of the woods somewhere; sometimes it meant full scale hydroponic laboratories with "grow lights" and all the trimmings.

Of course, no mention was ever made of possible Paraquat spraying in the US. That would have caused riots in the streets. The price of marijuana skyrocketed while the price of cocaine and heroin, because of a glut, dropped substantially — it eventually was cheaper to get high on crack cocaine than marijuana. The enormous amount of drug money flowing through Mexico fed the growing opposition to the PRI, which was getting stronger and louder, and the possibility of a political revolution in Mexico became a real threat to US security — prompting US authorities to tell the PRI to ease off. The assault on Mexican marijuana proved politically successful for the PRI, but only temporarily.

Chapter 7

The Terrible 1980s

In the 1980 election, Carter's only real chance to beat Reagan was to expose and exploit his irresponsible and irrational ultra-conservative position on the drug war, particularly in terms of marijuana, but after four long years of avoiding the issue he was not in a strong position to criticize Reagan. The Reagans, specifically Nancy, had made their anti-drug views known but it was not a real campaign issue. The mood of the country favored relaxing the draconian anti-marijuana laws and several states had already done so. Had Carter not backed away from his support of decriminalization, the pro-marijuana groups would have had those four long years to openly debate the issue. Since that was not the case, Carter could not really depict Reagan as a right-wing extremist. That left the door open for extreme right wingers, like the "Moral Majority," to take center stage and even afforded them a degree of credibility. Carter essentially had deserted his party's liberal wing, and more conservative Democrats deserted him; they crossed party lines en masse to vote for Reagan.

The election and reelection of Ronald Reagan to the presidency was more a matter of Democrat incompetence than a show of support for Reagan's policies. Although well intentioned, Jimmy Carter was ineffective and really did not do much — worst of all, he divided the Democrats, making it easier for Reagan to win. Reagan's reelection in 1984 was even easier after Walter Mondale, Carter's vice president and Democrat Presidential nominee, announced in his acceptance speech at the Democratic convention that he was going to raise taxes. (They would have to do so, because during Reagan's first term the national debt had more than doubled — and by the end of his second administration the National Debt almost tripled, rising from $845,116,000,000 on January 1, 1979 to $1,662,966,000,000 by December 1984, and reaching $2,857,430,960,000 by September 1989 — the largest percentage increase in the history of the national debt. But that was no time to say so.)

Reagan's economic policies were atrocious and devastated the working class. "Supply Side" economics, better known as "trickle-down" economics, failed to stimulate the economy as Reagan and his supporters promised. Instead, it created long-term mass unemployment. When the air controllers went on strike and Reagan fired them, he sent a message to employers to hold the line on wages. Working-class people quickly discovered that their jobs were not as secure as they once had thought. Then Reagan decided to buy steel from the Japanese to build a nuclear submarine, putting thousands of US steel workers out of work (at a steel mill less than 10 miles away from where the submarine was being built).

Reagan used borrowed money to pay for his vastly escalated war on drugs, extended unemployment benefits, and massive military build-up — while he severely cut the government's tax revenue. He impoverished the working man and woman under the guise of making American-made products more competitive on the world markets (which basically meant keeping wages relatively low). Known as the "Great Communicator," Reagan should more appropriately be remembered as the "feel-good president," because pumping up a primitive sense of patriotism was all he accomplished. In actuality, there was very little substance to Reagan's economic or social policies; principally, he dramatically increased the national debt and devastated the job market.

Since the ability to get and use an education is tied to the level of economic activity, we can judge our level of progress by the population's level of education. In the US, 7.8% of the population benefits from 4+years college; 1-3 years college, 27.4%; high school graduates are 43.2%; those with less than a high school education are 21.6%.[112] Today, less than 10% of the population has a college education and 20% of Americans are considered functionally illiterate. That compares very poorly to the rest of the developed world and one of the implications is that

---

112. *The World Almanac*, 1992, Pg. 213

the economy is not expanding fast enough to produce an environment conducive to social progress.

Ironically, when Ronald Reagan was asked which former US President he most admired, he cited Calvin Coolidge. Unfortunately, their administrations were also very much alike, representing the interests of big business, espousing trickle-down economics, and increasing the gap between the haves and have-nots dramatically. Both demonstrated some contempt for organized labor. Clearly, Reagan's handling of the Air Traffic Controllers strike mirrored the way Coolidge handled the 1919 Boston Police strike: both refused to negotiate in good faith and both refused to rehire the striking workers. In his legislative and may-oral career Coolidge has been described as exhibiting "honesty, party loyalty and completely unspectacular ability" and his Massachusetts governorship "would doubtless have passed unnoticed but for the Boston police strike," which came in Coolidge's first term as Governor. Actually, the sentence, "There is no right to strike against the public safety by anybody, anywhere, anytime," brought Coolidge to national fame.[113] However, Coolidge's pronouncement did not reflect the law and does not prevent government employees from exercising there legal right to strike. Coolidge, known as "Silent Cal," epitomized a do-nothing president; his greatest achievement as president was to reestablish the public's confidence in the office after his Republican predecessor, Warren Harding, had totally destroyed it.

REJUVENATION OF AMERICA'S DRUG WAR (1980S)

Ronald Reagan certainly did not get elected by making drugs a major cam-paign issue; the   state of the economy (specifically, high interest rates) was the major thrust of his campaign. However, as president he almost immediately reju-venated Nixon's war on drugs. To counter what he described as Florida's wide-open illegal drug trade, Reagan established the Florida Drug Task Force. That turned out to be a major effort and for the first time included the US military. While Reagan campaigned in 1980 with a promise to get government out of peo-ple's lives and pocketbooks, he instead initiated severe banking regulations that

---

113. In a message to Samuel Gomper, president of the American Federation of Labor (AFL), to whom the striking police appealed. Van Doren, Charles, editor. *Webster's American Biographies.* Merriam-Webster, Springfield, MA: 1984, p. 221.

allowed Big Brother even greater access to personal bank accounts and information about banking transactions, all under the guise of attempting to curtail the laundering of drug money.

In truth, many banks were laundering drug money, especially in Florida, a drug capital at that time. But Florida was also benefiting from the laundered drug money; the state was experiencing an extremely robust economy and an enormous building boom. All of that abruptly stopped when Reagan's new banking regulations became effective, in part because under the new regulations banks were required to immediately report cash deposits and transfers of over $10,000 to the Internal Revenue Service.

Although Reagan's new banking regulations made it harder for US banks to launder drug money, news of government's expanded powers sent shock waves across the country. Americans shuddered at the invasion of their Constitutional right to privacy (with the new USA Patriotic Act that was swiftly enacted in 2001, using Sept. 11 as an excuse, those shudders have become convulsions). To avoid attracting the attention of the IRS or creating a paper trail, people began using cash whenever possible and limited the amount of money they deposited in banks. That diminished the funds available to banks to lend out. This may be part of the reason why, during the 1980s, banks and small businesses (including family farmers) went belly up at an extraordinary rate. The overall effect of Reagan's stringent banking regulations was to force money out of the banks and out of the legal economy. Several years later, in 1993, economic statistics noted a sharp decline in personal saving accounts compared to those in other industrial countries. Reagan also tried to rejuvenate Nixon's idea of using the chemical Paraquat to destroy marijuana fields — not in foreign countries but here in the United States. Fortunately, it was soundly rejected by the states and the agricultural industry.

Reagan also called for a drug-free working environment and initiated a federal drug testing policy to discourage federal employees from using drugs; and on the pretext of reducing accidents and improving productivity, he encouraged the corporations to do the same. Since drinking on the job has always been a bit of a problem but never was targeted for this type of "clean-up" activity, the rationale is highly suspect.

More likely, he was simply initiating an economic war against those who used illegal drugs — infringing on their Constitutional right to privacy and hampered their ability to earn a living. If safety had been a real concern, Reagan would not have slashed OSHA's funding (the Occupational Safety and Health

Administration) and undermined their ability to enforce safety laws. People have routinely been injured, even died, because of faulty equipment, chemicals and generally unsafe practices. The principal reason why conditions and safety in the workplace improved was that juries were finding corporations legally and financially accountable — making it more expensive for employers to ignore unsafe equipment and conditions.

Certainly, the use of intoxicants at work raises many serious issues. Different types of work require different qualities from workers. When an accident occurs, it should be thoroughly investigated. If human error is suspected, the individuals involved should be tested for the presence of legal and illegal "drugs." If it is proven that an intoxicated individual(s) contributed to causing the accident, he or she should certainly be fired and prosecuted. But simply using "drugs" as a scapegoat will never lead to the truth about any accident.

That scenario is considerably different from the drug testing "witch hunt" Reagan espoused, which assumes that illegal drugs are totally responsible for people's irresponsible or careless actions. That view unrealistically presents the notion that people who do not use illegal drugs are perfect. Accidents do happen, and we are not perfect people. Mistakes are a part of human nature, unpleasant as the admission may be. Mandatory drug testing does not prevent accidents, and if you cannot distinguish users from non-users without a urine test or a drug-sniffing dog, then there may not be much of a problem. Taking mandatory drug tests in order to get and keep a job is antithetical to the "liberty" so loudly and proudly hailed as the essence of America; it only makes a mockery of the US Constitution and the human rights we are all supposedly guaranteed.

If we test any workers, the President, vice president, members of the US House and Senate, the Joint Chiefs and the Supreme Court should be first in line. What these people do affects all our lives and they should expect to be held to a higher standard than they impose on everyone else. They should be subjected to drug tests, alcohol tests, and IQ tests, lie detector tests and psychological evaluations. They should also be tested for signs of senility.

Reagan increased the DEA's budget every year and in 1983 he proposed an additional 200 million tax dollars to hire 1200 more agents (a 25% increase) with the intent of setting up a permanent drug task force on the east and west coasts and along Mexican Border. The call for more money was not received well by Congress — not with the unemployment rate hovering at 11%. In fact, when Reagan made that proposal in his State of the Union Address he intentionally paused, expecting a favorable response — applause, or even a standing ovation?

but the audience responded in total silence and Reagan was noticeably disappointed.

In late 1983, the government reported the results of Reagan's escalated war on drugs. Three times as much cocaine and twice as much marijuana and heroin had been confiscated, but there was no discernable decrease in the amount of illegal drugs available on the streets.

A sluggish economy and Reagan's own budgetary constraints hindered his anti-drug efforts during his second term, especially since they'd proven ineffective — the war on drugs deteriorated into little more than saber rattling. Reagan circumvented Congress's refusal to increase funding by expanding Nancy Reagan's "Just Say No" campaign, which he financed with a $10 million donation from Saudi Arabia's royal family — after agreeing to sell them military aircraft.

When Nancy's anti-drug campaign started attracting too much criticism, Reagan's corporate supporters, primarily the alcohol, tobacco, oil, petrochemical, lumber and pharmaceutical companies profiting from the illegal status of Cannabis, established the Drug Advisory Council and later the Partnership for a Drug Free America (PDFA), which they financed by diverting money they owed in taxes as tax deductible charitable contributions. In fact, both these organizations were little more than fronts that protected their corporate identities while producing anti-drug propaganda to protect their corporate sponsor's profits.

Is it not somewhat suspicious that an organization dedicated to warning people about the danger of using illegal intoxicants (which, combined, kill under 8,000 people every year) never mentions the danger of using their sponsors' legal intoxicants — alcohol (which kills 150,000 people every year), tobacco (which kills about 400,000 every year) or FDA-approved prescription drugs (which kill about 100,000 people every year)? And, is it not somewhat strange that the PDFA has never solicited contributions from the general public?

Faced with a recession, declining tax revenues, and possible budget cuts, but determined to continue on the same course, Reagan proposed and Congress enacted into law the egregious policy of giving law enforcement a financial incentive to go after drug offenders. It allowed law enforcement agencies to keep the proceeds of sales of confiscated property in drug-related convictions; this was promoted as way to defray costs and reduce the taxpayer's burden. What it actually did was corrupt law enforcement from the top down and encouraged the most predatory tendencies.

Drug arrests quickly became law enforcement's top priority, and since the mid-1980s the number of drug related arrests skyrocketed. Two-thirds of the prison population is there on drug offences and people convicted of violent crimes, even murder, are released early to keep drug offenders locked up — all because of the billions of dollars worth of private property that law enforcement agencies gets to keep. The actual financial boon to the agencies did not last long, as many cities reduced the official police department budget to offset the amount expected to be "earned" by confiscating property — which meant that now, the agencies *had* to arrest people who had something to lose.

The murder of millionaire Don Scott in his Malibu, California, home showed just how far law enforcement would go. Scott and his wife Frances owned a piece of property adjacent to a national forest. Apparently, the National Park Service had already contacted the Scotts about purchasing their land in order to enlarge the national forest, but Scott was not interested in selling. A combination of agencies looked at the property — worth $5 million to the National Park Service — and decided Scott might be engaged in cultivation and selling of marijuana. At the trial it was revealed that the Scotts and their property had been under surveillance for 30 days before the actual raid. With a warrant to search for evidence of marijuana cultivation, on October 2, 1992, L.A. County Sheriffs (operating outside their jurisdiction) and five federal agencies (including DEA) raided the Scotts' home in the middle of the night. Probably believing the house was being burglarized, and hearing his wife scream "Don't shoot me, don't kill me," Mr Scott came down the stairs with a gun. Apparently, he did not drop his gun fast enough when ordered to do so by the police; they shot and killed him. In the investigation that followed, the Ventura County District Attorney, Michael Bradbury, concluded that the police had lied to obtain the search warrant, that there had never been any marijuana cultivation on the property, and that the raid was motivated by a desire to forfeit the multimillion dollar ranch. Despite the DA's dramatic conclusions, no officer was ever indicted or even lightly disciplined.

That same year, 1992, a "60 Minutes" report indicated that suspicion alone was the criterion used by law enforcement agencies to confiscate money and property suspected of being used to purchase, transport, or conceal illegal drugs. "60 Minutes" reported that the police had confiscated a little under $10,000 from a man at an airport, essentially because a ticket clerk notified them after seeing the man was carrying a large sum of cash. There was no evidence that he was involved with illegal drugs, but he fit their concept of a possible drug dealer so the police searched him and confiscated the money — claiming they *suspected* the money was going to be used to purchase illegal drugs. In the same report, "60

Minutes" also told the story of an executive jet confiscated because a box belonging to a passenger was found to contain illegal drugs. In both cases, the police charged and arrested only the money, not the individual — arresting the individual would have invoked protection of his civil rights. But charging an inanimate object with a crime is lunacy, and to recover his money the victim faced the costly and almost impossible task of proving his money innocent in a court of law.

Both these incidents demonstrate the predatory abuse of power, not justice. There is no justice without the presumption of innocence. The confiscation of private property caused so much outrage that the US Supreme Court, often accused of ignoring Fourth Amendment rights when "drugs" were involved, was finally forced to take action. Unfortunately, they did not outlaw the practice; they only made it harder for law enforcement.

THE COLOMBIA TRAGEDY

Reagan visited Colombia in the early days of his presidency, hoping to get the country's cooperation in the anti-drug crusade. Of course, the Colombian officials he was talking to were the very same people profiting from the drug trade. It would be mighty expensive to induce them to try something else. In truth, the majority of the food, clothing, schools and medical services in Colombia came from the drug dealers, not the government. The visit was a political embarrassment for Reagan, and he retaliated by initiating an economic war against Colombia. He cut off all foreign aid and ordered US Customs inspectors to conduct detailed searches of all passenger and luggage arriving from Colombia. All of that put a damper on US tourism to Colombia, as well. He also apparently had the Central Intelligence Agency depose the political leadership of Colombia, as they had done in Chile in 1973, when Allende was thrown out. By the mid 1980s, a new regime beholden to the US government was installed in Colombia and they were willing to engage in a war against their own people, simply to re-qualify for US foreign aid. The drug war in Colombia quickly turned into a civil war, which is still financed today by drug money and US taxpayer money — a civil war that will continue until the US government comes to its senses and ends its own irrational drug war.

Reagan did essentially the same thing in Panama, using the Justice Department to file charges against Panama's General Noriega, declaring him a drug dealer. When Noriega would not resign his position and immediately surrender himself to US authorities, the Reagan administration intentionally destroyed Panama's economy in an attempt to pressure Noriega into resigning. That situation escalated during the Bush Administration to a full-scale military invasion of Panama. In June 1992, the (very conservative) US Supreme Court decided that the United States has the right to kidnap foreign citizens on foreign soil and bring them to trial in the United States for violations of American law — and that gave a green light for an invasion. Noriega did eventually surrender to US authorities, specifically the DEA.

It is highly doubtful any international court would uphold the US Supreme Court's authority to make such a decision. In essence, what the Supreme Court did was sanction the ability of the local bully (the US government) to terrorize the neighborhood. The United States government subsequently put Manuel Noriega on trial, convicted him, and has imprisoned him ever since.

The Reagan administration's drastic increase in military spending came at the expense of social programs. Military strength is not what has made America powerful or influential; the world does not respect a bully. Our power and influence derived, until recently, from our wealth of natural resources and the consumer-based economy that has provided us with the best standard of living on earth. A consumer-based economy invests in a cycle that replenishes itself: industry expands, jobs are created and a middle class creates more and more market demand for products; military spending is more like pouring resources down a hole.

As for the ill-founded claims that Reagan was the best president America ever had or that he was somehow responsible for the demise of the Soviet Union and communism, they just are not true. The Soviet system was set for a sea change regardless of whatever outside influences were brought to bear. It is inconceivable that any president who conducts a war against his own people, like the "war on drugs," could ever be considered by future historians as one of the best presidents — despite Reagan's once 68% approval rating.

THE FIRST GEORGE BUSH PRESIDENCY

The Bush administration also dramatically and vindictively escalated the drug war, and the reason became quite obvious years later when the Bush family's heavy investment in the pharmaceutical industry became public. According to the New York Times, George H. W. Bush served as a member of the Board of Directors of the Eli Lilly Pharmaceutical Company, a position he was given by his long time friend and former Yale University classmate James C. Quayle (Vice President Dan Quayle's father), who owned a controlling interest in Eli Lilly.[114]

Actually, the Bush family fortune, originally created by George's father, Prescott Bush, was also invested in Abbott, Bristol, Pfizer, and other pharmaceutical companies. A Wall Street banker, Prescott Bush became wealthy trading with Hitler's cronies even during World War II. Three of Prescott Bush's companies were seized by the US government under the Trading with the Enemy Act because they were selling fuel to and laundering money for the Nazis. In 1952, Prescott Bush, a Republican, became a US Senator, representing the State of Connecticut; he retired in 1963. George Bush has lobbied on behalf of the pharmaceutical industry throughout his political career, even as vice president — in 1982, the US Supreme Court ordered Bush to stop lobbying the IRS on their behalf. By the way, Eli Lilly & Co. owns the patent rights to Methadone, the only government-approved treatment for heroin addiction; that may well have come about due to the efforts Texas (R) Congressman George H. W. Bush, 1966-70. Methadone was originally developed under the name "adolphine" in the 1940s by the Nazis as a synthetic pain-killer.

That relationship is principally why George Bush's undersecretary for Health and Human Services and Chief of the Public Health Service, James Mason, in 1991 denied the applications of 300 AIDS patients seeking legal access to marijuana under the federal Compassionate Marijuana Use Program. Marijuana had proven far more effective and less debilitating than AZT, the federally-approved drug for treating the symptoms of AIDS.

As far as the government was concerned, marijuana was the last medicine they would allow AIDS patients to try, and even Marinol (Lilly's patented synthetic Tetrahydrocannabinol) was severely restricted. Marinol did not prove effective at reducing the nausea associated with chemotherapy; even so, in April 1992, the Bush Administration announced it was ending the Compassionate

---

114. *New York Times*, May 19, 1982. p. A-1.

Marijuana Use Program and would no longer permit the medicinal use of marijuana (or even maintain the fiction that it would), and formally denied AIDS patients legal access. Closing that program was clearly not an example of benevolent government.

While the Compassionate Marijuana Use Program was cancelled, the US government continued supplying marijuana to a dozen medical marijuana patients who had previously taken the government to court and won legal access. The marijuana was and still is produced and supplied by a government operated facility at the University of Tennessee which for decades has been studying marijuana. There were only a dozen medical marijuana patients because lawyers do not want cases that only seek compliance, not monetary compensation; even when they win on principle, they are usually not compensated for their time or expenses. The overwhelming majority of medical marijuana patients, already heavily burdened with enormous medical bills, simply could not afford to retain a lawyer to fight for their rights to legal access to the medicine they needed.

In January 2002, a decade later, researchers at the Mayo Clinic confirmed Marinol's ineffectiveness,[115] stating that a marijuana-like drug (Marinol) was less effective than standard treatment (that is, marijuana) in helping cancer patients fight appetite loss and weight loss.

THE MEDICINAL MARIJUANA ISSUE

America's "war on drugs" has gone far beyond the bounds of reason; we are being driven by trumped up fears and ignorance, based on the commercial interests of corporations. Morphine, cocaine and marijuana did not acquire their illegal status because they were seriously considered dangerous; they were outlawed by people who were persuaded to act out of bigotry and fanatic moralism. These substances have remained illegal because a few giant corporations want it that way, and the pharmaceutical industry and the government bureaucracy (federal, state and local) that long ago learned to use the drug war to pad their annual budgets.

The bureaucracy has blatantly distorted, misrepresented and even lied about the threat of illegal drugs to protect their jobs and future. Many govern-

---

115. *Minneapolis Star-Tribune.* January 26, 2002.

ment regulators (particularly FDA officials), after retiring from government service, go to work for companies in the industries they once regulated. After distorting the truth, bureaucrats try to justify keeping these intoxicants illegal, particularly marijuana, by telling us we do not know enough about their long-term effects to legalize them; perhaps 5000 years of marijuana use, without a single death directly attributable, is not enough evidence. The bureaucracy is using vastly different standards to judge what it has labeled "drugs" as opposed to pharmaceutical-industry produced "medication," and alcohol. It's not well publicized, but FDA-approved prescription drugs, used to excess, kill between 70,000 and 140,000 in the US every year.

Medical researchers have continuously charged officials with failing to fund or with discrediting research that demonstrates the medicinal benefits of marijuana, and they have criticized the police for refusing to make high-quality confiscated marijuana available to medical researchers. The truth is not welcome, particularly about the medicinal benefits of marijuana; and as it becomes public knowledge, the drug war and the people who enforce the law lose the respect of the people. The champions of the drug war will do and say anything to squelch the use of Cannabis for any purpose.

Fortunately, they are losing that propaganda war and although they have successfully limited researchers and their discoveries, medical researchers nevertheless have time and again demonstrated marijuana's medicinal prowess. Marijuana has proven effective at relieving the nausea associated with chemotherapy and has been found to repress the blindness and pain associated with glaucoma and suppresses the severity, recidivism and spread of herpes.

The knowledge and use of Cannabis (marijuana) for its medical properties are well documented.[116] The definitive guide to the ancient use of plant drugs is Dioscorides Materia Medica, written in AD 80, which was the standard for well over 1,500 years, described the medical applications and preparation of over a thousand substances including hemp and opium.

Cannabis is not a cure all, but it is an extraordinary non-toxic medication that relieves the pain and discomfort associated with a variety of common human ailments. Cannabis was used to treat dysmenorrhea, neuralgia, gout, epileptoid convulsions, senile insomnia, rheumatism, convulsions, mental depression, insanity, uterine hemorrhage, migraine headaches and asthma. Marijuana first appeared on the Official US Pharmacopoeia, a highly selective listing of the

---

116. *High Times,* p. 233.

most widely accepted drugs, in 1839, due to Dr. Wm. B. O'Shaughnessy's research in India. Between the 1840s and 1890s, tincture of Cannabis was one of the most often prescribed medications in America — probably second only to aspirin. Drugs do not usually appear on these pharmaceutical listings without having undergone many years of practical application with proven safe results. One company, Gremault & Sons, even marketed a ready-made marijuana cigarette especially for asthma sufferers. Eminent physicians in Europe and America touted marijuana's therapeutic benefits — among them Queen Victoria's personal physician, Sir John Russell Reynolds, who reportedly prescribed Cannabis for more than thirty years and considered it "one of the most valuable medicines we possess."[117] Does this mean that Queen Victoria was a pot-head?

The list of prominent probable marijuana users — including several former US presidents and the Queen of England seems to be growing, and it did not seem to hurt them. However, over the objection of the American Medical Association (AMA) and despite prominent doctors and volumes of scientific medical reports touting its therapeutic value, it was removed in 1937 from the Official US Pharmacopoeia, pursuant to passage of the Marijuana Tax Act.

Since that time, neither the government, pharmaceutical companies or doctors have acknowledged Cannabis's beneficial properties, and although the pharmaceutical companies have introduced thousands of new drugs, few, if any, have proven any more effective or even as good as Cannabis — it has been suggested that 70% of over-the-counter drugs and 30% of the prescription drugs would not be necessary and could not compete with the effectiveness of legal medical marijuana.

Our "cops and robbers" mentality on this issue is causing needless pain, suffering and death by denying people the proven medicinal benefits of Cannabis. Unfortunately, because the government has intentionally tried to squelch knowledge of Cannabis' medical benefits, most people suffering from ailments that marijuana is known to relieve are unaware of it. Even if doctors are aware of marijuana's medicinal benefits, they cannot prescribe it — although many of them find it appropriate to "mention" it to their patients. The physician's application must be approved by the FDA, DEA and the National Institute on Drug Abuse.[118] Despite the lack of information, the article said that 44% of the oncolo-

---

117. Reynolds, Russell J. Dr. *On the Therapeutic Uses and Toxic Effects of Cannabis Indica.* Lancet: March 22, 1970, p. 637.

118. Ostrow, Ronald J. *Los Angeles Times*, May 1, 1991, p. A-11.

gist responding to their survey, said they had recommended marijuana to relieve the nausea associated with chemotherapy.

Many doctors, however, avoid patient-initiated discussion because they are afraid of being lured into making some self-incriminating statement. Intimidated by the government's threats of prosecution and/or possible loss of their prescription writing privileges, they are forced to prescribe much harsher and far more dangerous pharmaceutical drugs, which despite extensive testing and FDA approval are not always the miracle drugs their manufacturers claim. Patients are being over-medicated, and they suffer unexpected reactions and complications and even die — not because of the illness that sent them to the doctor, but from the harsh pharmaceutical drugs the doctor prescribed. Such "medications" may, for example, destroy the liver, and the death will be attributed to liver cancer — if no autopsy is performed, the pharmaceutical companies do not get the blame.

Most pharmaceutical drugs do not, in fact, promise a cure or everlasting life — they simply enable patients to live with their medical conditions without needless pain and discomfort. That is what marijuana does; but marijuana does it better, less expensively, and it does not produce unwanted side effects. Patients do not die from using it. It is only medically prudent to administer the least dangerous treatment first. Only after that proves ineffective is the use of more dangerous drugs appropriate — and even then, marijuana appears to help patients deal with the debilitating aspects of those much harsher pharmaceutical drugs.

> In strict medical terms marijuana is far safer than many foods we commonly consume. It is physically impossible to eat enough marijuana to induce death. Marijuana, in its natural form, is one of the safest therapeutically active substances known to man.
> — *Francis L. Young.* Administrative Law Judge, USDEA, September 6, 1988

Since they cannot talk about it, we will never know how many people are actually treating their ailments with marijuana, nor do we know which ailments they are treating; and that means that the medical community is deprived of potentially important knowledge. It also means that the patients are forced to pay exorbitant "street" prices for Cannabis, unless they live in one of the few states that allow patients to grow marijuana for personal medicinal use.

OPIATES, THE MOST EFFECTIVE PAIN KILLER

A similar problem exists in the world of painkillers. Although we've known for centuries about the superior pain-relieving properties of opiates, we have barely begun to utilize them intelligently or humanely. For the many people who suffer from excruciating pain, a judicious daily dose of opiates could give them some deserved relief; and in some cases, it would enable them to get enough exercise to prevent their muscles from atrophying and making them more ill and more dependent.

But the same draconian mentality that bans marijuana prevented hospices from operating in America until the mid-1970s. Hospices were developed in Europe and operated there several decades before they were able to operate in the United States. A hospice is essentially a residential setting where people with terminal illnesses are, often with the help of morphine, able to live out the last few weeks or months of their lives with dignity and without undue pain or suffering. Hospice patients are not trying to prolong their lives — that's what doctors and hospitals are for. They are avoiding last-ditch efforts with experimental drugs or surgery that might cause them pain, prolong their dying or even induce a vegetative state. If necessary, they are given enough morphine to relieve pain but they remain functional and mobile, enabling them to take care of themselves and interact with the people around them. Many hospice patients are able to dress themselves and make their own breakfasts until the day they die; it is a far more dignified and humane way of dealing with death and is much less expensive than a hospital.

COCAINE: A RELIABLE LOCAL ANESTHETIC

Medically, cocaine is recognized as an extremely effective numbing agent or local anesthetic. It was first used in 1884 by Dr. Carl Koller to perform delicate eye surgery. Sigmund Freud used it to cure his patients' morphine and alcohol addiction problems. Cocaine was also used to treat depression, digestive disorders, tuberculosis, asthma, and disorders of the central nervous system. However, very little experimentation has been done with cocaine. It was not introduced to the "enlightened" medical community until the mid-1850s and by 1914 it was essentially declared illegal under the Harrison Anti-Narcotics Act. Admittedly, to some extent that happened because many of Freud's controversial psychiatric theories were being discounted because of his own addiction to cocaine. The use of cocaine, either personally or professionally, became a professional liability for physicians and psychologists alike, especially Freud. Nonetheless, given its proven beneficial effects, one would think that proper research could teach us how to take advantage of cocaine's medical properties while avoiding or controlling the negative effects.

COPS AND ROBBERS — HOLLYWOOD'S INFLUENCE

Even the most principled and well-intentioned people are susceptible to corruption when the risk is small and rewards are great enough; it's human nature. Elected and law enforcement officials at every level are especially susceptible when the laws they are given to uphold are irrational and irresponsible. The police, after all, don't make the laws or pass judgment; they simply enforce the law. The results of Alcohol Prohibition are just one of the glaring examples.

The drug war is another. Throughout the 1970s–early 1990s the news was full of reports of corrupted police — missing evidence, missing confiscated drug money and missing drugs, taken out of supposedly secure police property rooms. Even the heroin confiscated in the most publicized drug bust in history, and described in the book and film *The French Connection,* mysteriously turned into powdered sugar before the trial. Where did the real stuff go? In the mid-1980s, a dozen Florida narcotics officers were convicted of ripping off a drug dealer for millions of dollars worth of cocaine and murdering several people in the process. In 1989, almost the entire narcotics squad of the Los Angeles County Sheriff's Department was suspended for selling illegal drugs. Rumors that the police always had the best illegal drugs, confirmed by reports by a former officer on CBS Nightly News in June 1992, suggest the pervasive use of illegal drugs by police. Did they actually consume, or sell, the cocaine and heroin they claim to have destroyed?

The problem of misjudging the dangers of drugs, drug users and drug dealing was exacerbated by the film and television industry. Hollywood uses drug hysteria to sell movies and TV shows the way William Randolph Hearst did to sell newspapers in the 1920s and 1930s. They use imaginary car chases and break-ins and shoot-outs to punch up the action. "Cop shows" produce good ratings and are cheap to produce, since police departments willingly provide equipment and facilities when the police are portrayed in a positive light. These violent shows, strating as early as the 1950s with *Dragnet* and *Highway Patrol*, shaped America's attitude toward drug users and dealers by portraying them all as the dregs of society. Sadly, examples of entrapment, coercion, manhandling, planting of evidence, and disregarding constitutional rights have been presented as acceptable, even expected, behavior as long as it gets drugs off the streets.

Real police officers adopted the Ramboesque mentality Hollywood created, probably encouraged by their superiors who wanted confiscated property. The number of actual arrests went up and so did charges of police brutality. America has started to look more like a "police state" than "the land of the free." The situation exploded in March 1992, with the beating of Rodney King by several LAPD officers (which a bystander caught on videotape), and less than two months later the officers were found not guilty. Although there were obviously racial overtones to resulting riots, it was more a revolt against the misuse of police power. In June of that year, Amnesty International characterized the United States as the world's leading violator of human rights and specifically identified the Los Angeles Police Department and the California prison system as flagrant violators.

One might think the police and courts had more than enough to worry about and would be pleased to eliminate victimless crimes from the list of laws they are sworn to enforce. But, the more we criminalize drugs, the more money is directed at fighting crime; and that means more jobs, more promotions, more overtime, and more money in the pockets of those whom we hire to go after the criminals

In California, the yearly number of marijuana arrests increased by almost 500% between 1954 and 1960, from 1,156 to 5,155. By 1966, the figure more than tripled to 18,243 and by 1968 it jumped again to over 50,000.[119] Nationally, the arrest figures for simple possession of marijuana skyrocketed, from 18,000 in 1965 to 220,000 by 1970; by now, nationwide arrests are averaging about 725,000 a year. In 1980, there were 401,982 arrests for possession of marijuana compared to 88,900 arrests for prostitution and 87,000 gambling-related arrests. We are now turning people into criminals at the rate of almost one hundred an hour. The following data can be derived from the FBI Uniform Crime Report.[120]

---

119. Brecher, p. 422.

Marijuana Arrests in the US, by Year:

2001	723,627
2000	734,498
1999	704,812
1998	682,885
1997	695,200
1996	641,642
1995	588,963
1994	499,122
1993	380,689
1992	342,314

It's counterproductive. If we spent that much time, energy and money every year helping people instead of hurting them, we could wipe out poverty and crime in a year. Treating drug dependency as a criminal problem is expensive, ineffective and inhumane; it's far more rational to treat it as a medical affliction and a sign of personal trouble that might be addressed through counseling. At least, these people could remain productive members of the society.

The United Nations estimates that 141 million people around the world use marijuana. This represents about 2.5 percent of the world population.[121]

TODAY'S REALITIES ARE DIFFERENT THAN IN 1937

In 1937, as the winds of war again began to gust in Europe, the overall demand for American products, especially weapons, began to rise, creating many more jobs. However, as demand increased, inflation reared its head (See: Ameri-Trust Graph — late 1930s and early 1940s). Wage and price controls during the war years (1942–46) stabilized prices but when the war ended, babies were

---

120. "Marijuana Violations for Year 2000 Hit All Time High, FBI Report Reveals," October 22, 2001. *NORML News*, available online at http://www.norml.org/index.cfm?Group_ID=4363. Statistics for 2001 are available in *Crime in the United States 2001*, from the FBI online at http://www.fbi.gov/ucr/cius_01/01crime4.pdf.

121. United Nations Office for Drug Control and Crime Prevention, *Global Illicit Drug Trends 1999* (New York, NY: UNODCCP, 1999), p. 91.

booming, increasing the population along with the demand for consumer goods, and the inflationary spiral (rising prices) took off. Perhaps if hemp had been an option, the other raw materials available to industry would not have been under so much pressure and prices could have been kept down. Industry did adapt quickly to the raw materials that were legally available (primarily cotton, wood and petroleum), but many needs were chasing a finite flow of raw materials.

When the products we need and use every day are made from a limited, in fact dwindling, reservoir of natural resources, we inevitably drive up the cost of producing those goods. Instead, we should take advantage of the alternative resources available to us. Why squander cotton, wood, and petroleum (and their byproducts, like plastics and paper products), which are no longer quite so abundant or cheap? Why not bring back hemp?

Outlawing hemp forced everyone to focus on the development and utilization of petroleum, which led to an unwise dependence on trade relations with many parts of the world that we do not control. It has hastened the destruction of the forests, devastated the environment, and contributed to five decades of inflation. Fortunately, many of these problems can and will be resolved by re-implementing our cultivation and utilization of hemp.

WE'RE WASTING OUR NATURAL RESOURCES

Not only are we wasting our natural resources, we are undermining the ability of the planet to support its human population. The biggest waste of forest resources is their use for paper and packaging products — an area where hemp could be substituted quickly and easily.

Had it not been for the timber industry's effort at replanting, the US was on track to wipe out its forests by 2000 (according to the USDA's bulletin #404, in 1916!). Trees simply do not grow fast. It takes between five and twenty years to grow a tree and most paper products (newspapers, paper towels, toilet paper, cardboard boxes and other packaging) have a life expectancy of about 24 hours. Trees should be saved for building homes and furniture with a life expectancy of twenty, fifty, a hundred years or more.

Newspapers are just one example of how we are wasting our natural resources. Packaging is another. Merchandise is shipped in boxes packed inside bigger boxes, and the bigger the box on a supermarket shelf the more exposure that product gets, the better chance of it selling. And let's not forget all the paper that business uses: invoices, statements, letters and advertising. The paperless office was a pleasant fantasy, but there is no sign of it arriving anytime soon.

As the worldwide demand for wood byproducts grows exponentially, particularly in the last twenty years, the world's forests are being devastated. In addition, many large forests around the world are dying from the effects of acid rain caused in part by our extensive use of fossil fuels and petrochemicals. The forests are the lungs of the planet, and we need those trees to convert carbon dioxide into the oxygen — more than we need them for paper towels.

Such concerns apply to all kinds of packaging products. McDonald's started packaging hamburgers in styrofoam containers (derived from petroleum) instead of just wrapping them in paper in the mid-1970s. The price of gasoline was already through the roof due to the oil embargo, and the proliferation of new industrial uses for petrochemical products competing for the raw material hardly helped keep prices down. In early 1988 McDonald discontinued the use of these foam containers, but even today hundreds of thousands of restaurants still use similar foam containers for take-out orders. The production of this type of foam also has been implicated in depleting the ozone in the atmosphere, which may be causing increases in melanoma (skin cancer) cases.

THE BENEFITS OF USING HEMP TODAY

Hemp can help. Hemp grows fast. The large-scale cultivation and utilization of hemp would enable us to cut down fewer trees and would increase the amount of vegetation on the planet — that would contribute to improving the quality of the air we breathe. Switching to hemp in place of various fossil fuel products could decrease air and water pollution and reduce the impact on the atmospheric ozone. Wood and petroleum can be conserved for uses that only they serve best; but it is possible to reduce their use significantly.

Unfortunately, we've paid little more than lip service to the idea of reducing our consumption of these resources, because the government has failed to develop alternatives to either petroleum or wood-based products. The government encourages recycling, but that is a waste of time and money as long as we continue to squander petroleum and wood resources on products with a short life expectancy. Although helpful, recycling is simply not a rational or practical solution to a problem of this scale — it is labor intensive and not cost effective. Resolving the problem lies at the point of manufacturing, which means developing environmentally safe and economically sound substitutes for the petroleum and wood-based products we currently produce and use. Hemp, Cannabis, is a fast-growing "renewable" resource that clearly makes sense as the basis for paper- and various other products.

Until 1940, hemp-based products were the worldwide standard that everything else was judged against. Paper, cardboard, fabrics, plastics, fuel, building materials and lubricants of all kinds, products we use every day, could easily be made from hemp or hemp oil, and at a much lower cost than we currently pay. In fact, in many instances the quality of the products would go up. Hemp is one of the most versatile and fastest growing plants on the planet. Its long fibers are the strongest natural fiber known; yet it has also long been made into the world's finest cloth. Hemp-based paper lasts three times longer (225 years) than wood-based paper (75 years) and does not yellow. Hemp-based cardboard boxes are stronger than wood-based cardboard boxes. Even hemp-based building material (plywood sheeting and manufactured dimensional lumber) would produce homes that last longer and hold up to the weather better.

The obvious starting point in re-implementing hemp as a viable resource would be the production of hemp-based paper, cardboard, and packaging products. We can produce four times the amount of paper pulp per acre from hemp[122] than from trees, and we don't have to wait a minimum of five years for it to grow. Hemp grows to maturity in three or four months, and two (sometimes three) crops a year can be harvested off the same parcel of land, year after year. Hemp also does not require the highly toxic non-reusable and non-recyclable chemicals (sulfuric acid, to break down the organic glue called lignin and chlorine bleach to whiten the paper) that are needed to break down wood fibers into pulp,[123] nor does it require chemical pesticides. (Because of the ever rising demand for paper products and despite environmental concerns, the US government currently allows paper mills to simply dump non-recyclable sulfuric acid into rivers and streams.)

Tree-free hemp paper, by contrast, can be made without sulfuric acid, chlorine bleach or any toxins,[124] because the hurds (found inside the stalk of the plant) can be broken down with simple caustic soda, which can also be recycled.

---

122. USDA Bulletin 404, 1916, confirmed in "New Billion Dollar Crop," *Popular Mechanics.* February 1938, p. 144-A.

123. Herer, p. 21.

124. Conrad, p. 70

We already know how to use hemp for a wide range of paper and packaging products from toilet paper to cardboard and everything between. Hemp can be used to insulate homes, for wallpaper and for fiberboard for the construction. Books, documents, and artwork produced on hemp-based paper last three times longer and do not yellow. It is also stronger, and that is why, worldwide, paper money has always been made from hemp-based paper (a.k.a. rag bond — linen), including paper money in the US.

Hemp has also been developed already into a building material. Compressed Agricultural Fiber, CAF, is a sheeting material in the same genre as plywood, particle board, composite-board, and Masonite; it is strong, long lasting, termite free and less expensive. Because of hemp's long strands, it can be made into substitutes for laminated wood or composite beams. The construction industry is already using more and more composite materials, but these composite materials are still wood-based — either wood chips or sawdust mixed with a petroleum-based binding material. In fact, all of these composite materials can be made from hemp and hemp oil by-products, and they would not destroy the environment in the process.

In the 1960s, the world's largest furniture manufacturing plant was built in Ukraine, and it was designed to use hemp as the principle raw material[125] the way the US has been using particle board — it's much less expensive than solid wood and is acceptably hard and durable. It's not meant to replace fine hardwood furniture, but it is quite suitable for mass producing affordable furniture and cabinets.

OUR MISCONCEPTION OF LINEN

Most encyclopedias and dictionaries today describe "linen" as being made from Flax. Traditionally, fabrics made from hemp have also been known as linen.[126] In fact, linen is made from several of the soft bast fibers -- flax, hemp, and nettles, and mainly because of economic considerations often consisted of a combination of these fibers. It is practically impossible to identify whether a fin-

---

125. Bentsianova, I.Y.; Veksler, G.M.; Markov, L.R.; Melamed, S.N.; Petrienko, P.M.; *The Manufacture of Wood-particle Board from Hemp Soutch.* Derevoobrabat. Prom. 11(4);9-10 (April 62); ABICP 33:474 — Courtesy of the Institute of Paper Chemistry.

126. *Encyclopedia America*, Americana Corp, New York: 1956, vol. 17, p. 422.

ished piece of linen fabric was made from flax or hemp.[127] Actually, the majority of linen comes from hemp.[128] Flax is unquestionably a more flexible fiber, even stronger, and is generally preferred for fine linens, but it is harder to grow and there are some strains of hemp, like Italian hemp, that are superior to flax for fine fabrics.[129]

The important differences lie in the type and quality of the seeds and how the matured plants are retted. Retting (rotting) is the microbial decomposition of the stem of the plant, to release the fibers. This is accomplished either by leaving the mowed-down stems in the fields in the damp fall or by submerging them in water – water retting produces higher quality, lighter colored fibers.

Hemp yields about twice the fiber per acre as flax,[130] but even more relevant is the fact that flax is "hard" on the soil, absorbing most of the nutrients, which is why it was not recommended to be grown more than once in ten years on the same parcel of land.[131] That was not so important in colonial times when land was plentiful, but today it is. It also requires a good deal of attention and manual labor. Weed control is also a problem with flax and it is also susceptible to a variety of diseases, including races of wilt, canker, rust and blights.[132] Hemp, on the other hand, is "good" for the soil and requires very little attention. Its deep penetrating roots breakup and aerate the soil; it does not attract insects, chokes off weeds, and it can be grown on the same parcel of land over and over again. In many parts of the world hemp has been or was grown on the same parcel of land for well over a hundred years.

Both flax and hemp fibers, with a tensile strength up to 80,000 pounds per square inch,[133] are twice as strong as cotton. Textiles and cordage made from hemp fibers are much stronger and will last much longer than those made from cotton fibers. Furthermore, cotton crops are vulnerable to insects — and the boll weevil and his friends can only be eradicated with expensive and polluting petrochemical-based pesticides. The cultivation of cotton accounts for half of all the

127. Rosenthal, Ed. *Hemp Today.* Quick Americam Archives, Oakland, CA: 1994, p. 9.

128. Herer, p. 18.

129. Rosenthal, p. 8.

130. Robinson, B. B. 1943. Hemp. *Farmer's Bulletin no. 1935,* USDA

131. Rosenthal, p. 10.

132. *Ibid.,* p. 19.

133. *Encyclopedia Americans,* 1956, Vol.11 p.168.

agricultural chemical pesticides used in this country. Hemp does not attract insects and does not require chemical pesticides.

Cotton no longer has the economic advantage of the cotton gin or slavery it once enjoyed, and although it has enjoyed almost 200 years of research and applied technology, today it is not cheap to produce compared to hemp. With a bit more research, existing hemp technology can be further developed to give us a wide range of hemp-based fabrics from delicate summer wear to the sturdiest of jeans, upholstery fabrics and carpeting. The original heavy-duty Levi pants were made for the California 49ers out of hempen sailcloth and rivets – the pockets wouldn't rip when filled with gold nuggets panned from the sediment.[134]

The economic and environmental benefits would more than compensate for the initial costs of re-tooling parts of the textile industry. All that is needed is to end the criminal sanctions against the use of Cannabis as a raw material.

As for petroleum, alternatives are already in the works. Ethanol, methanol and alcohol all burn substantially cleaner and cost less than petroleum. Late in World War II, the German army used alcohol to fuel its vehicles, including tanks. The US used methanol in the same period as fuel for bombers and jet fighter planes, and hemp oil was used to lubricate those engines. Today, most race cars and high performance cars run on methanol or pure alcohol and to improve air quality, several states have passed legislation that forces the big oil companies to include ethanol (made from corn stalks) in the gasoline they sell. Actually, both the combustion and diesel engines were originally designed to run on biomass fuels, derived from vegetation, not fossil fuel (petroleum). And hemp can provide that.

Henry Ford was operating a biomass cracking plant at Iron Mountain, Michigan, in the 1930s specifically to produce biomass fuel to run a fleet of automobiles.[135] Hemp is by far the most efficient plant for such uses; it is the leading source of methanol (one acre of hemp will produce 20 barrels of fuel), ten times better than corn stalks — its nearest agricultural competitor. Cannabis is at least four times (possibly as much as fifty times) richer in biomass cellulose than its nearest rivals, corn stalks, sugarcane, kenaf, and trees.[136] Petroleum is also being used to run our power plants (or worse yet — coal). Those generators can

---

134. Herer, p. 6.

135. *The Drug Cartel, The Control for World Economics*: Len Bauman Productions, Los Angeles, CA: 1993

136. Solar Gas, 1980 — Omni, 1983 — Cornell University; Science Digest, 1983.

be operated on hemp-based charcoal or methanol; hemp contains no sulfur to pollute the environment. In fact, the Pyrolysis process used to convert fossil fuels into gasoline is exactly the same process employed in a biomass cracking plant.[137]

Ford abandoned his Iron Mountain biomass cracking plant but in the short time that it was operating his researchers produced a number of chemicals commonly used by industry, explored various applications for hemp and hemp oil, and demonstrated the versatility of Cannabis by producing an automobile made almost entirely of hemp — a picture of which was published in 1941 in *Popular Mechanics Magazine*. The body of the car was made of hemp-based molded plastic which was ten times stronger than steel. The car itself weighed 1000 pounds less than a metal version, which means it could run more miles per gallon. Even the fuel the car ran on was made from hemp — meaning that operating costs were substantially lower. Can you visualize an America where vehicles operate on clean burning hemp-based methanol produced in the US, by local workers? It is a practical, environmentally beneficial, economically responsible vision and moving in that direction will dramatically reduce the US dependency on foreign-owned oil.

ANYTHING OIL CAN DO, HEMP CAN DO BETTER

Practically everything that is currently made from petroleum or petrochemicals could be made from hemp or hemp oil — all kinds of plastic and foam packaging, lubricants, suntan oil, toothpaste, shampoos and conditioners, all kinds of lotions, and fuel for our cars and trucks — even the vehicles themselves.

Cannabis (hemp) is the perfect raw material. It is extraordinarily versatile, its long fibers are exceptionally strong, it is long lasting and environmentally safe, and it is one of the fastest growing plants on the planet — growing as high as thirty feet tall in three or four months. It is also very hardy; it does not need groomed land or pesticides; it grows on any terrain — mountains to swamps — and requires very little care. Cannabis is even good for land and soil reclamation, as its long roots (up to seven feet) aerate overworked soil. It breaks up compacted soil while preventing erosion and mud slides, with the concomitant loss of watershed[138] after heavy rain or forest fires.

---

137. Herer, p. 44.

The laws that have kept hemp illegal are artificially protecting the petro-leum, petrochemical and forest industries. But since Cannabis was outlawed in 1937, there have been dramatic changes. The petroleum companies no longer own the wells that produce the oil they are processing, so they are realizing much reduced profits. In addition, they are paying exorbitant transportation and exploration costs. And the supply is not infinite.

Because the cost of oil and gasoline keeps going up, the petroleum industry is on the verge of losing its primary market, the automobile industry. The search for alterative fuels and alternative technology (fuel cells and solar power) is pro-gressing. Gasoline will become obsolete, one way or another.

Politics As Usual? A Condemnation Of Political Realities

Politics is more show than substance and elected officials generally have to please the industry lobbyists who make huge contributions to their election or reelection campaigns — not the little guy who merely gave his vote. That inher-ent conflict of interest is realized in the credo politicians live by: "The first job of a politician is to get (re-)elected." That is why corporations get most of the tax breaks.

The problem, of course, is that the best interests of the country as a whole are not being served. The economic gap between the haves and have-nots keeps growing larger and larger. The middle class has shrunk, and the majority of American families today are heavily in debt.

Our government is controlled and manipulated by the same wealthy elite, basically the Hamiltonian Federalists, we saw earlier. Money determines the pecking order. One of the most alarming groups today is "The Federalist Society for Law and Public Policy Studies,"[139] as documented in a white paper for the People for the American Way Foundation by its President Ralph G. Neas. The Federalist Society was founded in 1982 by students at Yale and the University of Chicago Law School; initially, it was nurtured by law professors such as Robert Bork and Antonin Scalia; it is not a political party. They promote an ultra-con-servative elitist philosophy and, according to the Washington Times' *Insight Mag-*

---

138. Herer, p. 47.

139. Neas, Ralph G. *The Federalist Society and the Challenge to a Democratic Jurisprudence.* Institute for Democracy Studies, January 2001 p. 8, 14.

azine, they are the "single most influential organization in the conservative legal world"[140] and within the Republican Party. Six of George W. Bush's first 11 nominees to the influential federal court of appeals have been Society members (Jeffrey Sutton, Michael McConnell, Priscilla Owen, and Carolyn Kuhl among others).[141] Also according to Neas, "The leading voices of the Society share an ideology that is hostile to civil rights, reproductive rights, religious liberties, environmental protection, privacy right, and health and safety standards, and would strip our federal government of the power to enforce these rights and protections." Essentially, The Federalist Society is attempting a takeover of the federal government. The Society boasts of a membership list of over 40,000 lawyers, policy analysts and business leaders including 5,000 law students at roughly 140 law schools. The players may be different, but the philosophy is identical.

There is nothing illegal about what the Federalist Society members are doing, but they are creating a predatory relationship between the money interests and the general public — class warfare. But survival requires a symbiotic relationship between the wealthy/elite, the government, and the majority of the people making up the society. There are no winners when it comes to class warfare.

It is the political parties that make public policy, select candidates for public office and get laws enacted. Who are the parties responsible to? The Democrat/Republican oligarchy actually represents the interests of the wealthy elite, and while some details shift over time, the two parties end up being two sides of the same coin and not much has really changed. Now, the Democrat/Republican oligarchy is apparently losing its influence with the average voter, who feels ideologically disenfranchised. That is why so few eligible voters turn out and that is why there is an increase in the number of "3rd party" choices — Libertarians, Greens, and dozens more. People are becoming more issue-oriented and are starting to look elsewhere for leadership and for rational, effective answers to our social, economic, and environmental problems.

---

140. Wagner, David A. "When Conservatives Lay Down the Law." *Washington Times' Insight Magazine*, August 10, 1998.

141. *Ibid.*

ECONOMICS: HARDLY AN EXACT SCIENCE

Economists use many theories and tools to justify their various conclusions, but the very variety of conclusions that have been drawn — in response to practically every economic event — shows how imprecise and subjective the "science" of economics is. Indeed, politicians hire economists not to suggest policies that would stimulate economic growth, but to manipulate statistics and justify their political agenda. Nonetheless, in the aggregate, good laws and good economic decisions will likely enable a society to prosper. Conversely, an economic decline (short of objectively recognized external calamities, such as a series of natural disasters that wipes out all the resources) generally indicates that more wrong choices are being made. Those choices could come in the form of people using their money and influence to force society down one road instead of another, or the enactment of laws (both positive and negative) that affect the way the society operates. Good laws encourage a prosperous economy, and anything less than that simply means we're doing something wrong — and when we do more wrong than right, we pay dearly for it.

We study economics hoping to acquire a better understanding of the factors that affect every aspect of our lives, particularly the quality of life and the standard of living. Unfortunately, economics is imprecise, incomplete and uses unreliable and misleading; statistics. For example, the monthly unemployment statistics only represent the number of people collecting unemployment insurance. They do not include the people who have exhausted their unemployment benefits and still can't find a job, or who became discouraged and gave up seeking a job altogether. In hard times, the real figure could actually be three times the number reported by the government.

In the above chapters some of the economic turning points of American history have been analyzed from a standpoint different from the usual ones; by considering some factors that are often overlooked, we may not have hit on exact explanations for events but hopefully will stimulate a fuller consideration of the factors that shape history and the evolution of society.

FORCED MORALITY — ATTEMPTING TO CHANGE HUMAN NATURE

For as long as civilization has existed, moderate use of recreational intoxicants has been an integral part of social customs. Wine and beer go back thousands of years. Marijuana developed as the intoxicant of choice in the poor, less developed nations of the world, because it was essentially free and readily available. It was also used by such notables as George Washington, Thomas Jefferson and Queen Victoria; if not as an intoxicant, then surely as a medicine or as a smoking agent.

Some would argue that we are never going to stop people from using recreational intoxicants. Whether harsh policing methods or a benevolent "Drug Czar" would make a difference is open to question. If we were truly interested in reducing the problem of drug abuse, the common sense thing to do would be to make an honest and unbiased assessment to determine what are the effects of the less dangerous and mildest drugs, and enable people to make educated choices about using or not using them. We certainly have a problem at hand, but it is mostly a social problem, not a drug problem *per se*. This book looks at Cannabis and its use as a drug through the lens of history, social interactions and group self-interests.

The preamble to the US Constitution charges our elected officials with the responsibility "to promote the general welfare." That doesn't mean creating a welfare state; it means creating an atmosphere conducive to economic growth, including a healthy and productive populace.

It is naive to think the US government considers the use of illegal intoxicants especially marijuana, a threat to America or the health and well-being of America's youth. In fact, the drug war merely justifies expenditures, hiring, and promotions, and the bigger the perceived problem the more money and resources they can justify throwing at it. The only other reason for the "war on drugs" is to keep Cannabis illegal, as a favor to corporate America — specifically the oil and petrochemical companies, the liquor and tobacco industries, the forest and cotton industries and especially the pharmaceutical companies.

In discussing the rights of Americans, Professor Steven Duke, of Yale Law School, says,

> The core difference between America and totalitarian regimes is that Americans have rights to make wrong choices; rights to do things that are not good for them. They also have a right to do things that are not good for other people.[142]

---

142. Duke, Steven B. *America's Longest War*. G. P. Putnam's Sons, New York: 1993, p. 146, 158, 161.

The great thinker John Stuart Mill saw the situation clearly, back in the 19th century. He objected to laws in some American states that prohibited the sale of alcohol, calling such regulations a "gross usurpation upon the liberty of private life" and an "important example of illegitimate interference with the rightful liberty of the individual."

Mills said,

> The only purpose for which power can be rightfully exercised over any member of a civilized community, against his will, is to prevent harm to others. His own good, either physical or moral is not a sufficient warrant. He cannot rightfully be compelled to do or forbear because it will be better for him to do so, because it will make him happier, because, in the opinions of other, to do so would be wise, or even right.[143]

---

143. Mill, John Stuart. *On Liberty*. John W. Parker & Son, London: 1859, p. 22.

INDEX